THE NEXT BIG IDEA

Also by Carol Kennedy

Business Pioneers (Published in hardback as *The Merchant Princes*)
Guide to the Management Gurus
Managing with the Gurus
ICI: the Company that Changed our Lives
Mayfair: A Social History
Harewood: the Life and Times of an English Country House
The Entrepreneurs

Carol Kennedy

THE
NEXT BIG IDEA

RANDOM HOUSE

BUSINESS BOOKS

Published by Random House Business Books in 2002

1 3 5 7 9 10 8 6 4 2

Copyright © 2001 Carol Kennedy

Carol Kennedy has asserted her right under the Copyright, Designs
and Patents Act, 1988, to be identified as the author of this work.

First published by Random House Business Books in 2001

Random House Business Books
Random House Group Limited
20 Vauxhall Bridge Road, London SW1V 2SA

Random House Australia (Pty) Limited
20 Alfred Street, Milsons Point,
Sydney, New South Wales 2061, Australia

Random House New Zealand Limited
18 Poland Road, Glenfield,
Auckland 10, New Zealand

Random House (Pty) Limited
Endulini, 5a Jubilee Road, Parktown 2193, South Africa

The Random House Group Limited Reg. No. 954009

www.randomhouse.co.uk

businessbooks@randomhouse.co.uk

A CIP catalogue record for this book is available from the British Library

Papers used by Random House are natural, recyclable products
made from wood grown in sustainable forests. The manufacturing processes
conform to the environmental regulations of the country of origin.

ISBN 0 7126 8449 2

Typeset in Baskerville & Gill Sans by
MATS, Southend-on-Sea, Essex
Printed and bound in Great Britain by
Biddles Ltd, Guildford and King's Lynn

CONTENTS

ACKNOWLEDGEMENTS

I am grateful to the following publishers and publications for permission to use quotations or other referenced material: Nicholas Brealey (*Organizing Genius* by Warren Bennis and Patricia Biederman and *Digital Capital* by Don Tapscott, Ticoll and Lowy); *Fast Company* for the IBM Speed Team case study, 'Faster Company,' in its May 2000 issue; the *Financial Times*; David Wilson of Texere (*Blood, Sweat and Tears* by Richard Donkin; *Surfing the Edge of Chaos* by Richard Pascale, *Open Minds* by Andy Law, *Future Revolutions* by David Mercer and *Weaving the Web* by Tim Berners-Lee); Penguin Books (*Business@the Speed of Thought* by Bill Gates).

My thanks go also to W. Chan Kim and Renée Mauborgne, professors of strategic management at INSEAD, for permission to summarise their 'six utility levers' findings from articles published in the *Harvard Business Review* and the *Financial Times*; to Belbin Associates for permission to quote from Meredith Belbin's *The Coming Shape of Organizations*; to Michel Syrett and Jean Lammiman for permission to draw on their reports *Innovation at the Top: Where do directors get their ideas from?* and *Entering Tiger Country: How ideas are shaped in organisations*, and for access to some of their research for *Management Development: making the investment count* (Economist Books, 1998). Michel was also of inestimable help in shaping Chapters 2 and 10 and a source of sustained encouragement and inspiration throughout, as was my great mentor and friend, the late George Bull, OBE. Dr. Bruce Lloyd, professor of strategic management at South Bank University, London, was an unfailing source of advice and encouragement, as was Clare Smith, my ever-helpful editor at Random House Business Books. Cathy Castillo and Barbara Buell of Stanford University Graduate School of Business opened doors for me and were an invaluable source of access to key members of the faculty.

The following distinguished thinkers and academics generously gave of their time for interviews and discussions: Richard Pascale, Gary Hamel, Charles Handy, Kenichi Ohmae, Professor Sumantra Ghoshal of London Business School, Professors Jeffrey Pfeffer, Garth Saloner, Robert I. Sutton and Michael Ray of Stanford University Graduate School of Business; Professor Ronald A. Heifetz of the John F. Kennedy School of Government, Harvard University; Don Tapscott; John Seely Brown. Eric D. Beinhocker of McKinsey and Co. shared his valuable insights into the work of the Santa Fe Institute on living systems. Bill Drobny of Barclays Global Investors in San Francisco explained his system for getting projects delivered on time. Martin Bluck of General Electric's Global Xchange, formerly known as GE Information Systems, was immensely helpful in outlining GE's latest big ideas in the application of technology to the company's famous Work-Out system. Mark Goyder of the Royal Society for the Arts, Manufactures and Commerce helpfully brought me up to date on the Tomorrow's Company project.

Any errors or omissions in my treatment of their contributions are mine alone, but I have made every effort to ensure there are none. The Recommended Reading list fills out many other sources I found of great help in writing this book.

Carol Kennedy, London, August 2001

PREFACE TO THE PAPERBACK EDITION

2001 was a difficult year to be writing a book about the ideas that management could usefully learn from the new economy – except to learn from mistakes. Throughout the early part of the year dotcoms were in free-fall, affecting in collapsing domino fashion even well managed companies like Cisco, left with a stack of inventory as orders were cancelled.

Then came September 11. The devastating attacks on the World Trade Center and the Pentagon, planned for years by a well-concealed global terrorist conspiracy, delivered a massive blow to the confidence of the world economy. But September 11 did not, as many predicted on September 12, change everything. The world economy picked itself up and went on climbing slowly out of near-recession.

Finally came the unmasking of Enron, a blazingly innovative business that seemed to break the boundaries of conventional thinking in the way it traded and made markets in everything from natural gas to bandwidth. Until, that is, the Wizard of Oz's curtain was ripped down by whistleblowers and we saw how the illusion had been worked – by shifting debt off the balance sheet into 'partnerships' that existed only to hide Enron's losses and acquire more assets to bolster its share price.

What can be learned from these three seismic events

in terms of better management ideas? The bursting of the dotcom bubble and that icon of the new economy, Enron, reinforced what I was being told by keen-eyed observers of Silicon Valley the year before; that the old principles of sound management are worth a ton of cool new Internet business models. Business plans have to be properly put together and costed, people managed wisely and financial controls consistently monitored. Dazzling extrapolations of profits and shareholder value are bound to meet a more sceptical response in future: even General Electric has faced hard scrutiny over how it famously managed to hit its growth targets every quarter for 20 years. In financial discipline, as several wise heads were already predicting in the fall of 2000, some old ideas are due to come around as the next big ideas.

September 11 demonstrated in the most savage way that the industrial West now needs to be forearmed as well as forewarned to deal with the kind of catastrophe it would once have dismissed as unthinkable. All those mantras of the 1990s about managing for discontinuity look absurd in the face of what happened on September 11 – literally, out of a clear blue sky. On the most practical level, businesses need above all to have data backup in secure places: one financial house in the Twin Towers that held a complete backup system in New Jersey was able to resume operations within hours of its main offices being vaporised.

On a wider canvas, September 11 also demonstrated the power of ideas at their most fundamental and frightening; medieval religious fanaticism harnessed to 21st century technology and training. Advanced nations can no longer delude themselves that the rest of the world only needs to improve itself materially to be stable and content: destructive ideas need to be fought with creative ones. There has to be a philosophy beyond the mere satisfaction of material wants.

I suggested in the introduction to this book that big ideas might be on the way out, both in business and in global politics following the collapse of communism. History, as September 11 showed, has a habit of confounding such predictions; something the US pundit Francis Fukuyama discovered after he wrote a book about the triumph of Western democracy hubristically titled *The End of History*. In geo-politics, al-Qaeda has lethally proved that some very old big ideas are as undead as Dracula.

In business, although the search for new ideas continues – in the UK, most actively for the better management of public services such as healthcare – the one-size-fits-all approach of big concepts like re-engineering has almost certainly had its day. A tech-nology-led business environment that is still evolving its revolutionary new tools enables more choice and experimentation in management ideas, both in the way businesses are run and in the markets they offer customers. The dotcom crash has not brought the new economy to an end, as futurist Alvin Toffler says, any more than the Industrial Revolution came to an end 'because some London textile plants shut down in the 1830s.' It has just presented us with the opportunity to learn, re-establish old management skills and open ourselves to the next wave of ideas, whether big or small.

Carol Kennedy, London, May 2002

INTRODUCTION

THE LURE OF
THE BIG IDEA

Management, born as a profession with the twentieth century, has for most of its lifetime been in love with the Big Idea. Just as with politics, its practitioners have perennially sought the road to salvation, the magic formula for prosperity, some grand vision that would rally people behind them. Since the century's two biggest ideas that aimed to transform society, fascism and communism, turned into monsters that engulfed the world in revolution and total war, we should perhaps be thankful that today's political leaders have more mundane agendas, even if voters become apathetic as a result and pundits complain about a lack of vision.

In business, too, there are signs that big visionary theories may have had their day. Right from its birth in the 1900s, professional management has been seduced by the Big Idea, from Frederick W. Taylor persuading industry that it could be run with the science and precision of a stopwatch to the Taylorism of the 1990s known as business process re-engineering. Throughout the century management gurus have continued to search for ways to make business more efficient and workers more productive, swinging their focus from process to people and back again. If the ideas haven't been as big as those in politics, they haven't been as disastrous either, but the constant drive for better performance has often been counter-productive in human terms, and the obsessive short-term cost-cutting of the 1990s resulted for many businesses in a sort of 'corporate anorexia' (a phrase coined by the gurus Gary Hamel and C.K. Prahalad) which prevented them from healthy regrowth when their markets came back.

Until around 1980 the stream of Big Ideas was a relative trickle, perhaps one or two in a decade, then it turned into a flood. Out poured tens of thousands of books and magazine articles, a dozen Harvard, Stanford and Massachusetts Institute of Technology professors became multi-millionaire gurus and ceaseless waves of change washed over the world's biggest industrial companies. The catalyst was one book, *In Search of Excellence* by Tom Peters and Robert H. Waterman, which encapsulated the promise of world-beating performance in eight core practices that the authors decided were shared by the best companies in America. Although two-thirds of those companies fell from grace within five years, the book still sells in its original, unrevised form because enough people find that the eight mantras still work, though much modified by the hectic competition and change of the new economy.

The formula of *Excellence* was irresistible, and ever since its low-key launch in 1982 – it caught on by word of mouth among chief executives – few managers have been immune to the lure of the magic bullet, the hope that this time, just possibly, the latest 'thought leaders' of management theory will have found the password to better performance, bigger quarterly profits, massive shareholder value.

If only. It's not just a case of the latest business blockbuster promising seven steps to heaven on the airport bookstalls, but Big Ideas do filter down from the books and the business schools to the management consultancies, those exponential money machines that girdle the world with their change programmes (many of which fail or don't last) and their promises of a better

tomorrow. Their bills are enormous. Some organisations have never recovered from the attentions of
consultants, as James O'Shea and Charles Madigan's
book *Dangerous Company* revealed in the late 1990s, while
others, like the BBC, continually reinvent the wheel with
successive generations of management throwing out the
last consultancy Big Idea and calling in the mighty
McKinsey yet again. It's all rather like horoscopes in the
popular press: for a short time they give the illusion of
accurate guidance, but if they prove wrong there's
always another one the next day.

But things are changing. It seems only yesterday that
e-commerce, even the Internet, was something new, on
the fringe of the economy, the preserve of Bill Gates's
Microsoft and a few techie companies in Silicon Valley.
Suddenly, and with terrifying speed, it has engulfed
every type of business organisation. The smallest metal-
basher in Birmingham making minor motor components knows about market exchanges on the Web, e-
business is an indispensable part of the most venerable
old-economy companies, and a whole new business
language is in daily use, from 'dotcoms' to 'clicks and
mortar'. In November 1999 the magazine *Forbes Global*
listed around twenty of the extraordinary business
innovations since 1990, among them:

- Tim Berners-Lee completing the World Wide Web;
- the Web browser invented at the University of Illinois
  and commercialised by Netscape;
- Jeff Bezos launching the e-commerce revolution with
  Amazon.com;
- technology start-ups in the US rising fortyfold from
  $2bn to $80bn a year.

With so much of business now moving at Internet
speed, it's hardly likely that the old cycle of the Big Idea
– or, more unkindly, management fad – would survive.

In the 1980s a lecturer at the Cranfield School of Management, Hugh MacDonald, put the life-cycle of a management fad at between 11 and 13 years from its first inception at an academic's desk in Stanford or Harvard Business School or MIT through the obligatory article in *Harvard Business Review* to the lecture circuit and seminar and into the consultancies and business, eventually to be worn out or discredited and tossed aside when the next new theory came along.

Richard Pascale, a respected guru who formerly taught at Stanford, likes to carry with him a chart he compiled for a conference held by the European Forum for Management Development in Prague in 1997. It is headed 'Ebbs, Flows and Residual Impacts of Business Fads, 1950–1995', and it records 34 theories or fads over those 45 years, from Decision Trees in the 1950s to Benchmarking in the 1990s. Over the first 20 years there are only nine fads; all the rest, apart from Decentralisation, are packed into the 15 years from 1980 to 1995, and all but three of those – Continuous Improvement and the Learning Organisation, Re-Engineering and Benchmarking – burst into life in the 1980s, none lasting more than a year or two. When MacDonald made his 11–13 year calculation, he was already way out of date.

Pascale's ideas and books have lasted longer than most. In the early 1980s he co-invented the 'Seven-S' strategy of hard and soft management skills for McKinsey to explain Japan's surging industrial competitiveness (respectively: structure, strategy, systems; staff, skills, style and shared values); in 1990, his book *Managing on the Edge* identified a decade early the fatal risks of complacency in successful organisations that were to send Sainsbury and Marks and Spencer into a tailspin. But for a successful guru/consultant among the top five in the world, he is refreshingly clear-eyed about the magic-bullet fantasy of management ideas. The Big

Idea has become an industry in itself, a self-nourishing nexus comprising academia, publishing and the conference circuit, each demanding a new eye-catching theory that can create the revenue streams until the cycle starts all over again.

Business schools and consultancies aid and abet this cycle for their own reasons, as this book explores later, but the industry is chiefly promoted by publishers and conference organisers, who in turn put pressure on gurus to come up with Big Ideas at regular intervals, preferably once a year. Pascale told in a 1997 interview of visiting his New York publisher with a book proposal based on his latest work. The editor expressed interest, then added: 'But can you put your argument in one sentence?' When Pascale replied that he might be able to do it in four, he was told to go away and rethink it. This is the Hollywood blockbuster approach: give us the high concept in ten words or less.[1]

Pascale takes this problem seriously. Many perfectly sound management theories don't work in practice, he argues, because they get 'simplified down to the quick fixes of airport literature'. Gurus become seduced by publishing contracts and lecture circuits into offering soundbites and seven-steps-to-heaven approaches instead of carefully researched studies.

Why do most Big Ideas have such a short shelf-life? Hugh MacDonald suggested there was a deadening effect when the elixir syndrome ('this is a single solution to all our problems') wore off, plus a distancing syndrome made up of lack of commitment ('we have so much to do, we cannot spare the time') and the delegation of leadership to the information systems people or consultants. The basic preconditions for success, he maintained at the time that business process re-engineering (BPR) was being dreamed up at MIT, were:

- correct motivation;
- realistic expectations;
- effective processes;
- involvement of the right people;
- sustained commitment at the right levels.

John Seely Brown, chief scientist at that great ideas-incubator Xerox PARC (Palo Alto Research Center) and one of the wisest heads in Silicon Valley, says that each of the three Big Ideas that dominated the 1990s – quality, BPR and knowledge management – required a 180-degree turn in quick succession. The first and third had much in common, depending on people as a source of best practice and knowledge. The process movement was essentially top-down and operated from the centre outwards rather than bottom-up and inwards from the peripheries. It was no coincidence, he says, that one of the most successful areas for re-engineering proved to be the hierarchical military. Re-engineering gave the fatal impression of rating process over people (F.W. Taylor's big mistake back in 1900) and of valuing structure over creativity. It was, though no one could foresee it at the time, the worst possible preparation for the knowledge-based, people-based, creativity-fuelled economy of the new millennium.

After more than a decade of this, wrote Seely Brown in the spring of 2000, it was hardly surprising that many managers felt they had been spinning in circles and developed a suspicion of any new idea being promoted by consultants. He takes a more positive view: that each change in direction did involve progress of some sort, and that 'the followers of these movements may have been ascending a spiral staircase, not merely turning in place'. As a result, certainly in the US, there was a huge surge of productivity that seemed for a long time to be defying the old wisdom that a boom economy cannot last. 'The process movement offered an organisational focus that the quality movement, for all its qualities, lacked. And knowledge management, for its part, can be seen as something of a response to process engineering that supplemented it by overcoming its organisational tunnel vision.' The succession of ideas, Seely Brown concluded, reflected and was driven by a logic that 'lies deeper than fads and fashions – so deep, in fact, that it is often hard to see'.[2]

It's comforting to think that each Big Idea has contributed something to management wisdom, though corporations are all too capable of making the same mistakes again and again. But it is also true that business today is so full of tensions and contradictions – the need to be both global and local, for example, to recruit creative individuals and at the same time foster teamwork – that no prescriptive idea can last for long, or fit all the fast-moving conditions under which companies find themselves having to work. This situation, naturally, has not left the ideas merchants lost for buzzwords. The art of balancing such polar opposites has been christened 'paradox management'.[3]

The most distinguished advocate of paradox management is Charles Handy, the Irish-born thinker who has been the nearest to the great Peter Drucker in anticipating the social tides that will influence business. In 1994 he published a book entitled *The Age of Paradox* in the US; in Britain it had the quirkier title of *The Empty Raincoat*. In it he analysed fundamental dilemmas of our time, chiefly the paradox of a rich society in which economic growth reduces people to the status of ciphers, and of corporate wealth that results in fewer jobs, and therefore less wealth, for individuals. These paradoxes have yet to be managed, or even properly confronted.

Of course there is nothing new about managers dealing with conflicting pressures and directional pulls – that is what management has always been about. In every manager's office at Lego, the Danish toy manufacturer, an engraved wall plaque lists 'the 11 paradoxes of leadership', including 'to be a visionary – and to keep one's feet on the ground' and 'to be dynamic – and to be reflective'.[4]

The most transformational ideas in management have not merely come out of the business lecture circuit and best-seller lists; they have been grounded in industry and launched into orbit by industrial necessity. In his history of work, *Blood, Sweat and Tears*, the *Financial Times* writer Richard Donkin recalls how F.W. Taylor's scientific management principles of work study were propelled out of the confines of the steel industry and a few technical papers and became a global phenomenon.

In 1910, a US lawyer named Louis Brandeis took the railroad barons to court on behalf of consumers to fight freight price increases. When they claimed that 'practice, contact and experience' justified them in raising revenues in order to maintain efficiency, Brandeis challenged them with Taylor's 1903 paper 'Shop Management', a dry account of his methods that few had read. Brandeis had spoken to Taylorist disciples who were practising his stopwatch measurements, cutting out wasteful practices and raising productivity all over the place. Managers could use these methods to set new working practices, saving massive amounts of time and money. The *New York Times* gave headline treatment to Brandeis's claim that the railroad companies 'could save $1m a day' through scientific management.

When, a year later, Taylor published his *Principles of Scientific Management* in magazine articles, they swept the world from Germany to Japan and maintained their influence for another generation. 'If Henry Ford had repeated the formula, narrating the effectiveness of his new moving assembly line in 1913, his book would have sold millions,' says Donkin. But Ford was a practical pioneer in more basic ways: as well as transforming manufacturing through mass production, he paid his workers $5 a day at a time when car workers averaged $11 a week, and cut the working day from nine to eight hours. Industry was never the same again.[5]

It was an industrialist, too, not a guru, who launched decentralisation upon the world – Alfred Sloan at the infant General Motors in 1919. Sloan did not write his own book until 1964, but *My Years With General Motors* was a formative influence on some of the world's top managers. Peter Drucker began his own phenomenal career as the guru of gurus in 1946 by studying Sloan's work at GM and writing his seminal *Concept of the Corporation*, the first modern management handbook.

In this book I have attempted to show how Big Ideas are born or are deliberately manufactured, and how many of the best and most durable have come out of the noise, stress and grime of the manufacturing workplace rather than the academic's study. But we live and work in a different world in the twenty-first century, and the ideas are changing in their scope and ambition. This has huge implications for the guru and consultancy industry that has grown exponentially since 1982. When anyone can log on to the Internet and access new management thinking online, there is clearly a new freedom and fluidity in the ideas marketplace. There is, for example, free access to some business school sites such as Wharton and INSEAD and the *McKinsey Quarterly* site, the latest articles in the *Harvard Business Review* can be downloaded for a fee, and it is possible to find out what Tom Peters, the world's busiest and most prolific guru, is writing and speaking about at www.tompeters.com, without paying hundreds of pounds for a conference seat.

We also live in a business world increasingly influenced by the start-up mentality. Even big old-economy businesses are starting up new e-ventures and adopting the mindset to go with it. Start-ups have a different way with ideas. They try something, see if it works and, if it does, adopt it. If it doesn't, or if it works for a time and is then overtaken, they dump it and move on to the next thing. This is not slavishly following fads but is a practical approach to the best way of running a business, in the same way that Silicon Valley businesses tirelessly reinvent and reinvigorate themselves. This book explores some of the hot-button ideas being tried out as it was written, and some of those likely to follow. But, given management's enduring love affair with the Next Big Idea, it also identifies a few candidates for that role, at least one of which is being shaped every day in the world outside business, in the streets and at disaffected shareholder meetings, in Internet chatrooms and among thoughtful people who worry about the future.

Like invention, the only worthwhile Big Ideas are those mothered by necessity.

NOTES

[1] Golzen, Godfrey: 'The Next Big Idea', *Human Resources*, March/April 1997

[2] Seely Brown, John: 'Practice vs Process: The Tension That Won't Go Away', *Knowledge Directions*, Spring 2000

[3] Overell, Stephen: 'And now for something completely paradoxical', *FT*, 19.1.01

[4] ibid.

[5] Donkin, Richard: *Blood, Sweat and Tears*, Texere, 2001

CHAPTER ONE

MANAGEMENT IN THE LABORATORY

The first and still the most enduring Big Idea in management was born in 1883 at the Midvale Steel Works in Philadelphia when Frederick Winslow Taylor first clicked his stopwatch to time an industrial process. This simple action by an obscure young engineer, foreman of the machining shop at the foundry, was to revolutionise the practice of management and send reverberations down the decades into almost every cranny of the industrialised planet. Re-engineering, the last truly Big Idea to sweep the business world, was essentially pure Taylorism hitched to the electronic tools of the 1990s. Taylorism remains with us in every industry that relies on standardised processes, from burger bars to car assembly plants, hotel training manuals to supermarket shelf-stacking. The Big Idea was efficiency delivered by the timed study of work, or as Taylor himself put it, 'the one best way' to perform every industrial task.

In 1883 Taylor was an opinionated, restlessly inquisitive 27-year-old, nicknamed 'Speedy' for his obsession with cutting time in whatever he was doing. As a 16-year-old schoolboy at Phillips Exeter Academy in Exeter, New Hampshire, he had been impressed by a teacher's habit of timing how long it took the students to solve an algebra or geometry problem. The boys were told to raise their hands and snap their fingers for attention when they had finished, and the mathematics master, George 'Bull' Wentworth, would unobtrusively check his watch. He thus knew how long it took the average pupil to do his homework.

Since starting at Midvale in 1880, Taylor had been keeping notes himself on how long it took the men to perform a range of tasks; now, in 1883, it occurred to him for the first time to break down and time each element of a job to see how its efficiency could be improved. His intention was not quite as dehumanising as it has been portrayed in industrial history; as well as raising the productivity of labourers, he also sought to improve their pay, and to make each man 'first class at some job'. The stopwatch experiment, which officially gave birth to 'scientific management', as Taylor was to call his system, enabled a workman by the name of Henry Noll to raise his loading of pig iron into a rail car nearly fourfold, from 12.5 tons a day to 47 tons. When the same technique was applied to bricklaying it succeeded in nearly trebling the daily number of bricks laid.

Taylor's Big Idea has proved by far the most influential of the last hundred years, giving rise successively to a whole family tree of efficiency-driven theories: assembly-line production (simultaneously with Henry Ford just before World War One), time and motion study (1920s), work study (1950s), just-in-time (1970s) and re-engineering (1990s). Elements of it inspired such comparative practices as benchmarking and performance measurement, and even the quality movement, the other enduring Big Idea of twentieth-century management, started as a statistically driven method of eliminating production variables that Taylor would have recognised with professional enthusiasm. Equally influential was the reaction that Taylorism provoked by being associated with a mechanistic, command-and-control approach to managing people. By the 1930s the seeds were sown of an opposing family tree of management ideas connected with workplace consultation, motivation, empowerment, self-organising teams and flat, non-hierarchical organisations. Without Taylor, in fact, the whole twentieth-century management advisory industry might never have developed as it did. Fittingly enough, he eventually became America's first true management consultant.

Taylorism was a global idea. It captivated newly industrialising nations around the world. After the publication of his *Principles of Scientific Management* in 1911, the Japanese took to it avidly, as they would to quality management over forty years later. The French Popular Front government discovered it in the 1930s as a way of kick-starting stalled industry during the Depression, to the fury of the French labour unions, which called it 'the American cancer'. Mussolini's Italy embraced it with enthusiasm, as did Hitler's Third Reich from 1933, eventually turning the methodology of efficiency to such dreadful ends that a post-war German historian described Adolf Eichmann, the master administrator of the death camps, as 'a perfect Taylor engineer'.[1]

Taylorism also inspired the work of the first British management consultant, Lyndall Urwick, who had read Taylor's articles in the trenches of Flanders, and it was the driving force behind the massively concentrated US war production effort after 1941, both in its application to rapid training techniques and the high-speed production of equipment. The two world wars, with their need for rapid, wholesale reconstruction of civilian industry, had enormous influence in spreading Taylor's gospel of efficiency around the globe. Peter Drucker, the godfather of present-day management theory, asserted in *Post-Capitalist Society* (1994) that Taylor's influence was the prime factor in victory over both Germany and

Japan. Today almost every standardised unit of the industrial or service sector can be traced back to Taylor's breakdown of processes, from the making of a Big Mac (identical from Buffalo to Beijing) to the manual that instructs a Marriott hotel employee in the best way to make a bed.

Taylor predicted of his work: 'In the past, the man was first. In the future, the system will be first.' In his lifetime he was reviled, especially by the American labour unions, for stripping workers of the need for skill and judgement that gave them satisfaction in their work. 'After Ford and Taylor got through with them,' writes Taylor's biographer Robert Kanigel, 'most jobs needed less of everything – less brains, less muscle, less independence.' Coming full circle, and despite the achievements of the industrial psychologists whose theories on human relations in the workplace had triumphed as a reaction to Taylorism, re-engineering in the 1990s failed precisely on the same grounds: people were made dispensable to processes.

When Big Ideas are misunderstood

It is just beginning to be discovered, however, that it was the application rather than the principle of Taylorism that skewed Taylor's original intentions, which were neither to dehumanise working practices nor to maximise profits for the bosses but to increase productivity by means of a general improvement in the understanding of work processes among both managers and men. The progenitors of re-engineering, Mike Hammer and James Champy, have also consistently argued that their principles were misapplied, often in the blind pursuit of cost-cutting during the recession of the early 1990s.

Drucker has long believed that Taylor, rather than Karl Marx, deserves to rank alongside Darwin and

Freud in the trinity that shaped the modern world. 'Few figures in intellectual history have had greater impact than Taylor,' he wrote in *Post-Capitalist Society*. 'And few have been so wilfully misunderstood and so assiduously misquoted . . . Taylor's reputation has suffered precisely because he applied knowledge to the study of work. This was anathema to the labour unions of his day, and they mounted against Taylor one of the most vicious campaigns of character assassination in American history.' Applying knowledge to work, he noted, was now acknowledged as the only way to raise productivity in the post-industrial world. Drucker was writing in 1994 with the authority of the thinker who first coined the term 'knowledge worker' back in 1969.

Taylor certainly made no effort to convert organised labour to his theories, but he had just as little use for the owners, whom he called 'hogs'. He advocated that most of the savings generated through scientific management should go to the workforce, and that work study should be done in consultation, if not partnership, with the men on the factory floor. And although he believed that managers should be in charge, these were not nineteenth-century owners he had in mind, but professional managers with superior knowledge of the work processes.

Taylor remains the single most influential figure in the development of management thought. If one pursues the analogy of the two family trees of Big Ideas, the second springing from the first, the list of biblical 'begats' would run something like this.

Scientific management (conceived *c.* 1883, first published as a series of papers for mechanical engineers including 'Shop Management' in 1903, then in magazine form as *Principles of Scientific Management* in 1911). Taylor's work, introduced into scores of companies by several of his assistants who became consultants in their own right, was already something of a cult in industry when it attracted the interest of another efficiency-obsessed engineer, Frank Gilbreth. His methods paralleled but differed from Taylor's in being motion-based rather than time-based: he had been apprenticed as a bricklayer and had devised a way of vastly raising bricklaying performance by breaking down the job into its physical elements and eliminating every non-essential motion. By this means he reduced the number of movements needed to lay a brick from eighteen to five, doubling a skilled man's output from 175 to 350 bricks an hour.

Gilbreth called his method **motion study**. When the two men finally met in 1907, Taylor offered to collaborate with him, but Gilbreth was already planning his own book with his wife Lillian, later to become the first outstanding woman engineer in America, carrying on her husband's work after his premature death in 1924. The Gilbreths became almost as famous in the efficiency field as Taylor himself, not least for the eccentric training of their twelve children, one of whom wrote the humorous memoir *Cheaper by the Dozen*, which became a popular film in 1950 starring Clifton Webb. In the 1920s and beyond, the Taylor and Gilbreth approach became conflated into **time-and-motion study**.

After World War Two the discipline evolved into **work study** and in many large corporations such as ICI was partly used as the basis for bonus and incentive schemes. Sir John Harvey-Jones, chairman of ICI between 1982 and 1987, started his career with the chemical company in the work study department in 1957 and quickly came to feel that the system lacked any understanding of human motivation, although he confessed to finding the 'method study' side a valuable management tool as he rose up the company.

There is some debate over whether Henry Ford drew on Taylor's work in developing the **assembly line** for the Model T in 1913, thus ushering in the age of mass production. The Ford system seems to have been evolved through trial and error by a team of in-house engineers.[2] Ford certainly never acknowledged any influence by Taylor, and Taylor, who had already worked in the car industry for five years and was advising Packard while Ford was gearing up his production line, spoke disparagingly about Ford's 'cheaply and roughly made cars'. Between them, however, Taylor and Ford shaped twentieth-century industrial production methods until the advent of electronic technology.

Taylor's early death in 1915 at the age of 59 launched a continuous management search for improved efficiency and performance which has produced almost all the Big Ideas based on comparative data and measurement, from ***benchmarking*** to ***business process re-engineering***. The biggest and most sustainable of these ideas, ***quality control***, originated in the analysis and elimination of variables in production by the US statistician Walter Shewhart. Because of a lack of interest within US industry, it was refined and exported to Japan in 1950 by Shewhart's disciples W. Edwards Deming and Joseph Juran. It, too, was a measurement-based methodology and might have remained as mechanistic as Taylor's stopwatch had not Japanese management style introduced the essential element of team-based responsibility by inventing quality circles. While Juran sniped at Deming for his statistics-based approach and developed something called Company-wide Quality Management (CQM), a third quality guru, Philip Crosby, denounced the entire movement as suffering from more emphasis on procedures than on philosophy. Crosby has always been against such 'box-ticking exercises' as ISO 9000. 'Techniques and systems don't accomplish anything by themselves,' he maintains. 'Management has to do that.'

Two other Japanese Big Ideas which were perfect examples of Taylorism refined in the workplace came out of the motor industry – specifically, out of the Toyota car company. These were ***lean production*** and its key component, ***just-in-time*** supply, or 'kanban', which eliminated the need for costly inventory. How these developed and the effect they had outside the industry for which they were designed are examined in the next two chapters, along with the extent to which durable management theories have originated in industry rather than in the business schools or consultancies. Indeed, even Western Electric's Hawthorne experiments of 1927–32, which established the humanist school of workplace relations, were started not out of altruistic psychological motives but as a way to bump up sales of lighting equipment and subsequent profits.

The Hawthorne plant in Chicago has gone down in history as a result of the Harvard psychologist Elton Mayo's discovery that productivity rose whether lighting intensity in the works was raised, lowered or remained the same. The difference, Mayo decided, could only be attributed to the workers feeling good about being consulted. But later research established that Mayo doctored the findings to fit his own theories about motivation, ignoring the conclusions of the company's own researchers that the opportunity to earn extra cash played a key part in the productivity surge.[3] And the 'Hawthorne Effect' was always more honoured by academics and management theorists than by production managers in the workplace. As Richard Donkin writes in his history of work, *Blood, Sweat and Tears*, 'Hawthorne had done enough to make a case for the human relations school of management, but would the evidence convince a sitting jury beyond reasonable doubt? Sadly, all these years after, the jury still appears to be out.'[4]

At the time, however, Mayo's work begat an influential family of motivation experts from university psychology departments, headed by Abraham Maslow, inventor of the **hierarchy of needs** theory, and Frederick Herzberg, who analysed the springs of working satisfaction and coined the term **job enrichment**. Maslow, a behavioural scientist from New York, devised a ranking order of needs in the shape of a pyramid rising from the basic physical requirements of food, warmth and shelter to aspirational ones of fulfilment and peer esteem. His key perception was that nothing is absolute – as soon as one 'need' is satisfied, the achievement loses its importance to the worker. Peter Drucker took the theory further to demonstrate that economic incentives become devalued because they are eventually taken for granted and are viewed as entitlements. But Maslow's single book, *Motivation and Personality* (1970), published in the year he died, remains a classic among HR professionals.

Herzberg, who was still working as a professor of management at the University of Utah well into his seventies, separated the concept of needs into 'hygiene' or 'maintenance' factors – those necessary for a reasonable standard of living, including salary and job security – and pure motivation factors – recognition, esteem, job satisfaction and a sense of achievement. The three most important elements, he discovered from a study of two hundred engineers and accountants in Pittsburgh, were responsibility, progress and personal growth or self-development, which he dubbed the 'Abraham factor' after the biblical patriarch. Jobs could be 'enriched' by designing Abraham factors, such as more accountability, into them, he reasoned. The concept has since flowered into **empowerment**, a doctrine identified with the Harvard guru Rosabeth Moss Kanter and her work analysing success factors in big corporations.

A common thread in all the motivational discoveries of the past half-century can be traced back to the thinking of Douglas McGregor, hugely influential in his day on a generation of management students (including Charles Handy and Warren Bennis) at the Massachusetts Institute of Technology (MIT), but largely ignored since his premature death in 1964. McGregor's **Theory X and Theory Y** of management styles contrasted command-and-control with self-management, and the belief that workers shied away from responsibility and had to be coerced in order to get anything done with the belief that people value and respond to being given responsibility. It reflected Taylorist versus humanist philosophy, and is still all too recognisable in companies and public-sector management today. Few businesses, even now, except in parts of the new economy, are run on true Theory Y lines of participative management and self-organising teams, although thirty years after McGregor's death it was revealed that he had designed a Theory Y detergent plant for Procter and Gamble in Atlanta in the 1950s, and that it had performed so spectacularly in productivity terms that the company kept it secret from the world for forty years.[5]

Apart from the enlightened P&G manager who commissioned McGregor, very few people in McGregor's lifetime agreed with his theories. Even Maslow, with whom he shared many beliefs about human needs, decided that Theory Y did not work adequately when it was briefly tried out in a California aerospace factory in the late 1940s. In Silicon Valley today, of course, every firm is run on the knowledge and enterprise of individuals, and semi-autonomous teams and cells are regarded as the best model of people management.

Leadership models – from battlefield to sports field

The world wars, particularly the second, exerted a powerful influence in shaping ideas about management and business leadership, which became identified in many ways with the analogy of the commander at the top taking his troops forward to victory. Many demobilised officers went into industrial management after 1945, reinforcing this image. In 1948 a keynote speaker at a conference of 1,200 British managers in Sheffield was Field Marshal Sir William Slim, victor in the Burma campaign against the Japanese, who argued that the principles of modern military leadership were an ideal model for industry. Until sporting analogies took over in the 1990s, along with the emphasis on team leadership and coaching, wartime heroes from Nelson to Montgomery remained a powerful influence on business leadership, not only in terms of setting strategy and leading by example, but in the loyalty they inspired in their followers. Even Warren Bennis, today's grand old man of leadership studies, was inspired to his life's work by his experiences as a 19-year-old US army lieutenant serving under a company commander who instilled in his men supreme confidence in their own abilities.

In fact, the top-down, structured command view of military leadership is more properly associated with a peacetime army than one in the stress and turbulence of war, which demands 'competent leadership at all levels', as the Harvard professor and leadership guru John P. Kotter wrote in 1990, adding: 'No one has yet figured out how to manage people effectively into battle; they must be *led*.'[6] Competent leadership at all levels is much more in tune with today's movement away from hierarchy and a belief in the power of project groups and teams. Interestingly, military practice is now tending to follow that of business rather than the other way round. The British army has moved towards developing cross-functional teams and a more flexible command structure as the nature of military operations has changed from shifting large masses of men and equipment (the key priority up to the Falklands and Gulf wars) to the deployment of rapid-response groups, as in Bosnia and Kosovo.

Leadership was not the only business application that came out of World War Two. Strategy and strategic planning were also born in a military cradle. Strategic studies carried out by the US army air force in the war were later adapted to business use by the Ford Motor Company under its then president Robert McNamara, who was to become Secretary of Defense in John F. Kennedy's administration in 1961. Business schools latched onto the subject after two Princeton academics, J. von Neumann and O. Morgenstern, published a paper in 1953 on the resolution of conflict in politics, war and business. In 1962, the Harvard economic historian Alfred D. Chandler published *Strategy and Structure,* a hugely influential study of major US companies and their development between 1850 and 1920, in which he argued the importance of setting the strategic direction for a firm before framing the structure of its organisation.

H. Igor Ansoff, a Russian-born mathematician who had worked in the post-war Rand Foundation analysing military problems, definitively established strategy as a business study with *Corporate Strategy* in 1965. He divided the subject into two concepts: pure strategy, the direction followed by a company in a particular area such as product development, and grand strategy, a statistical rule by which the firm could decide how to apply pure strategy in any given situation. Today, although Ansoff's body of work in the field entitles him to be called the gurus' guru of strategy, the starriest name is Harvard's Michael Porter, who took the subject into the marketplace in the 1980s. He identified the five forces driving competition in an industry; set out how firms could choose their competitive strategy in response, based on differentiation, cost or niche supremacy; and introduced the concept of the value chain within the organisation as a tool to control costs and enhance differentiation. The Internet, which effectively blows up the cost/niche/differentiation matrix by allowing businesses to pursue both low-cost and focused strategy, is now rewriting all the rules and may well result in many Big Ideas of the last fifty years becoming history.

Even before the Web captured the globe, the value of strategic planning had undergone several stages of critical scrutiny. Ansoff rewrote large chunks of *Corporate Strategy*, realising that many companies had attempted to use the tools too mechanistically. The Canadian management thinker Henry Mintzberg also cast a beady eye on the subject in *The Rise and Fall of Strategic Planning* (1994), which, like Ansoff's *Implanting Strategic Management* (1990), argued that each firm should use a flexible, adaptive approach to strategy according to its circumstances and environment, rather than trying a one-size-fits-all application. In 2000, 89% of US companies were still rating strategic planning as their top management technique, according to a survey by the consultancy Bain and Co. In Europe the top choice is apparently benchmarking, used by 77% of companies in 2000.[7]

Here today, gone tomorrow

When it comes to compiling a list of the really Big Ideas of the century, the fact that jumps out at you is how few they are in number and how even fewer have lasted, aside from *scientific management* in all its

variations, ***motivation theory*** and ***quality control***.
Strategy and strategic planning is not really an idea but
a business essential that probably didn't have a name
before the 1960s. Dozens of lesser theories had their few
months or years of fame and then faded. Who now talks
of Management By Objectives, or the Experience
Curve, or Time-Based Competition? It doesn't mean
they were bad ideas, and they have contributed to the
sum of management knowledge, but they did not
change the business world.

Learning from successful companies became a craze
with *In Search of Excellence* in 1982. Case studies continue
to form the core of most best-selling management books,
but look what happened to Peters's and Waterman's 43
excellent companies on which they based their eight key
principles: two-thirds lost their haloes within five years,
though Bob Waterman points out, fairly, that these were
stockmarket judgements, not necessarily reflecting the
underlying strengths of the business. Still, some of their
eight principles remain bible-strong – they were the first
to advise companies to be 'close to the customer' – even
if others, like 'stick to the knitting', are no longer so
useful.

But learning from 'best practice' doesn't really qualify
as a Big Idea. What else have we got? In recent years the
emphasis has been on a new approach to people
management that taps their knowledge and experience
of the business for the corporate good. The linked ideas
of knowledge management, intellectual capital and
the learning organisation are all intended to make
employees feel more valued. However, depending on
how they are applied, they could end up simply making
the employee feel more of an exploitable 'human
resource' than before, and even more disposable if he or
she has given up a precious store of expertise to some
central data system.

If the Big Idea is fading, it may well be as much due

to a cynicism among employees about management fads as to the new suck-it-and-see ways of managing associated with technology-based start-ups. ***Re-engineering*** was a classic example of a big, efficiency-based idea, a direct descendant of Taylor's stopwatch measurement that destroyed itself in practice by riding roughshod over human beings. Even at the height of its popularity on both sides of the Atlantic, re-engineering was failing in two-thirds of the companies where it was being applied – mainly, it must be said, as a cost-cutting instrument to cope with the recessions of the early 1990s.

Streamlining processes, cutting out wasteful hand-ons and reducing cycle times all had a useful part to play in change programmes designed to make the company leaner, fitter and more productive of its assets. More often than not, though, they resulted in an anorexic business that was unable to grow when the economic cycle turned favourable again. Many thousands of careers were laid waste in mass redundancies, much valuable knowledge was lost and bitterness sown. No wonder that, as yet another change programme was imposed by a new CEO, middle managers responded with the cynical mnemonic BOHICA – 'bend over, here it comes again'. The idea was to bend like a palm tree before the gale, springing back safely when it had passed, as every storm does.

If Big Ideas with some merit in them failed for lack of being thought through, did the blame lie only with the managements that bought them from consultancies or learned about them from gurus and seminars? In Chapter 2, we examine how, in the last half-century, management ideas have increasingly been manufactured and marketed like some Hollywood blockbuster. And, like Hollywood blockbusters, some have invariably turned out to be turkeys.

Powerpoints

- Scientific management or Taylorism became the biggest idea of twentieth-century business, laying the foundation for all performance-measurement tools and industrial techniques that rely on standardisation.
- Big Ideas can be fatally misunderstood and mis-applied, as happened with much of Taylorism and its latter-day spawn, business process re-engineering.
- The 'family tree' of scientific management includes time-and-motion study, work study, the assembly line, statistically controlled quality management, lean production, just-in-time and, of course, the notorious business process re-engineering.
- In reaction to Taylorism, a whole school of thought developed to study human motivation, opposing command-and-control 'Theory X' with participative 'Theory Y' and leading to empowerment and self-managed teams.
- Since World War Two, leadership models have moved from the military commander to the sports coach and mentor. Strategic planning, another military legacy, is having to be remade for an Internet world.
- Few Big Ideas have lasted more than a year or two, and faith in them is fading as a result of misapplied techniques like BPR, cynically used by many companies to justify recession lay-offs.

Notes

[1] Kanigel, Robert: *The One Best Way*, Wiley, 1996

[2] Wren, Daniel A. and Greenwood, Ronald G.: *Management Innovators: The People and Ideas That Have Shaped Modern Business*, Oxford University Press, 1998

[3] ibid.

[4] Donkin, Richard: *Blood, Sweat and Tears*, Texere, 2001

[5] Waterman, Robert H. Jr: *Frontiers of Excellence*, Nicholas Brealey, 1994

[6] Kotter, John P.: 'What Leaders Really Do', *Harvard Business Review*, May/June 1990

[7] Bain and Co., www.Bain.com

CHAPTER TWO

THE MAKING OF A BIG IDEA

Where do big management ideas germinate, and how do they become powerful movements within business? For two-thirds of the twentieth century, the biggest ideas were born in the minds of inventive engineers or statisticians like F.W. Taylor and W.E. Deming, trained observers of the human condition such as Abraham Maslow and Frederick Herzberg, or practical men on the shopfloors of industry, often working in anonymous teams. Some still emerge from the business professor's study – Gary Hamel, Charles Handy, Michael Porter, Richard Pascale and Rosabeth Moss Kanter have been responsible for some of the most important management concepts of the last decade – but since the 1960s consultancies have become prime forcing-houses for new theories, through which they can then attract clients and large revenue streams. Boston Consulting Group made its name with the experience curve and the famous Boston Matrix (dividing business units into cash cows, dogs, stars and question marks for the purpose of cash allocation among them), while McKinsey gave birth to Peters and Waterman and their excellence principles that launched the management guru boom in 1982.

Industry, particularly the motor industry, has been a rich source of new management ideas since 1913 – think of Henry Ford's engineering team developing the assembly line, Alfred Sloan spreading General Motors' decentralisation principle across industry, Toyota evolving lean production and just-in-time and General Electric under Jack Welch promoting its Work-Out system of problem-solving and innovation between shopfloor and management, not to mention Six Sigma quality management, which GE borrowed from Motorola and buffed up into a whole corporate culture – yet the boundaries between academics, consultants and practitioners have never been fixed or simple. The last twenty years have seen an increasingly insidious movement of key thinkers between the three areas.

Take Andy Grove, for example. Grove's concept of the 'strategic inflection point' – a watershed development in the history of any organisation which, if not understood and acted upon, will lead to that organisation's irreversible decline – is generally associated with his business role as former CEO and now president of Intel Corporation. Yet the thinking behind it, and his best-selling book, *Only the Paranoid Survive*, owes as much or more to his underlying academic links as visiting professor of strategic studies at Stanford University, where he leads a major teaching programme.[1]

Arie de Geus, a currently fashionable thinker on the subject of the corporation as living organism, is still pigeon-holed as a practitioner because of his long career as head of planning at Shell, where he pioneered scenario techniques. But his most valuable work in the field has taken place in an academic context at London Business School, both before and after he formally left Shell.

Richard Pascale, Gary Hamel and Charles Handy – originators of such key ideas as challenging complacency in successful organisations, identifying core competencies and the 'shamrock organisation' that foreshadowed the whole outsourcing boom – achieved their most prominent success as independent consultants, packaging and selling those ideas to client companies through their own professional channels, and in the lucrative field of conferences and best-selling books. Yet their roots lie in academic work for leading business schools, and in many cases, such as Hamel with London Business School, they are still connected to their former parent institution. Even the legendary Bruce Henderson, founder of the ultimate ideas consultancy Boston Consulting Group (BCG), had his perspective shaped by a stint at Harvard Business School before he joined Westinghouse and later Arthur D. Little, the engineering-based consultancy, from which he split to form BCG in 1964.

In similar fashion, the research projects that lead to Big Ideas can originate with individuals from all three backgrounds. The project that led to the first business blockbuster, *In Search of Excellence,* was the result of a substantial investment by McKinsey and Co. After decades of unchallenged success, McKinsey faced serious competition for the first time in the 1970s with the growth of Boston Consulting Group. McKinsey identified the key battleground as that of ideas and new concepts, launching a number of research projects of which the excellence programme was just one. Peters and Waterman, then senior McKinsey consultants, may have led the research and profited hugely from the success of their book, but they also enlisted the support and research of Stanford's Richard Pascale and Harvard's Anthony Athos. Pascale's comparative research into US and Japanese companies in the 1970s, which produced a seminal book called *The Art of Japanese Management,* had already resulted in the famous McKinsey 'Seven-S' framework, dividing management skills into 'hard' and 'soft' categories (structure, strategy and systems; staff, skills, style and shared values). Both

Peters and Waterman were on the team that developed the concept and they made it a centrepiece of their own book.

In an almost exact mirror image of this germination pattern, business process re-engineering – the ultimate consultancy-led concept of the 1990s – first started to coalesce at the Massachusetts Institute of Technology in a programme of research into 'management in the 1990s', which ran from 1983 to 1987. Its primary study was the impact that information technology was likely to have on organisations and managers in the coming decade. Techniques for organisational change that the programme examined included tools for determining added value and non-added value in business processes, benchmarking and process cycle time reduction. Many of these tools had originated with a work study engineer at ICI in the 1950s called Currie, but their wider value had been overlooked by being lumped together under the work study or time and motion label.

Two consultants at Computer Management Group, Geoff Elliott and Robin Holland, later perceived the similarity of techniques used in business process redesign, total quality management, change management and organisational development. 'All four approaches to change are supported by the same tools and techniques, for example, process modelling, work flow analysis, competency modelling, failure mode analysis, etc.,' they wrote. 'There are 100 or so creative problem-solving techniques which are constantly being used to underpin and support change within all four of the approaches.' Elliott and Holland went on to suggest that a single framework for change was emerging from all these disciplines, and the MIT programme, known as MIT90s, began to sketch out that framework.

Among its so-called 'jewels' were 'the importance of a deep understanding of business processes by management' and 'successful organisations and transformations depend on leadership, sharing of management's vision, and effective human resource management practices'. (The latter was to be notably ignored in the practice of re-engineering.) There were five levels of 'IT-induced transformation' to what MIT termed, for the first time, 'business process re-engineering'. These involved business network redesign, business processes and value process models, and, again, 'leadership and human resource management issues', which were conveniently overlooked. Central precepts were 'processes are organisational assets and must be treated as assets' and 'rethink the core of the business'.[2]

Among the research participants was an MIT mathematician called Michael Hammer. A few years later, in 1990, he pulled the concept out of the academic papers, wrote it up using the sort of hard-hitting language a business readership would respond to and published a seminal article in *Harvard Business Review* called 'Re-Engineering Work: Don't Automate, Obliterate'.[3] The quasi-industrial term caught on and a small IT-based consultancy called CSC Index saw an opportunity to capitalise on the idea. Its CEO, James Champy, joined Hammer in writing the book that founded the consultancy boom of the early 1990s, *Re-Engineering the Corporation*. It sold over a million copies in the English language alone, and in worldwide terms may well have outstripped *In Search of Excellence* as the best-selling management book of the century. Hammer, whose aggressive lecture style echoed his name, was soon a mini-celebrity on the conference circuit. (A typical saying of his was: 'We're not talking about cutting the fat from an organisation. We're talking about grinding it up and frying it out.')

Both the excellence and BPR stories illustrate how the origins of any business idea become woven into a net that spans academic research, consultancy perspective and practitioner experience. Most projects that spawn these ideas, however, go through a series of common stages where they are 'manufactured' for consumption by the business customer. It is worth exploring each of these stages in turn.

Stage one: the research

The first determinant is the sponsor. In an age when state sponsorship for research is in sharp decline on both sides of the Atlantic, most big research projects are sponsored by a consortium of employers or under-pinned by consultancy funds, and the choice of case studies and thrust of the research will be heavily influenced by this. Leanness as a management concept, for example, originated with the publication in 1990 of another piece of MIT research conducted in the late 1980s by a team led by James Womack. It emerged into the bright light of day as a book called *The Machine That Changed the World*, which soon became something of an industrial bible. Conducted over five years, the research was undertaken by an international academic team, each of whose members had an employment background in industry. It compared the production methods of the Japanese automotive industry, led by Toyota which was experimenting with just-in-time concepts, to the mass-production methods used by Western car companies since the days of Henry Ford at River Rouge.

The research team was funded by a $5m grant raised by a consortium of 36 car companies, each of which was allowed to contribute no more than 5% of the total funding. The team studied 90 auto assembly plants in 15 countries and in 1989 found that it took on average more than twice as many man-hours to produce a car in a European-owned plant in western Europe than in a Japanese-owned plant in Japan. Womack's researchers also found that Japanese-owned plants located in North

America took 25% longer to produce a car, and American-owned plants in North America took 50% longer. Furthermore, they found that cars produced in European-owned plants in Europe in 1989 had, on average, 50% more defects, as reported by owners in the first three months of use, than cars manufactured in Japan.

'Lean production' was the term coined by Womack's team for the production system used in Japanese-owned car plants. The researchers identified four key characteristics:

- eliminating all unnecessary production processes;
- aligning all steps in each process into a continuous flow;
- realigning workers into cross-functional teams dedicated to a specific process;
- continually striving for improvement.

Their main finding, however, quickly latched onto by employers across all sectors of industry, was that under this system fewer employees were needed to get the same number of cars to customers.[4]

Stage two: the message

If the basic methodology of the research comes from the team as a whole, the twist that 'brands' it for the business marketplace – in this case, the analogy of leanness – comes primarily from the perspective of the individual or individuals leading the research. It is here, in theory, that the difference between practitioners, academics and consultants should be most pronounced, but it doesn't necessarily happen that way. UK consultants Michel Syrett and Jean Lammiman, in their research for Roffey Park Management Institute on how ideas take shape within organisations, found that in developing 'high' management concepts, senior managers in industry were heavily influenced by the subject of their first degree or professional qualification. It was their ability to use this perspective to make previously unrelated connections or analogies with the challenges facing their business that was the source of their creativity.

The chairman of Mazda UK, for example, chose a metaphor from his studies as a biochemist when explaining how he turned round the company in the early 1990s with a programme of slow adaptation rather than sudden change. He likened the process to that of melting ice – the frozen state of the organisation – by gently heating it over a low Bunsen burner flame. 'You cannot use a powerful flame because then the liquid will evaporate. Once I had created a new set of structures through kaizen ['continuous improvement'], ISO9000 and investment in people, then I refroze the organisation into its new format, only to warm it up again when the occasion demanded.'[5]

The same springs of creativity apply to Big Ideas produced by business academics. Rosabeth Moss Kanter, the main champion of empowerment as a Big Idea, was an associate professor of sociology at Brandeis University before she moved to Harvard in 1973. Her first book, *Men and Women of the Corporation*, was primarily a social study rather than a management guide, and won an award for the best US book on social issues. The research behind her later best-sellers, *The Change Masters* and *When Giants Learn to Dance*, was also focused principally on social issues: the establishment of equal opportunities and diversity and resistance to change. Empowerment as a management concept was developed from this perspective.

The recent theory of 'spiritual intelligence' developed in lectures and books by the US-born psychologist Danah Zohar, now working in the UK, takes quantum physics as its starting-point and is based almost wholly on a perspective Zohar acquired while studying physics and philosophy at MIT, and from her postgraduate work at Harvard in philosophy, religion and psychology. Around the same time, elsewhere in the Harvard warren, a young anthropologist called Karen Stephenson, inspired by the work of her famous predecessor Margaret Mead, wanted to take an anthropologist's view of the intellectual and emotional circuits underlying interrelationships in commercial organisations. She termed it the hard wiring behind the soft assets of human or knowledge capital. 'I wanted to extend the social anthropological work Margaret Mead had undertaken with primitive tribes in Papua New Guinea to corporations, and when the disbelieving scientific department at Harvard asked why on earth I would want to do that, I replied that in many ways the executive working for a large corporation is as exotic a creature to study as the member of a primitive tribe.'[6]

Her colleagues remained baffled and cynical about the project, but a decade on, Stephenson's vision has been vindicated. Now working at UCLA and at the Theseus Institute, a business school located in Sophia Antipos technology park in the south of France, she has turned a study of primates into a new analysis of corporate networking.

Drawing on a seam of research into the natural sciences increasingly being mined by business writers (see Chapter 5), she argues that social practices such as grooming, used to maintain group cohesion among chimpanzees, gibbons and other pack animals, are mirrored by those practised by employees in large organisations. The human equivalent of grooming includes activities such as gossip, small talk and playing games. Whether these take place in a commercial organisation or a personal social circle, they are as important to a group's cohesion as grooming is to the animal pack, Stephenson contends. Furthermore, the size of the animal pack seems to be related, among other things, to its collective memory capacity, which in turn is prompted by the ability to remember who reciprocated in the grooming process. Among humans, Stephenson has concluded that there appears to be a limit to the number of simultaneous memory links the brain can handle, and this in turn determines the optimum size of an effective team or work unit.

Stage three: the testing ground

Once the angle, concept or basic premise of the Big Idea has been defined, it is usually shaped and tested on the ground using a variety of collective methods.

Karen Stephenson refined her theories about grooming into a usable and practical business tool by working in close collaboration with the IBM Advanced Business Unit to observe how networks control the daily life of corporations. Using staff at IBM as the basis for a pilot study that was subsequently validated in other commercial organisations, she found that certain key individuals in these networks, through conversing in corridors and at the water cooler or coffee machine, play a critical role in downsizing, succession and mergers, effectively deciding who stays and who goes. Particularly important are the gatekeepers, managers who link the various parts of the business together through a small number of critical relationships; also the pulse-takers, managers whose cross-functional responsibilities allow them to know what everyone in the organisation is thinking or feeling. The work Stephenson conducted with IBM also provided her with the technological support to pilot and develop Netform, a software tool which enables organisations to trace the unseen relationships that lie behind an effective business. This has given her a platform from which to launch, like most successful gurus, her own independent consultancy business.[7]

Other academics use the sounding-board potential available to them as participants in open or in-company programmes run by their school. At London Business School, Lynda Gratton's 'glocal' concepts for managing human resources in global corporations, blending local and central strategies, were shaped in collaboration with members of a global business consortium programme that included Standard Chartered Bank, British Telecom and Lufthansa, and which Gratton ran in the late 1990s. Alden Lank, a professor at IMD, the international business school based in Lausanne, Switzerland, shaped his ideas about corporate governance in family-owned enterprises almost entirely out of a popular IMD programme called Leading the Family Business.[8]

There are also the MBA courses. They may not always admit it, but nearly all academic gurus test their theories in the MBA classroom before going into print with them. An indication of how important this is to both teacher and student came out of a recent survey of 1,200 alumni conducted by the Cranfield School of Management, a premier UK business school. Most alumni felt that conventional executive courses at the school failed to reproduce the 'cutting edge learning that they experienced while studying for the MBA'. They did not see these sessions as a one-way learning process. As Cranfield's Caroline Buller explains, 'Their model of learning is based on the MBA brainstorm in which they contribute to the theories being expounded. They do not want well-polished presentations based on well-polished theories. They want the professor to explore dangerous territory and ideas on the cutting edge, where they can make their own contributions to emerging concepts and be present while they emerge.'[9]

An indication of how systematic this process of in-school testing is becoming is that major schools are launching 'centres' based on key issues that bridge

research, teaching and consultancy. A good example is
the Foundation for Entrepreneurial Management, set
up in 1998 by Michael Hay at London Business School.
Its three divisions co-ordinate research and publishing,
teaching and materials development, and business
practice initiatives that test and disseminate the conclusions among LBS's corporate sponsors. A by-product
of its work is the Innovation Exchange, a forum for
companies to share ideas with LBS staff, supported by a
library, relevant articles and books, research, a quarterly
newsletter and an interactive Web site. It was launched
with a heavyweight champion in Sir Anthony Greener,
then chairman of Diageo, and by 1999 could boast 150
members.[10]

Consultancies have also long used their client companies as testbeds, particularly in the case of Big Ideas
that went on to make a difference to business. The first
breakthrough for the fledgling Boston Consulting
Group was the discovery – taken for granted today, but
revolutionary in its time – that a manufacturer and its
workforce become more productive as they gain experience. BCG's founder Bruce Henderson first gained this
insight from studying how manufacturing plants calcu-
lated bids for client contracts. The study was undertaken
for a client that had been with BCG from its inception.
Henderson then tested out the idea with a larger client
with multiple plants – Texas Instruments, an electronics
firm that hired BCG in the late 1960s to analyse its production costs. BCG's consultants plotted costs against
production experience and discovered that Texas
Instruments' costs fell consistently in line with its semi-
conductor division gaining experience. Every time TI
doubled its production experience with a particular
component, its costs fell on average by around 20%. Out
of these studies, very similar to the kind of work Karen
Stephenson has done with IBM, came the famed 'experience curve' model that first put BCG on the map.[11]

As pressure has grown on consultancies to produce a steady stream of bankable ideas to keep them competitive, the process of germinating, shaping and testing has become more internally confined and less based on practical research in the marketplace. Gemini has established a 'thinking room' in its Morristown, New Jersey headquarters where consultants sit in isolation booths with headphones on, thinking deep thoughts. Andersen Consulting, before it metamorphosed into Accenture, set up a 'thought leadership' centre near its technology base in Palo Alto, Silicon Valley. McKinsey is sifting the results of a series of research programmes on such subjects as growth, globalisation and the future shape of companies. Many consultancies have appointed knowledge officers to ensure that corporate learning circulates freely within the firm; many more, such as Accenture, have for some time been using computerised intranets that allow their consultants to tap into the organisation's collective wisdom from wherever they might be in the world.

Smaller companies are trying to compete by carving out special areas for the development of new ideas. Bain, for example, is concentrating on loyalty and leadership. But the danger for smaller consultancies is that if one of their ideas becomes big enough, it will be captured and branded by the giants with their massive resources. This happened to CSC Index with re-engineering: Andersen Consulting (as it then was), McKinsey and Gemini all invested heavily in their own versions and swamped CSC, despite the fact that its CEO, James Champy, was the founding guru of the subject with Mike Hammer.[12]

Stage four: launch and roll-out

The methods by which ideas originate and are tested may differ in academia, industry and consultancies, but where the guru business is involved, the process of

launch and roll-out is as standardised as the method of
assembling a Big Mac or getting a new feature film out
to the nation's cinemas. In fact, the process is not unlike
that of launching a Hollywood blockbuster, which
follows a predetermined path of distribution, marketing,
trailering, advertising, reviewing and premiering. The
big business idea goes through seven similar stages:

- The article in *Harvard Business Review*, the essential
  shop-window for every new management idea,
  leading to
- the book (and video, Web site and CD-Rom), leading
  to
- keynote addresses on the international conference
  circuit, including perhaps an appearance at the
  prestigious Davos World Economic Forum in
  Switzerland, leading to
- boardroom sessions with key corporate clients or
  sponsors, leading to
- in-company consultancy work, leading to
- an independent business and more research, leading
  to
- the sequel (publishers and booksellers lean on gurus to
  produce a book at regular intervals, and as Tom
  Peters has proved, it doesn't even have to support
  your previous theories).

All this to be repeated over the same cycle – two to three
times is the most that all but world-class gurus with a
strong research staff can manage.

Of these stages, the article in *Harvard Business Review* is
the sought-after gateway to success. Every publisher,
every international conference organiser, every major
consultant and a sizeable majority of corporate leaders
reads or at least flicks through *HBR* to see what's new
and who's in it. Sales of the journal's reprints reflect
some of the biggest management ideas of the century:

Theodore Levitt's 'Marketing Myopia' (1960), Frederick Herzberg's 'One More Time: How Do You Motivate Employees?' (1968), Michael Hammer's 'Re-Engineering Work: Don't Automate, Obliterate' (1990) and Gary Hamel and C.K. Prahalad's 'Competing for the Future' (1994), which introduced the theory of core competencies, were all record reprint sellers in their day, the last two going on to best-sellerdom as books. W. Chan Kim and Renée Mauborgne from the French business school INSEAD, originators of two recent concepts known as value-based innovation and fair process, were unknowns until a pair of articles in *HBR* in 1997 catapulted them onto the lower rungs of gurudom, although they have yet to produce a high-concept management book, the stage in the process that really launches both idea and originator into business orbit and a highly lucrative second career as conference speaker. (The top gurus can now command six-figure dollar sums for a high-profile conference, and have been known to demand Concorde tickets as well, adding thousands more to the cost of their pearls of wisdom.)

By this stage, of course, the ideas that had been at the cutting edge of new thinking a year before are fast becoming business orthodoxy. But it is now that corporate clients fall over themselves to buy the ideas, and when gurus and consultancies begin to get their real payback. As a result of their work on core competencies, competition and innovation, for example, Hamel and Prahalad wield an influence and a client list to make even the McKinseys of this world take notice. By the mid-1990s, Prahalad's corporate clients included names of the calibre of Eastman-Kodak, AT&T, Honeywell, Philips, Colgate-Palmolive, Motorola and Whirlpool. Hamel's list also featured Motorola along with Rockwell, Alcoa, Nokia, Ford and Dow Chemical. His recent work on innovation has brought him the custom of Royal Dutch/Shell – also a client of ex-Stanford professor Richard Pascale, now cultivating the field of 'living systems' and ecological analogies for business. Sometimes you wonder how a company like Shell has time to explore for oil, it's so busy with various gurus' workshops and entrepreneurial ventures, all of which become case-study grist for the gurus' next big books.

Who gains most from this two-way exchange is a moot question. Organisations have always fought shy of quantifying how or what they gain from bringing in top-dollar gurus to reinvent themselves. There is no doubt, however, that working with leading-name organisations enables the gurus to regenerate and revivify their own ideas in the marketplace.

Pascale based much of his research into corporate regeneration in the late 1990s on work he conducted in the wake of his 'S-curve' theories with large, well-established organisations such as Shell, Sears and the US army. 'As a researcher it might seem easier to look at the kind of organisation that might appear in fashionable books on business excellence,' he told a European management conference in 1997. 'Our purpose in looking at these three organisations over a long period of time – these particular organisations have very good data on themselves stretching over decades – is that you are looking at them both during times of ascendancy and in times of decline. You are better able, in these circumstances, to identify the changes that really count.'[13]

Indeed, the tendency for the top academic gurus to set up on their own rather than rely on either their school or a consultancy to package and market their ideas has been the defining characteristic of the last decade in this area. Schools have gone along with it, buying back their former top stars with offers of visiting professorships and chairs because access to these stars is one of the major reasons companies work with business schools rather than with consultancies. George

Rabstejnek, president of Harbridge House, a consultancy founded by former teachers on Harvard executive education courses, made the point in 1992: 'We are far better equipped to handle the process of analysing companies' needs, but we cannot compete with the brand image of schools like Harvard and Stanford, and that image is nearly always linked to the reputation of the faculty.'[14] Fear over loss of faculty brand image is a major issue for the new 'virtual' business schools like Cardean. What happens when it is not a case of exclusive access to Gary Hamel in a live class, but rather that he or any other big academic name is on tap across the globe at the click of a mouse?

Maintaining this brand image is what prompts schools to put up with a situation in which they have little or no control over what their top professors do, even if they wind up successfully competing with their own in-house staff. Sustaining a steady stream of new ideas is what gives business schools the edge over consultancy firms, but the link between them and the originators of those ideas grows more tenuous with each passing year. As the director of the UK's Cranfield School of Management observed at a conference in 1998, 'The best schools are just as likely to be competing with McKinsey and Andersen in the next decade as they are with themselves – and while these companies have not come up with as many ground-breaking ideas as we have, they certainly have much more command and control over their intellectual capital.'[15]

Stage five: transferability and sustainability

The way gurus rely on big corporate clients for financial leverage and the mining of material for their next Big Idea raises two questions that are the acid test of a Big Idea in the long term: is it transferable and is it sustainable?

There is no doubt, for example, that lean production methods, as outlined by Womack and his team in *The Machine That Changed the World*, revolutionised car manufacturing in the early 1990s. Among the many Western companies that benefited from adopting Toyota's lean techniques were Chrysler, BMW, Volvo and Ford. Where leanness began to fall from grace was when it started to be applied outside the auto industry. As Christian Berggen, a Swedish expert in work organisation, argued in 1993, 'The sweeping assertions of Womack, Jones and Roos are based on their belief that car manufacturing still is the premier industry, just as it was in the early 1960s; and that methods to promote productivity in the auto industry will of necessity do the same in other sectors. This view is certainly open to discussion. What, for example, do capital-intensive sectors like the petrochemical or paper-making industries, or research-intensive sectors like pharmaceuticals, have to learn from the almost obsessive focus on hours per unit produced, so evident in the *Machine* book?'

The reputation of Womack's theories was not helped by the fact that Western economies went into a dramatic decline within a year of his book being published, and 'leanness' along with re-engineering was grasped at by senior managers eager to give themselves intellectual respectability for the purely cost-driven decision to downsize their workforces. Nor did it help that Rosabeth Moss Kanter, in a parallel but separate study, promoted leanness as part of her analogy of business competition as the 'corporate Olympics'. In her reading, leanness was synonymous with fitness, but this was using the term in a way Womack never intended.

The truth is that Womack, while (perhaps unwisely) happy for his theories to receive a mass circulation outside the car industry, never intended them as justification for downsizing. Indeed, he argued, though perhaps too late, against excessive staff cuts on the grounds that such a policy runs in flat contradiction to the 'kaizen' (continuous improvement) philosophy on which lean production is founded. Responding in 1996 to widespread criticism of the way leanness was being applied, he retorted: 'Because lean methods are much more efficient, fewer employees are needed to get the same number of products to customers. Management has two fundamental choices at this point: lay off workers or find new work by speeding up product development and finding new markets. The second choice is clearly the correct one because otherwise management is asking employees to co-operate in the task of eliminating their livelihoods.'[16]

At about the time that leanness was entering its early stage of disillusion and decline as a Big Idea, two university professors – one American, the other from New Zealand – were casting doubt on one of the apparently most durable ideas ever developed by a management consultancy, the Boston Matrix.

Over a period of five years, Professors J. Scott Armstrong and Roderick Brodie tested 1,015 students from management schools around the world, nearly half of them MBAs with at least two years' business experience under their belts, by asking them to make a hypothetical investment decision based on the system of rating businesses as stars, dogs, cash cows or question marks. The students were asked to select one of two different companies as investment opportunities – one firm that was profitable and the other not, although this was not immediately evident. The professors deliberately labelled the profitable firm a 'dog' and the unprofitable one a 'star'. Up to 87% of the students chose the unprofitable company labelled 'star'. Armstrong and Brodie concluded that 'the BCG matrix interferes with profit maximising' because it was too often adopted unquestioningly, leading to distortion of business judgement by companies which tended to use it simply as a validation of their predetermined strategies.[17] The British academic Andrew Campbell, of Ashridge School of Strategic Management, has gone further and damned the Boston Matrix as 'the most damaging concept managers have been sold in the last 25 years'.[18]

More recently, some scepticism has been expressed about the fashionable use of the physical sciences to provide management analogies, such as the links drawn by Karen Stephenson between pack animals and social behaviour in the workplace, the parallels suggested by Danah Zohar between management decision-making and quantum physics, and the much larger canvas painted by Richard Pascale in which complex adaptive systems as observed in the natural universe are applied to corporate performance. The assumption behind all such scientific parallels is that research into the physical sciences is an absolute touchstone for other disciplines. But the distinguished scientist Richard Dawkins argued forcefully in the *Harvard Business Review* early in 2001 that while different fields might offer fruitful insights into business, the value of a non-business discipline could only provide a framework for thinking about old problems in new ways, not a practical model.

Dawkins, professor of the public understanding of science at Oxford University, counselled managers to think for themselves and cautioned them against picking up evolutionary ideas 'in a simple way'. Hardly any of the research on alpha male primates was relevant to humans, he argued. He also challenged the fashionable analogies between corporate strategy and nature's way of adapting to the environment. 'Natural selection, you see, does not anticipate the future. It has produced beautiful, elegantly "designed" organisms that fly and swim and do all sorts of terrific things. But it remains in essence a response to a current environment. By contrast, humans are accustomed to planning ahead. A company, for example, puts up with five years of loss because it is gambling on getting a new share of the market in five years' time. Nature never does that. Natural selection is totally blind to the future.'[19]

Transferability, whether from one industry to another or one academic discipline to another, is, of course, closely linked to sustainability. The re-engineering boom of the early and mid-1990s briefly transformed CSC Index, a smallish and previously little-known consultancy, into the hottest firm in the business. The consultancy's own survey figures suggested that within a year of the publication of the book its founder James Champy co-wrote with Michael Hammer, *Re-engineering the Corporation*, 69% of US companies and 75% of European companies had undertaken re-engineering projects. Another survey by Price Waterhouse found that 70% of Fortune 500 companies and 68% of UK companies had adopted the technique. The revenues of CSC Index doubled as a result.

But as described elsewhere in this book, BPR as an implementable strategy proved short-lived. Widely criticised for its failure to address the human cost of an entirely process-oriented redesign of operations management, re-engineering was soon being re-engineered itself by both Champy and Hammer in sequels to their original work. Hammer founded his own consultancy and Champy left CSC Index for Perot Systems, an EDS subsidiary. Their reputations survived, and Hammer still thrives on his 1990s status, but the idea in its original form had died within five years of its launch as opinion turned against it and growth and innovation replaced 'rationalisation' as the key board-room concern. Hamel and Prahalad, in their 1994 book *Competing for the Future*, coined the term 'corporate anorexia' to describe the state many companies were left in after the bean-counters had driven downsizing to extremes, often under the cloak of re-engineering.

The fall of BPR is not only an illustration of the ever-shortening life expectancy of big business ideas, but of the vulnerability of niche consultancies if they cannot produce a steady stream of ideas. CSC Index was trodden underfoot by Andersen Consulting and other giant firms that seized upon BPR and branded various versions as their own, backing them with multi-million-dollar budgets. Having lost control of its one Big Idea, CSC was then seriously damaged by the revelation of a scam by two of its consultants to hype a book on market leadership (itself a revamped version of a Michael Porter theory) up the *New York Times* best-seller list by bulk-buying it themselves. In the late 1990s the consultancy was folded into its parent, Computer Sciences Corporation, and no longer exists independently.

Bigger consultancies are less vulnerable because they rely primarily on implementing second-hand ideas more effectively than their true progenitors – the business schools and independent gurus – would on their own. The Peters–Waterman project at McKinsey and the Hammer–Champy link-up at CSC Index are exceptional in their ability to generate and disseminate original ideas to match those produced by guru partnerships like Hamel and Prahalad or Kim and Mauborgne. Also, business schools make sure they groom successors for gurus who leave to set up on their own, whereas consultancies can be left vulnerable when their stars quit. When EDS decided to review its future in the late 1980s, it brought in Gary Hamel, the king of core competence strategy, to ask what made the company unique and where it should be heading.

Europe vs North America: a big divide on Big Ideas

The Big Idea as a bankable management resource is essentially a North American invention, and Europe and North America differ fundamentally in the way that management ideas are propagated and applied. European gurus such as Charles Handy, John Adair and Meredith Belbin, even those from the business schools like Manfred Kets de Vries from INSEAD, are less devoted to selling and rolling out their concepts, or to reshaping or transforming them every half-decade. Handy, in particular, in his recent string of books (*The Age of Reason, The Empty Raincoat, The Hungry Spirit*) has tended to develop his ideas away from business towards a more contemplative, social interpretation. Adair's model of business leadership and Belbin's framework for building teams composed of different roles have remained little changed in two decades and are still being applied by companies long after such fads as BPR and 'leanness' have been dropped.

The difference is partly because there is a higher proportion of independent business schools in Europe, i.e. not tied to any one country's university system. But even among those schools that are either based on the North American university model or which aspire to the guru-led culture which emerges from it, there is a tendency to play down the 'branded' Big Idea in favour of less dramatic but easy-to-implement concepts. As INSEAD's Arnaud de Meyer commented while he was dean of executive education at the French school, 'European schools do not emulate the philosophy that every five to eight years you need a quantum leap in thinking. Much of the research we conduct is undertaken with corporate partners with whom we have worked for years, if not decades. The concepts that emerge are less dramatic, more applied and implemented on a drip-fed basis rather than being rolled out in a dramatic splash.'[20]

Not that this means there is any less tendency for leading members of European faculties to cash in on independent consultancy work. If anything, the scrabble for consultancy has been greater in Europe because cash-strapped schools have been obliged to license such activity in an attempt to provide levels of reward that compete with those on offer in North America. But the consulting work undertaken by European academics is less about single ideas developed by the individual and more linked to an overall education framework promoted by their parent school. Peter Lorange, president of the industry-sponsored IMD in Lausanne, has stressed the need for a difference between the two approaches. 'Schools will need to follow a consulting firm's way of operating,' he commented in 1997. 'But while consulting firms have also performed high-quality research on critical issues, and while their *raison d'être* is often to help bridge the gap between strategic priorities and specific behaviours, the distinctive competence of business schools should be in engineering executive learning.'[21]

Not only are the boundaries between consultancy and academia becoming blurred, it is also happening between consultancy and industry, where companies themselves originate ideas capable of being propagated elsewhere. A company that comes up with a new management concept may spin off consultancy activities along with its other business-to-business services. The supreme example of this, and of an idea that has proved truly transferable across businesses as different as turbines and credit card management, can be found within the world's biggest and most restlessly inventive conglomerate – General Electric.

Powerpoints
- Most Big Ideas in recent years have come out of a mixture of academic, consultancy and practitioner research. They tend to be 'manufactured' for business consumption in five distinct stages.
- What determines the life and success of a Big Idea is

whether it can transfer across industrial borders and be adapted to changing environments.

- The current craze for drawing business lessons from non-business disciplines such as the natural sciences is only useful as a new way of thinking about business issues, not to be taken too far. 'Natural selection is totally blind to the future,' says Professor Richard Dawkins.
- Sustainability failed in the case of BPR because too many companies applied it to mask savage downsizing in the wake of recession, losing trust and credibility among their workforces.
- The Big Idea is a North American phenomenon; European business schools are geared to a more incremental approach, less so to marketing their theories commercially.

NOTES

[1] Grove, Andy: *Only the Paranoid Survive*, HarperCollins Business, 1997

[2] Author information from Hugh MacDonald

[3] *Harvard Business Review*, July/August 1990

[4] Womack, James: *The Machine That Changed the World*, Rawson Associates, 1995

[5] Lammiman, J. and Syrett, M.: *Innovation at the Top – Where Do Directors Get Their Ideas From?*, Roffey Park Management Institute, 1998

[6] Syrett, M. and Lammiman, J.: *Management Development: Making the Investment Count*, Economist Books, 1999

[7] ibid.

[8] ibid.

[9] Syrett, M. and Lammiman, J.: *MBA*, Vol. 1, No. 4, March 1998

[10] Syrett and Lammiman: *Management Development*

[11] O'Shea, James and Madigan, Charles: *Dangerous Company*, Nicholas Brealey, 1997

[12] *The Economist*, 'Trimming the Fat: a Survey of Management Consultancy', 22.3.97

[13] Pascale, Richard: 'Effective Management Development: Linking People, Processes and Performance', European Federation for Management Development (efmd), Prague, 14–16 June 1997

[14] Syrett and Lammiman: *Management Development: making the investment count*, Economist Books, 1999

[15] ibid.

[16] Womack, J.: 'The psychology of lean production', *Applied Psychology*, an International Review, 1996

[17] O'Shea and Madigan: *Dangerous Company*

[18] Jackson, Tony: 'Today's insight, tomorrow's fad', *FT*, 25.6.98

[19] Dawkins, Richard: 'What is Science Good for?', *Harvard Business Review*, January 2001

[20] Syrett and Lammiman: *Management Development*

[21] ibid.

CHAPTER THREE

WHEN NECESSITY BREEDS IDEAS

In 1988, Jack Welch was far from being the icon of industry, the world's most admired manager that he became ten years later. As a result of the restructuring of General Electric, a sprawling though profitable octopus of businesses associated principally with lighting and household appliances, to meet the criteria he had imposed on assuming the chief executive's chair in 1981 – be number one or number two in your business worldwide; fix it or close it – thousands of GE employees had been laid off and Welch had acquired the unwelcome nickname 'Neutron Jack', after the neutron bomb, which killed people but left buildings standing.

One September afternoon in 1988 at Crotonville, the company's centre for management development where the CEO could stand in an arena known as 'the Pit' and be challenged by his managers, Welch was bombarded with questions that should have been answered much lower down the management chain. People were being driven to do more with less for reasons they did not fully understand, and bureaucracy still reigned in many processes. When they complained, their managers blamed head office at Fairfield, Connecticut.

Leaving the Pit that day with Jim Baughman, the executive director in charge of Crotonville, Welch was in an angry mood, ready to bang heads together. Why weren't the GE managers sorting out problems and getting the new slimmed-down culture to work better? Why weren't the different levels of management talking to each other – or to the frontline worker? He told Baughman: 'We've got to change this. We've got to put the person who knows the answers to these frustrations in the front of the room. We've got to force leaders who aren't walking the talk to face up to their people.'

Baughman, a Harvard Business School alumnus, went away and designed, to Welch's specifications, a new kind of internal accountability and two-way communication between workforce and management that became known as Work-Out. The name was chosen to symbolise both the solving of problems and the transformation into a fitter organisation. Essentially it was an extension of the Crotonville principle – the CEO answerable in person to his senior staff – all the way through the organisation. A Harvard Business School professor who worked for GE as a consultant called it 'one of the biggest planned efforts to alter people's behaviour since Mao's Cultural Revolution'.[1]

Solving problems at the coal-face

Work-Out began in October 1988 with a series of New England-style 'town meetings' where the employees of a particular business, in groups numbering between thirty and a hundred, would spend three days offsite, in casual dress, discussing common problems and using their experience to propose solutions. Managers were kept out of these discussions until the third day, when they re-entered the conference room to hear the conclusions. They then had to make on-the-spot decisions on each proposal in front of the workforce. Any that needed further study had to receive an answer within one month.

The underlying aim of Work-Out was to shorten the

time and improve the quality of decision-making and to enhance GE's responsiveness to customers by using not only the collective intelligence of management but that of the entire company. Paolo Fresco, former vice-chairman of GE, once explained the philosophy thus: 'The traditional organisation asked maybe 5% of its people to do 95% of its thinking. What we have tried to do is get 100% of the people to do 100% of the thinking . . . the creative ability and contributing ability at all levels is tremendous.'[2] In GE's European businesses, ideas are mobilised through a series of management councils drawn from different divisions. At every council meeting, members are expected to bring a new idea from which other divisions can learn. At one, late in 1999, someone suggested 'reverse mentoring' – pairing senior managers with younger members of staff in order to bone up on the Internet and e-commerce. Within 48 hours, the idea had flashed around all GE's divisions in Europe.[3]

An immediate by-product of Work-Out was that many problems emerged as quickly solvable. These solutions became known in GE as 'picking the low-hanging fruit' – a phrase that has found its way into management textbooks to describe easy wins that build morale and confidence in change. Shopfloor workers were encouraged to speak up with ideas on how to simplify processes, improve equipment or clear bottle-necks in supply chains. One plant in the appliances division was getting periodic supplies of screws that broke whenever a bit was applied. Complaints to management were met with reassuring words, but the supplies continued to be unsatisfactory. Eventually a shop steward told a Work-Out meeting about the problem and suggested a solution: show the supplier exactly where the product was breaking down. He was flown to the supplier in another state, demonstrated the way to fix the problem, and there were no more bad screws. The shop steward was subsequently empowered to run his own part of the plant without supervision. Morale and efficiency soared.

Work-Outs spread rapidly through GE, proving just as practical a technique in the fast-growing financial services division of GE Capital as in the jet engines business, plastics, light-bulbs or NBC television. It then developed into 'Action Work-Outs' where the brainstorming and questioning of managers happened in the workplace rather than offsite, with the aim of producing a result in 24 hours, and into the 'Change Acceleration Program', where cross-functional teams with a range of knowledge and experience were empowered to solve specific problems. The key to the process, wrote Noel M. Tichy and Stratford Sherman in their account of the change years at GE, *Control Your Destiny or Someone Else Will*, was an insistence on emerging from every session with a list of immediately actionable items. At a turbine plant in New England, for example, there had been voluble complaints from hourly-paid workers about the milling machines they used. They were authorised to write their own specifications for replacement machines, to test and approve them and, when satisfied, to order $20m worth.

Productivity rose measurably as a result of Work-Out, with big gains often emerging from small investments. The head of GE Lighting in the mid-1990s, Chuck Pieper, reckoned that 70% of his division's productivity gains of $29m had come out of expenditures of $50,000 to $100,000 or less, 'figures within the budgetary discretion of folks well down the line'.

There were other innovative ideas to cut bureaucracy and free up decision-making, such as Quick Market Intelligence (QMI), an idea borrowed from Wal-Mart, in which salespeople were given weekly access to the CEO and his senior team to update them on customer trends, thrash out problems and make everyone in the organisation more customer-conscious. But Work-Out remained the core change process, and Welch went on to develop the principle into a vision of 'boundary-lessness' for the global group, designed to result in a free flow of ideas, information and best practice among all the businesses in GE – and eventually out to their suppliers to form a seamless whole in terms of satisfying the customer.[4]

GE's experimental ideas culture

Jack Welch liked to refer to GE as 'the largest petri dish of business innovation in the world'. It will pick and experiment with ideas from anywhere and polish them up for its own use, as with QMI. A notable example of the mid-1990s was its wholesale adoption of the Six Sigma quality measurement system originally pioneered at Motorola in 1987 when the electronics firm that had started with car radios in the 1930s was being eaten alive by quality-conscious Japanese competitors. George Fisher, then Motorola's communications chief, led a new approach to the company's various quality programs, which plainly were not delivering. The system worked out by his department offered a statistics-based, sustainable way to track how Motorola's performance was conforming to customer requirements.

It is a complicated system of performance measurement that has been memorably described as 'TQM [Total Quality Management] on steroids'. 'Sigma' represents the critical measure and 'Six Sigma' the goal of almost perfect quality: a statistically derived target of 3.4 defects for every million operations. In every case, measurements begin with the customer, and with the impact of improvements on customer satisfaction. The first step is to establish what the customer believes to be 'Critical to Quality', which may be different for each customer and hard to measure. Martin Bluck, head of

GE Information Services in the UK, explains the process by comparing it to different people's perception of the perfect cup of tea; you first need to establish, say, the extremes of temperature within which the perfect temperature is found, then to judge the 'acceptable' areas either side of perfection, and so on. The key is to begin by taking the extremes rather than the average. 'Most businesses look at the average, which is flawed,' says Bluck.

Six Sigma practice is credited with having saved Motorola over the ten years from 1987, raising its sales growth fivefold and its profits by nearly 20% annually over that time. In the process, Motorola developed its own squad of internal Six Sigma consultants, who then helped to spread the technique to other companies. Notable among these was Allied Signal, whose CEO Larry Bossidy had built his career at GE, who remained a valued friend of the GE chief and who convinced Welch of its value as a tool of corporate transformation. GE began to implement Six Sigma in 1995, taking it much further and introducing mandatory training for all its managers on three levels, using the martial arts analogy of green belt, black belt and master black belt. It is written into GE employees' contracts that they attend a course on Six Sigma and bonuses are paid on the achievement of targets linked to the process. Welch has 'driven it through the business by linking it to pay', says one senior British GE manager.[5]

In late 1998, Welch, who had long scorned the use of a personal computer on his desk, although other parts of the GE empire were gradually adapting to e-business, suddenly 'got religion', as colleagues put it, about wiring up every business in the group. It seems to have taken place as a result of watching his children shopping online for Christmas. In the space of a year, Welch imposed his conversion on the organisation, as he had done with Six Sigma, devising the concept of 'destroyyourbusiness.com', which nudged every business in the group into reinventing itself before it lost out to an e-conscious competitor. GE managers privately grumbled about the 'e-police' who monitored progress – some offices even put post-rooms out of bounds and watched to see that backsliders did not revert to old non-e habits like the mail and the telephone. The crash course worked: today, this oldest surviving member of the Fortune 500 transacts an estimated \$20bn a year, more than all the other B2B (business-to-business) marketplaces put together.[6]

Work-Out was quickly folded into the new culture, along with Six Sigma. At GE Information Services, for example, now rebranded GE Global eXchange Services (GXS), they sell custom-made e-commerce technology or 'solutions' as every technology service now likes to pitch it, using the Work-Out all-in-a-room discipline. Instead of GE staff alone, provider and customer meet to thrash out the problem to be solved and the solution to be applied. For one dotcom client, GXS ran a one-day workshop to identify the major problem: the original business of the company had been based on a paper catalogue which had been transferred to the Net, but there was a problem integrating orders which were now electronic into their order processing system, which was still geared to fax, telephone or paper. The company did not know how to get the linkage between its Web site and its order processing system.

GXS had an e-commerce toolkit to sell, known as Enterprise Application Integration (EAI), but the combination of Work-Out and Six Sigma (determining the customer's perception of value as well as its problems) enabled it to fit the appropriate technology solution in a much quicker time than would otherwise have been the case. The power of the Work-Out format in particular, says Martin Bluck, is that it imposes action immediately at the end of the session. 'It's getting the right people to understand the problem and get the authority to take a decision and execute it. We really do start by asking some very business questions, as opposed to technology questions.' Where suppliers and other business partners have to adapt their operations electronically, they are brought into the Work-Out sessions as soon as possible. GXS claims that the adoption of e-business along these lines has enabled it to deliver solutions in six to eight weeks instead of as many months.[7]

GE has enjoyed such adulatory management attention since Jack Welch began to work his economic miracle in the 1990s that it is not surprising that techniques such as Work-Out have had an international impact on corporate processes. Eagle Star, the 190-year-old insurance company, was the first major UK business to adopt it after enduring several years of failing performance following the collapse of the UK real-estate market in the early 1990s. A new chief executive, Patrick O'Sullivan, came in from the BZW merchant bank with the goal of changing Eagle Star's entire culture. Having previously worked for a subsidiary of GE Capital, the conglomerate's financial services powerhouse, O'Sullivan chose Work-Out as his tool for thawing out what he called the 'permafrost' – a layer of resistance to change from senior and middle managers. He insisted that key decision-makers were there at the end of the Work-Out process to listen to proposals for change from the staff. 'It has to be a yes or a no there and then, which has resulted in some healthy, heated debates,' he told the *Financial Times* in June 2000, two years after inaugurating the system. 'If it is a yes, then all the detailed aspects of the implementation are rolled out over the following eight to twelve weeks, and the changes happen. If it is no, then senior management have to give credible reasons why the proposals can't go ahead.'

To launch Work-Out within Eagle Star, O'Sullivan chose the liveliest and most innovative group in the company – the telesales team at Eagle Star Direct. 'They loved it,' he said. 'They worked on how to improve response time and significantly improve productivity. They came together for three-day Work-Outs and worked well into the night, skipping dinner and ordering in pizza. There was no extra pay, and these people usually got overtime. Reaction to that spread rapidly. I had some early wins through the process, and as a result it took off.' Later that year, 1998, Eagle Star and other former BAT financial services were merged with Zurich Financial Services to form ZFS, and O'Sullivan used Work-Out again to bond the two cultures, which had been very different. In 1999, about 25% of the merged group's general insurance businesses took part in Work-Out, making savings of £6m in the first year alone.[8]

Big Ideas from the car-makers

The fact that Work-Out originated at Crotonville, the first corporate 'university' (though only for management), is significant, because other companies with in-house educational centres have evolved similar problem-solving processes. In Britain, the car components firm Unipart effectively runs its own Work-Out in its 'Faculty on the Floor', a learning centre attached to 'Unipart U' and situated close to the production line. Unipart was an early pioneer of the learning organisation in Britain, introducing Unipart U in 1993 with the slogan 'learn in the morning, do in the afternoon'. Faculty on the Floor, launched in 1999, telescoped this, in the words of chief executive John Neill, to 'learning at ten o'clock and then doing it at eleven o'clock'. He called it 'learning at the speed of light'. Each Faculty on the Floor centre – there were four initially and fifteen were planned throughout the UK – has computer terminals dedicated to training and problem-solving in specific areas such as customers and products, core skills and production technology. Problems shared with other plants on the Web site can often throw up solutions and cost savings.[9]

Historically, the car industry has led the way in generating Big Ideas in the workplace, from Henry Ford's assembly line in 1913 through Alfred Sloan decentralising General Motors in the 1920s to the Toyota company in Japan evolving lean production and just-in-time in the 1970s. That was appropriate enough, since the car industry has been so dominant in twentieth-century economies, a benchmark of national virility for the leading industrialised countries. At one stage, until over-capacity and loss of competitiveness hit the sector, it was as if having a national car industry was as important to a country's status as a seat at the UN.

Ford's assembly line, which moved past the workers and in its pilot scheme broke down the assembly of magnetos into 29 distinct operations, one to a worker, was a Tayloresque efficiency breakthrough developed by a team of anonymous engineers under Charles Sorensen at Ford's Highland Park plant outside Detroit. Various influences have been cited as the inspiration for the assembly line, from a flour mill in Delaware to conveyor belts for grain at breweries, but a likely suspect is the system used by Chicago meatpackers to 'disassemble' animal carcasses. Ford, who had already declared his intention in 1908 to 'build a motor car for the great multitude', had watched the stockyard system in action and is reputed to have observed: 'If they can kill pigs and cows that way, we can build cars that way.'[10]

Taylor, on the other hand, had been breaking down working operations for decades by 1913, and his time-and-motion study disciples such as Frank (*Cheaper by the*

Dozen) Gilbreth were busy spreading the gospel well before World War One. Taylor had also 'Taylorised' other car plants such as Packard and Franklin by 1913, so these ideas were not only in the air but being practised in the industry, for all Henry Ford's dismissal of any Taylor influence on his innovation. All companies using them showed dramatic productivity gains and lower costs: between 1913 and 1914 the price of a model T Ford fell from $690 to $490. 'Both Taylor and Ford raised production, cut costs and reduced the judgement and skill needed by the average worker,' observed Robert Kanigel in his fascinatingly detailed biography of Taylor, *The One Best Way*. 'After Ford and Taylor got through with them, most jobs needed less of everything – less brains, less muscle, less independence.' The assembly line was a Big Idea, but Taylor's scientific management was bigger because it was infinitely more transferable, as Kanigel points out. 'The Taylorised workplace . . . appears everywhere, heedless of the lines between one industry and the next . . . Fordism was the special case, Taylorism the universal.'[11]

Alfred Sloan was a manager, not an inventive engineer like Ford, but his shaping of a slew of competing companies into the mighty General Motors in 1922 and the reorganisation of it into eight semi-autonomous divisions (five for cars, each targeted at a different market segment, and three for components) was the first big demonstration of US management in action, changing the face of the corporation. These divisions, the forerunners of strategic business units, were responsible for all their own operations except strategic policy and finance, which were controlled centrally. It was a model that would last well over half a century, until globalisation and electronics changed the nature of corporate power and decision-making. Nearly forty years after its publication in 1963, many chief executives will still cite Sloan's somewhat turgid memoir, *My Years With General Motors*, as the most influential management book of their career. The multi-divisional, decentralised organisation, pushing power out to the front line for the first time, came to be seen as the single most innovative change in corporate structure, enabling companies to grow in size and diversity, and Sloan's revolution became the basis for the first big management text on strategy, Alfred Chandler's *Strategy and Structure* in 1962.

As the ultimate process-driven industry, car manu-facturing was always a natural testbed for theories born of scientific management, starting with its most influential offspring, total quality management. A portrait of W. Edwards Deming, the US statistician who converted post-war Japan to a system for designing quality into the production process, still hangs in the lobby of the Toyota car company's headquarters in Tokyo, and it was on Japan's car assembly lines in the 1950s that Deming's concept of quality as the responsibility of every employee from senior manage-ment down proved itself the most valuable business tool ever invented. TQM was a natural partner for the Japanese philosophy of 'kaizen' (or 'kaisen'), or 'con-tinuous improvement involving everyone, managers and workers alike', as it was described by Masaaki Imai, the author who popularised it in the West. From designing defects out by the control of statistical variables and establishing ownership of quality goals by the teams who worked on the assembly lines, it was a short step to the control of waste – both of time in correcting defects and of resources in holding unnecessarily large stocks of components. This in turn led to two linked and massively influential industrial ideas: just-in-time and lean production, both born at Toyota Motors.

Toyota's chief engineer in the 1950s was a man named Taiichi Ohno, a disciple of Frederick Taylor's, as so many Japanese engineers had been since 1914. The story goes that Ohno was on a visit to the US after World War Two and was struck by the way in which stocks were automatically replenished as needed on supermarket shelves. From this, and the developing science of materials resource planning, Ohno evolved a system where supplies to car assembly lines were 'pulled' as needed by the shopfloor alerting the supplier through the use of 'kanban' – the Japanese word for a card or ticket to control material flows from one workstation to another further down the line. This bypassed the previous system of central control of inventory, and put production needs directly in touch with the supplier, eliminating the need to hold excess stocks in a warehouse.

'Lean production', as outlined in Chapter 2, was the enlargement of this in the 1980s in order to streamline more processes, to introduce the working of cross-functional teams and to produce a winning combination of greater productivity with fewer people. In another few years a further variation on this and other Taylorist principles would result in re-engineering, the biggest management fad of the 1990s and, like lean production, misused by too many companies seeking ways of cutting overheads to survive recession.

Knowledge management: the century's last Big Idea

If the car industry was the natural seedbed for process-driven theories, it also represented the acme of old-economy manufacturing, even as it embraced computer-aided design and robots on the assembly line. The remarkably prescient Peter Drucker foresaw as early as 1969, when goods and services still contributed two-thirds of America's gross national product, that the world was entering a post-industrial revolution in which, by the late 1970s, more than half that GNP would be provided by the 'knowledge industries' dealing in ideas and information. While crediting a Princeton economist, Fritz Machlup, with the term 'knowledge industries', Drucker was the first to introduce 'knowledge worker' and 'the knowledge economy' in his book *The Age of Discontinuity* (1969). As a predictive text, it is a good deal more impressive than Nostradamus's *Centuries*.

'The demand for knowledge workers in the future seems insatiable,' Drucker pronounced, pointing out that until the eighteenth century, the concept of knowledge had been quite separate from that of work, which was seen as the province of experience. He also gave F.W. Taylor, in the late 1960s at the lowest point of his reputation for allegedly denuding work of its dignity and skill, credit for understanding that productivity could only be achieved by applying knowledge to work processes. Taylor saw, wrote Drucker, that 'the key to producing more was to "work smarter". The key to productivity was knowledge, not sweat.' Drucker also foresaw potentially vast problems for society in managing the aspirations of knowledge workers, which would be very different from those of the unskilled or mechanically skilled. 'We will have to learn to manage the knowledge worker both for productivity and for satisfaction, both for achievement and for status . . . [This] is likely to be *the* social question of the developed countries for the twentieth and probably for the twenty-first century.'[12]

Knowledge management, or KM, perhaps the last big business idea of the twentieth century, was partly a response to this challenge – how to manage the talent resource within a corporation that, unlike other resources, could walk away at any time. Re-engineering compounded the problem with its wholesale culling of staff, many of whom later turned out to have been key gatekeepers of information. Along with this in the early

1990s came a growing realisation that organisations operating with very similar market strategies could only gain a sustainable competitive advantage through the collective knowledge housed, in all too volatile a fashion, in the brains of their workers, suppliers and other partners.

The quote from Lew Platt, former CEO of Hewlett-Packard, always rolled out in connection with knowledge management says it all: 'If H-P knew what H-P knows, we'd be three times as profitable.' Platt was acknowledging both the truth and the difficulty of KM. Charles Handy has estimated that the intellectual assets of a corporation are usually worth three or four times its book value, though the Swedish financial services group Skandia, a pioneer in knowledge management, puts it much higher, at between five and sixteen times book value. The phenomenal market cap valuation placed in the last few years on companies such as Microsoft, Intel and the investment bank Goldman Sachs, compared with their modest physical assets, represents the talent and knowledge housed within their walls, for which the market is prepared to pay sometimes beyond reason, as the collapse of the dotcom bubble in 2001 starkly revealed. Yet even with the multifarious electronic aids now available to tap, share and store information, knowledge management remains a frustratingly imprecise science, and its failure rate as a strategy almost matches that of re-engineering.

Basically, as the knowledge management expert Professor Amin Rajan has explained, a company needs a technological means of 'mapping' the knowledge held in its databases, filing cabinets and employees' heads. The simplest system would involve a corporate 'Yellow Pages' of who knows what within the corporation, a method of searching the Yellow Pages and a means of distributing the results through some form of intranet or groupware. As information is applied again to new situations it gains value as new knowledge and can be re-banked within the system. Businesses which exist on the sale of knowledge, such as management consultancies, operate like this on a global scale. McKinsey, for example, runs a Rapid-Response Team whose aim is to link within 24 hours across the globe any of its consultants facing a problem with others who might have special knowledge to solve it. The danger is that unless the process is expertly managed, as opposed to simply being installed, it can become little more than a store or exchange of information, which is not the same as applying it as knowledge.[13]

The company that did most to establish the value of KM as a practical business tool, and the first to attempt to quantify that value in corporate performance terms, is Skandia, the Stockholm-based financial services group. Skandia was embarking on an international growth strategy in the early 1980s and saw knowledge transfer within the group as a way of leveraging its start-ups in new countries. By 1991 it had recruited Leif Edvinsson as the world's first designated director of intellectual capital; he has since written books and established a high-profile conference speaking career on the subject.

Edvinsson evolved a methodology called Navigator for identifying and converting Skandia's organisational knowledge into performance, and since 1995 the group has published an intellectual capital report alongside its annual report and accounts which attempts to measure the value of its intellectual resources – that is, the gap in Skandia's equity between its book value and market value. No other company has yet matched this dedication to establishing some kind of accepted standard for knowledge management, though global giants such as AT&T, Dow Chemical and Monsanto have titles like 'chief intellectual capital officer' and 'chief knowledge officer' on their mastheads, and research-dependent companies in such sectors as pharmaceuticals are natural converts to protecting intellectual assets.

Among industrial giants, BP-Amoco set up a KM programme in the early 1990s in the exploration and production division, then led by the forward-thinking John Browne. They discovered that communicating by video link was a far more effective way of solving problems and sharing knowledge than by phone. For example, when a BP drilling vessel developed problems in the North Sea, the engineers on board were able to display the faulty equipment in front of a video camera and an expert in Aberdeen was able to diagnose the fault and give repair instructions, saving the expense of either flying an engineer to the site or delaying the vessel in port. BP also borrowed the US army's CALL technique of reviewing performance after every project and storing and sharing the information gained.[14]

After Browne, later Sir John Browne and now Lord Browne, became group chief executive, he inaugurated a knowledge management programme across the whole of BP-Amoco in 1996 and commissioned a taskforce of senior managers to identify best practice in the technique. Chris Collinson, a KM consultant to the group, says it has saved millions of dollars by sharing know-how. 'We have 150 business units in almost 150 countries, so there is tremendous potential for one isolated business unit to repeat things,' he said in early 2000. In a refinement of the Yellow Pages system, BP's intranet allows staff to create their own personal pages detailing strengths and expertise, and they are encouraged to join dedicated networks, of which the group now has nearly 300 worldwide.[15]

The power of ideas starts at the top

Ultimately, the real art of knowledge management lies less in the high-tech infrastructure than in persuading staff of the benefits of sharing what is often their prime bargaining asset in an uncertain career world. Assuming that management can 'milk' knowledge for the corporate good is to risk the worst sort of Tayloresque command-and-control image and defeat the ultimate objective. Research carried out by London University's Birkbeck College has found that one in five employees believe it is not in their best interests to share good ideas with colleagues or bosses. They prefer to hoard their knowledge for their own advancement, either by promotion or by moving to another employer.[16]

As always, the chief executive sets the tone, as Browne has at BP-Amoco and Sir C.K. Chow did at GKN. Born in Hong Kong, educated in the US and with experience of working in Japan, Chow brought a passion for knowledge and ideas-sharing to the venerable UK engineering group comparable to the way in which Jack Welch energised GE with his 'boundaryless' vision of exchanging best practice across his group's diverse businesses. GKN's solutions-sharing network was started in its 47 plants making constant velocity joints, a key motor vehicle component of which GKN produces 40% of the world's output. Each year about a thousand individuals from the CVJ (constant velocity joint) division attend formal workshop sessions to discuss new ideas, alongside more frequent informal discussions by email and telephone. The results have included productivity gains, breakthroughs in new products and dramatically reduced cycle times and inventory costs, affecting GKN plants as far apart as Germany, the US, Spain and the UK.[17]

Some of the greatest old-economy companies were built on this recognition of the power of ideas to solve problems and generate new products. 3M has long been celebrated for allowing its staff to devote 15% of working time to their own blue-sky projects and then to finding 'champions' in the management – resulting, famously, in the massive success of Post-it Notes. Its goal now is that 30% of sales should come from products brought to market in the last four years, and that 10% should come from innovations of the past year. Percy Barnevik's successor as chief executive at Asea Brown Boveri, Goran Lindahl, held that the key to the Swiss-Swedish engineering multinational lay in its 'brainpower'. Insofar as the 'learning organisation' – that icon of 1990s management thinking – actually exists, it is in the value placed by such business leaders on the infinitely renewable resource within the heads of their people, and the various attempts to structure and sustain it.

Now, at the beginning of a new century and a new kind of industrial revolution, ideas have become the most bankable of assets, the very currency on which business in the 'new economy' is built. Ideas for the testing are everywhere, of greater or lesser degree and durability. We don't yet know which ones will survive more than a few years; the dotcom massacre has shown that ideas are not enough without sound business plans and managerial skills. The age of Big Ideas may be vanishing with the demise of the big process-driven industries. The Internet makes everything fluid, a continuous flow of prototyping and piloting to find out what will work and what won't. This suits a younger generation that has seen some big management ideas fall spectacularly to earth and would rather invest in a spread of more modest techniques that won't wreak havoc if they fail to deliver. In the next chapter we will look at some of the hottest ideas in management currently circulating on both sides of the Atlantic.

Powerpoints

- GE became a powerhouse for management ideas with the 1988 introduction of Work-Out, a problem-solving, brainstorming technique in which workers could challenge managers for action face to face.

- Work-Out produced early wins and gave 'low-hanging fruit' to the management lexicon. It has developed into the sharing of ideas and best practice across GE's industrial boundaries and into other businesses.
- GE sees itself as 'the largest petri dish of business innovation in the world', experimenting with ideas from any source. It made Motorola's Six Sigma statistical discipline into a powerful, zero-defects culture.
- The auto industry has been a crucible of process-driven management ideas such as lean production, decentralisation, just-in-time and TQM. But some ideas did not transfer easily to other industries and were misapplied.
- Knowledge management, the last big twentieth-century contribution to management thought, was pioneered commercially by Skandia, which devised a system to quantify its benefits. But unless the human element is managed skilfully, it can fail for the same reasons as BPR.

NOTES

[1] Tichy, Noel M. and Sherman, Stratford: *Control Your Destiny or Someone Else Will*, HarperCollins, 1993

[2] Kennedy, Carol: 'Inside the Powerhouse', *Director*, September 1995

[3] Marsh, Peter: 'Original thought boosts the many interests of GE,' *FT*, 23.11.99

[4] Kennedy: *Director*, 1995; Tichy and Sherman: *Control Your Destiny*

[5] author interviews, GE Information Systems, 2000

[6] *The Economist*, 19.5.01; author interviews

[7] author interviews, GEIS

[8] *FT*, 30.6.00

[9] Groom, Brian: 'On-the-job lessons in savings and efficiency', *FT*, 17.9.99

[10] Kanigel, Robert: *The One Best Way*, Wiley, 1997

[11] ibid.

[12] Drucker, Peter: *The Age of Discontinuity*, William Heinemann, 1969

[13] Rajan, Amin: *Good Practices in Knowledge Creation and Exchange*, Create, 1998; *Observer*, 11.10.98

[14] Skapinker, Michael: 'Time to pass on the ripe fruits of experience', *FT*, 12.1.00

[15] Coles, Margaret: 'Sharing knowledge boosts efficiency', *Sunday Times*, 30.4.00

[16] *The Times*, 7.1.00

[17] Marsh, Peter: 'Profitable ideas that travel the globe', *FT*, 29.8.00

CHAPTER FOUR

HOT BUTTONS, COOL IDEAS

'The new economy is not about brawn, it's about the power of ideas,' says Vinod Khosla, a founder of Sun Microsystems and now a partner in Sun's original backers, the leading Silicon Valley venture capital company Kleiner Perkins Caufield and Byers. Khosla, now in his mid-forties, was an advance scout for the battalion of talented tech-heads from the Indian sub-continent who have taken over much of the high-ground technology battlefield around San Francisco's Bay Area. An electrical engineer from New Delhi and a Stanford MBA, he ran Sun as chief executive until 1986, when he joined Kleiner Perkins, relishing the risk factor in the venture capital industry as much as in his favoured leisure pursuits: sky-diving, whitewater-rafting and hang-gliding.

The risk-taking paid off in spades. Kleiner Perkins is a legend in the technology industry, having also backed Tandem, Compaq, Lotus, Intuit, Netscape, AOL, Excite, Genentech and Amazon.com, among a host of other successes. Its partners sit on the boards of several leading Silicon Valley companies and are hugely influential in putting deals together such as that between AOL, Netscape and Sun. If anyone knows about the power of ideas, Kleiner Perkins do, because their role goes far beyond the provision of finance. Khosla describes their role as 'a McKinsey for start-ups'.

If brainpower is the oil of the new industrial revolution, there is no shortage of theories and techniques bubbling away on how to drill for it, refine it and get it to the corporate engine-room. Knowledge management, creativity and innovation are the three grails every business strives to capture, and it is hard to achieve one without the others. Ideas about ideas – how to breed them, nurture them and turn them into viable business concepts – are among the hottest of hot buttons in management theory at the start of the new millennium. Spotting potential winners is the most difficult part of the process, and there is massive wastage. It is reckoned to take at least 3,000 good ideas to produce four workable new products, out of which one might be a market winner. Skyline, a US company that licenses ideas for toys to bigger manufacturers, found that out of 4,000 ideas it tested in 1998, 230 went forward to development and 12 were eventually sold, a return of one-third of 1% of the total research.

Skyline's experience is cited by Robert I. Sutton, professor of manufacturing science and engineering at Stanford University's engineering school, who emphasises the importance of accepting failure in his executive course Managing Innovation. 'A high failure rate is the only way to achieve a high creativity rate,' he maintains. 'Perfection can only be accomplished by using old knowledge in new ways.' Sutton quotes Soichiro Honda, founder of the car company: 'Success represents the 1% of your work that results from the 99% that is called failure.' Sutton's great hero is Thomas Edison, whose greatest contribution to science, he believes, was not so much the products that changed society like the electric light-bulb and the phonograph, but the 'invention factory' he ran in his laboratory in Menlo Park, New Jersey. Edison 'created a setting – and ways of thinking and working – that enabled his inventors to move easily in and out of separate pools of knowledge, to keep learning new ideas, and to use ideas in novel situations', explains Sutton. Edison habitually used old ideas in new ways. The phonograph, for instance, blended elements of past work on telegraphs, telephones and electric motors. In his 'invention factory', Edison would pack all his inventors into a single large room where they could not avoid discussing and exchanging ideas and work in progress.[1]

Idealab, a pioneer Californian incubator of start-ups, follows the same philosophy in the way it invents new businesses. The company's Pasadena headquarters operates in a 50,000-square-foot, one-storey building in which people are forced to run up against each other. Founder Bill Gross believes in 'cross-pollination' among everyone in the building. His own office is in the centre, with concentric rings of desks around it, those in the innermost circle belonging to employees working on early-stage start-ups. As the businesses develop, they move their desks further away from the centre, and once they achieve the critical mass of 70 employees, they leave and set up their own offices. Idealab also practises the fail-to-succeed philosophy, being prepared to invest in scores of potential businesses that flop in order to find the handful that will make it big. The company over-reached itself with rash investments in 2000 and has seen some early successes scythed down in the dotcom massacre, but it is still fizzing with ideas it claims will revolutionise the Internet.

The right creative setting: grunge or comfort?

There is a growing belief that ideas and creativity can be enticed out of people by placing them in the right environment. One of the first companies to experiment with this was the Swedish financial services group

Skandia, already a leading proponent of knowledge management. Skandia was the first company to build KM into its corporate processes, to quantify the asset value of knowledge in a special annual report and to set up the management position of chief knowledge officer. Skandia's Futures Center, situated at Vaxholm on an archipelago north of Stockholm and opened in mid-1996, is a purpose-built forcing-house for new ideas to which employees are despatched to mix with each other, think about directions in which the business could go, and 'help create the future faster'. The place has vast sea views, classical music playing softly and even the aroma of baking bread floating through its rooms to create an atmosphere of wellbeing and home comforts – supposedly good for the thinking processes. The rhythmic combination of the music and the sound of the waves outside is similarly thought to be conducive to creative expression. An old ship's steering wheel and antique typewriters serve as symbolic reminders of past ages' exploration and progress.

Typical of Skandia's methods is the two-day workshop that was held at Vaxholm soon after its opening. Twenty people, chosen to represent a cross-section of Skandia in terms of age, experience and location, were formed into five 'future teams', each with someone of 25-plus, 35-plus and 45-plus to facilitate cross-generational pollination. The ideas-creating workshop was based around the five drivers of Skandia's business environment: demographics, technology, the world economy, the insurance market, organisation and leadership. Several innovations emerged from the teams and went up to Skandia's top managers for evaluation.[2]

Andersen Consulting, which was recently separated from its sibling Arthur Andersen and forced to devise a new brand identity as Accenture, has a Chaos Zone and a Zen Zone on the top floor of its central London offices, designed along lines laid down by Edward de Bono, the man who has made a goldmine out of lateral thinking. The Chaos Zone, which is for the generation of ideas, is decorated in red and has desks and chairs on wheels to enable clusters of staff to regroup and brainstorm at will. The Zen Zone, designed for the calmer process of incubation, has bean bags and fishtanks in place of office furniture, scenes from nature and a sign declaring 'No meetings. No phones. No interruptions.' The two zones are linked by a working corridor called the Touchdown Bar, where people can sit and plug in their phones and laptops.

Sun Microsystems in Menlo Park, Silicon Valley, became aware that its engineers tended to gather in doorways and kitchens, have a quick chat and then return to their offices. Realising that these conversations could have creative value, the company designed spaces called Forums spreading out from the kitchen areas, where people could develop their thoughts in more comfort. There are also 'Sun rooms' designed for incubating ideas, some with ping-pong tables or stereo equipment, all with whiteboards. Ever since William Hewlett and Dave Packard devised the 'H-P Way', Valley companies have been noted for employee-friendly amenities such as free coffee, soft drinks, jars of jelly babies and places where the corporate brainpower can turn itself loose in conversation, often to productive effect. Sometimes it just needs observation of what's going on: when Oticon, the innovative Danish hearing aid manufacturer, realised that employees from different floors tended to gather on the stairwells for informal discussions, the company simply widened the stairs.

Large areas of whiteboard to scribble on tend to be a common factor in these designs for creative living, as are intimate clusters of chairs and tables to encourage the exchange of thoughts. When Albert Einstein was a professor at Princeton University in the 1940s, he had his office and the corridor leading to it lined in whiteboard so that he could scrawl down thoughts as they occurred. Three McKinsey consultants who wrote a book called *The Alchemy of Growth* about techniques for developing ideas into businesses spoke of Einstein's practice as ideal. Although they were never able to design a common workplace, being based in McKinsey's Sydney and Chicago offices, Mehrdad Baghai, David White and Stephen Coley made their own discoveries about the creative process. Working in two different continents while writing their book, they had to meet periodically at a midway point to bring the project together and brainstorm ideas. A resort in Hawaii proved the best logistical choice, and allowing for jetlag, they found their creativity reaching its peak on the third day. That was also when they got the most work done.[3]

A grandiose offshoot of the Einstein whiteboard environment has been developed by a subscription-only business development network in London called The Fourth Room. And what a subscription – the project was launched in 1998 by Michael Wolff of brand consultancy Wolff Olins at £10,000 a year. For this, companies with money to burn on creativity exercises for their senior executives get the use of an elegant Georgian house in Bloomsbury, the old literary quarter of central London, and the opportunity to network and brainstorm with each other at weekly breakfast meetings, monthly dinners and custom-tailored workshops. Discussions at the breakfasts and dinners are themed, dealing with such subjects as the threat of the Internet to old-economy companies, healing techniques and ways of becoming receptive to creativity.

The house itself is divided into networking areas with four rooms each representing a concept, such as 'The Room of Great Works', 'The Room of Great Reason' and 'The Room of Great Experience'. The 'Fourth Room' itself, styled 'The Room of Unknowing', is intended to be a place where managers can abandon thinking about work, analysis or their professional experience – all subjects for the other rooms – and let their minds roam free in the world of imagination. The room is filled with light from tall windows, the walls, floor and ceiling are brilliant white, and participants are encouraged to write or draw on them with coloured crayons as their consciousness dictates. The three partners behind the venture boast titles as new agey as the rooms: Head of Imagination, Head of Insight and The Pacesetter. Yet companies as substantial as American Express Europe, Safeway, Prudential, 3i and Abbey National have signed up. Whether The Fourth Room is just a boomtime luxury for some big companies, an eccentric display of management faddism or a solid contribution to the development of creative business strategy is something we may have to wait until the next recession to find out.[4]

The paradox behind all this concentration on the physical setting for creative work is that technology companies as outstanding as Hewlett-Packard and Apple were famously born in a comfortless garage, while Yahoo!, the Internet search engine, was devised in a grungy student trailer. Jeff Bezos, too, created Amazon.com and worked out its business plan in his garage. Carly Fiorina, the charismatic CEO who set out in 1999 to reinvent H-P, made the legendary garage where Stanford graduates William Hewlett and David Packard began their partnership in 1939 a leitmotif of her campaign both for internal and external use. In one TV commercial she was seen leaning against a ramshackle garage, promising that the company would continue to be true to its original principles, while H-P's internal culture-change programme was led by something called 'The Rules of the Garage'. These ran:

Believe you can change the world.

Work quickly, keep the tools unlocked, work whenever.

Know when to work alone and when to work together.

Share tools, ideas. Trust your colleagues.

No politics. No bureaucracy. (These are ridiculous in a garage.)

The customer defines a job well done.

Radical ideas are not bad ideas.

Invent different ways of working.

Make a contribution every day. If it doesn't contribute, it doesn't leave the garage.

Believe that together we can do anything.

Invent.[5]

Great Groups, hot groups – changing the world

Associated with the garage legend in promoting creativity and innovation is the Great Groups theory advocated by Warren Bennis, the world's best-known guru of leadership, or 'hot groups' as they are called in a similar study by Harold J. Leavitt, emeritus professor of organisational behaviour and psychology at Stanford University. Leavitt and Bennis have both been studying the workings of small, task-obsessed groups for some forty years. 'The hot group state of mind can occur anywhere and anytime, wherever and whenever people come together to do something they believe is worth doing,' writes Leavitt in a book co-authored with his wife, academic and consultant Jean Lipman-Blumen. Hot groups, he says, should not be confused with teams. The two may sometimes overlap, but on the whole hot group members are not good team players. 'The hot group as a group is almost never ready to salute and do whatever the organisation asks.'[6]

In their book *Organizing Genius*, Bennis and Patricia Ward Biederman write: 'All Great Groups aim to do more than fix a problem – they are out to change the world.' From the feature animation unit at Walt Disney to the top-secret World War Two airplane factory at Lockheed (the original 'skunk works'), Great Groups have accomplished extraordinary tasks against the odds. In the words of Bennis and Biederman, 'Something happens in these groups that doesn't happen in ordinary ones. Some alchemy takes place that not only results in a computer revolution or a new art form, but in a qualitative change in the participants. If only for the duration of the project, people in Great Groups seem to become better than themselves. They are able to see more, achieve more, and have a far better time doing it than they can working alone. Groups of the stature of PARC in its glory days and Disney Feature Animation are rare. But they could happen far more often than they do.'

Bennis and Biederman offer 15 top 'take-home lessons' of Great Groups, some positive, some cautionary:

1. Greatness starts with superb people (not only talented but intellectually original; people who 'want to do the next thing, not the last one').
2. Great Groups and great leaders create each other (Robert Oppenheimer showed no particular leadership ability before or after the Manhattan Project, but 'when the world needed him, he was able to rally inner resources that probably surprised even himself').
3. Every Great Group has a strong leader (whose ability lies in recognising excellence in others, 'curators' rather than 'creators').
4. Leaders of Great Groups love talent and know where to find it (they are people 'confident enough to recruit people better than themselves').
5. Great Groups are full of talented people who can work together (they don't need to be liked, but they do need to be respected).

6. Great Groups think they are on a mission from God (there has to be an element of crusade).

7. Every Great Group is an island – with a bridge to the mainland (they create a culture of their own and often have a great deal of fun).

8. Great Groups see themselves as winning underdogs (Steve Jobs always presented his Macintosh PC makers as the David to IBM's Goliath).

9. Great Groups always have an enemy (competition with an outsider tends to boost creativity).

10. People in Great Groups have blinders on ('the project is all they see').

11. Great Groups are optimistic, not realistic (they 'believe they can do things no one has ever done before').

12. In Great Groups the right person has the right job (when person and task are matched, passion ensues).

13. The leaders of Great Groups give them what they need and free them from the rest (brilliant people want above all a worthy challenge that stretches the whole of their talent, and they need to be able to spark off each other's ideas).

14. Great Groups ship (they meet deadlines, continually focus until the job is done).

15. Great work is its own reward.[7]

Perhaps the last is no longer as true in the age of stock options as it was for, say, the young scientists creating the atomic bomb to put an end to World War Two, but for many, solving problems and creating something new is the ultimate buzz. Warren Bennis believes problem-solving is the task for which mankind was evolved: 'It gives us as much pleasure as sex.' Historically, there are other common denominators in these high-achieving groups. Members tend to be young (twenties or thirties) and male, dress like students and share a fraternal college atmosphere. They have tunnel vision about the task in hand and will cheerfully go without food or sleep to accomplish some goal. They ignore their surroundings (so much for the carefully designed Chaos and Zen Zone syndrome) and happily work in offices that, as Tracy Kidder wrote of the computer company in *The Soul of a New Machine*, 'look like something psychologists build for testing the fortitude of small animals'. The reason why so many creative enterprises started in garages, Bennis speculates, is perhaps that unattractive surroundings act as 'an aesthetic blank slate that frees the mind to dream about what might be'.

By their very nature, coming together to get a critical project done, Great Groups or hot groups characteristically have a short life and tend not to be sustainable, but those who have been in them never forget them, if only because of their intensity. If corporations could bottle the spirit of Great Groups and dispense it on a repeat prescription, they would find the business equivalent of the elixir of life.

Disney Animation is one admired exception: it managed to reinvent itself twenty years after Walt Disney's death and recapture some of the group genius that created the studio's first great triumph, the 1939 classic *Snow White and the Seven Dwarfs* – a project that engaged 750 different artists. It did so under Michael Eisner in a number of ways, notably by deciding to release a new feature film every year and by breaking the group into project teams working on several films at once. To recapture that essential 'enemy' challenge of competing against an industry leader, today's Disney animators compete internally against each other's teams and also, interestingly, against their great predecessors, who made *Snow White*, *Bambi*, *Pinocchio* and the rest. Disney Animation is a rare example of Great Groups dynamics that survived, but the company as a whole also has a management flair for continually motivating staff by giving its best talents challenging new projects. For example, it took the cream of its theme-park creators and set them to develop the Disney cruise business.

Not every Silicon Valley veteran believes in the Great Groups magic. John Seely Brown, chief scientist at Xerox PARC and respected elder statesman of the Valley, doubts that there is any sustainable value in the Bennis theory. He knows from the Xerox experience that his starry group of innovators who dreamed up most of the basic tools of today's technology went on to do nothing significant in subsequent regroupings, despite having 'millions of dollars thrown at them'. Great Groups are not a paradigm, insists Brown, who finds Bennis 'poetical' on the subject rather than rigorously analytical. 'Few of the magic team leaders build an executive team with true diversity – in reality they are dictatorial. Most of Bennis's examples never had a repeat experience. They had the right secret formula at that one moment in time, but in a constantly changing world the question is how do you have an adaptive magic, how do you really foster authentic diversity – cognitive diversity, race diversity, gender diversity?'[8]

The cluster theory in creativity

Although Silicon Valley still pays lip service to the magic of the hot group in the garage, it knows that today's laid-back talents prefer comfort and a touch of fun in their working environment. Dorothy Leonard, a professor of business administration at Harvard, observes in her co-authored book about the creative process in groups, *When Sparks Fly*, that 'the office environment makes a powerful statement about the value the organisation places on creativity'. The right physical surroundings, she says, set in motion the group dynamics needed to spark off ideas: 'open communication channels among group members, well-designed places for brainstorming and noisy divergence, spaces devoted to incubation and reflection, easily accessible and well-equipped meeting places for convergence, flexible areas that invite reconfiguration by group members for creative activities, and accessible information technology that links people and ideas'.[9]

IDEO, a Silicon Valley firm whose business is designing high-tech gadgets from Apple's first commercial mouse to the Palm Pilot V, believes, along with Dorothy Parker, that 'nothing propinks like propinquity'. Built around hot groups and project teams partly modelled on the Hollywood production system, the company deliberately pitches its talents into brainstorming sessions in cramped places. 'Close quarters can charge the dynamics of a hot group,' writes general manager Tom Kelley in *The Art of Innovation*, his account of IDEO's working methods. 'Too much square footage, like too large a budget, can dissipate energy and discourage a more immediate and emotional connection between team members.' Kelley outlines IDEO's seven routes to a perfect brainstorm, such as: sixty minutes is the optimum length; begin with a fast-paced word game to clear the mind; focus on the problem; don't critique people's contributions and encourage lots of them. He also lists six surefire ways to kill effective brainstorming, including taking written notes of everything and holding the session offsite, which dilutes the creative buzz.[10]

By themselves, these things won't make people creative, but they are capable of supporting or inhibiting creativity. Outside the office, too, the 'cluster' factor works just as well for human creativity; the infrastructure of cities, with bars, pubs and clubs where young creative staff can mingle after work, persists in being attractive to creative and knowledge-based industries despite high rentals, commuting problems and other urban disadvantages. Philips, the Dutch electronics firm, moved some of its design staff from industrial Eindhoven to Amsterdam for this reason, and many creative businesses hang on to otherwise cramped, old-fashioned offices in London's Soho and Covent Garden because the area attracts the right sort of talented staff.[11]

The business environment itself can also powerfully reinforce or undermine a company's stated values. At Intel, Leonard points out in *When Sparks Fly*, CEO (now chairman) Andy Grove works out of a cramped cubicle in a rabbit warren of similar hutches; at Chaparral Steel, a US company noted for its innovative management, CEO Gordon Forward sits 'next door to the lockers where employees gather their hard hats before heading off to the mill'. Such visible 'open doors' to top management facilitate a free flow of information and communication – the first step to creativity, as well as making a positive statement about collective commitment and the absence of hierarchy.

'Creativity is a process that harnesses energy, allows knowledge to flow,' Leonard continues. 'We want physical environments that enable those flows. Knowledge, like water, flows along lines of least resistance.' In her chapter on designing the physical environment, she notes that a characteristic of many new offices in the US is a wide 'main street' corridor lined on one side with sofas and the ubiquitous whiteboards. In the UK, British Airways, under its former chief executive Robert Ayling, took the bold and expensive decision to create its entire head office at London's Heathrow airport in the style of an enclosed village called Waterside, with a 'high street', cafés, shops and even trees. Ayling himself had no conventional office, merely a space with sofas and chairs. The £200m project, whose quantifiable payback was hotly argued at board level before being approved, may take years to justify itself in productivity terms and did Ayling no good in the end – he was ousted in the spring of 2000 (for other reasons).[12] BA has also been overshadowed by a string of critical problems, not least the crash of a Concorde outside Paris in the summer of 2000, causing the suspension of the whole elite fleet and unforeseeable costs. As with politics, innovation in business thinking can take hard knocks from what Harold Macmillan, the British prime minister in the early 1960s, famously called 'events, dear boy, events'.

The supreme paradox in all this emphasis on creating opportunity for face-to-face encounters, creatively fruitful and sociable exchanges with colleagues, is that it is occurring in the age of technology, an age when we are supposed to be saving time and logistics by communicating via Lotus Notes, tele-conferencing, email and a score of other digital long-distance tools. Leonard and her co-author Walter Swap readily acknowledge that most of the creative physical environments so consciously designed rely heavily on electronic links and data storage technology. 'However, we find that all the technology in the world does not – at least not yet, and maybe never – replace face-to-face contact when it comes to brainstorming, inspiring passion or enabling many kinds of serendipitous discovery ... Face-to-face communication is the richest multi-channel medium because it enables use of all the senses, is interactive and immediate.'

Richard Scase, a professor at the University of Kent, thinks workplaces will in future become 'think-tanks to stimulate corporate creativity and innovation. Generating and managing tacit knowledge through colleague sociability will be a major challenge. A revolution in management practices will be required if sociability is to be combined with the Internet to achieve competitive success.'[13] Sociability, importantly, also promotes that critical sense of fun that is difficult to spark off a computer monitor among even the most technologically adept users of an intranet. Leonard and

Swap say that creative groups 'usually indulge in a lot of playground behaviour'.

One of the first things Nick Earle did in 1999 when Carly Fiorina appointed him head of Hewlett-Packard's new E-Services Solution (ESS) group at Cupertino, California, was to rip down the notices in H-P's corridors which prissily requested 'Please do not speak in the corridors – people are working'. Instead, Earle created a sense of levity by throwing foam rubber balls at staff across the open-plan dividers as he wandered around making calls on his mobile. 'What I am doing is really trying to get this spirit of fun and motivation,' he told Stanford University researchers preparing a case study on ESS. 'As a result, people will work until 11 at night. They work Saturdays and Sundays.'[14] Tom Kelley of IDEO advises letting hot groups 'play hookey' in an unplanned way – going to see a baseball game or a hot new movie, or a scientific exhibition that excites them. 'Sometimes the best inspiration for a team can be the Zen-like act of not doing any work at all.'[15]

Back to the playpen?

An element of play is agreed to be important in fostering creativity. Regressing to playground behaviour is actually part of the courses held at his own consultancy by one of America's leading academics in creativity and entrepreneurship. John Kao has been teaching these subjects at Harvard Business School since the mid-1980s and has a fittingly enterprising background: as well as an MBA from Harvard, he has studied medicine, gained a doctorate in psychiatry from Yale, played piano for Frank Zappa and produced the movie *Sex, Lies and Videotape* during a successful career in Hollywood. He runs biotechnology companies, a multimedia company and a creativity consultancy called The Idea Factory in San Francisco, which once featured on a BBC documentary about the consultancy business, showing managers playing with toys on a sandtable. Its meetings area is a room without walls, a space defined by tilted designer tables covered with paper ready for drawing. Kao likes to compare companies to jazz musicians, arguing that they can play variations rather than a standard score, but should have some structure to their interpretation. However, as *The Economist* pointed out in a 1996 profile, while he argues that firms should treat their creative workers well, how does he explain the fact that so many creative industries, led by Hollywood, 'thrive on fear and paranoia'?[16]

Michael Ray is professor of creativity and innovation at Stanford Graduate School of Business, where he has run a course called 'Creativity in Business' for Stanford's MBA programme since 1980. He is also professor of marketing, which betrays the practical, commercial edge behind his talk of the 'inner child' in everyone and his habit of interspersing classes with meditation exercises. Ray once worked in advertising for Foote, Cone and Belding in Chicago, after training in social psychology at Northwestern University, and he is now reducing his Stanford teaching commitments in order to spend more time running workshops for businesses such as Hewlett-Packard and Charles Schwab, and developing software to bring his classroom methods to the executive suite.

Ray, a man of engaging enthusiasm, teaches that individuals need to understand themselves and how they work before they can begin to tap the creative process. Creativity to him is not just a case of coming up with ideas, but of selecting which ideas to develop further; it has to be an ongoing thing, a way of life. Two of many techniques he uses are to ask his students to write down one thing they want to remember (and keep it in their wallets) and to identify one problem or obstacle that would, if solved, vastly improve their lives. In response to the first challenge, one former student, now a vice-president at eBay, wrote 'Remember what you want to do, and that time is limited.' Five years later he still has the frayed piece of paper in his wallet and says, 'it puts me back on track every time I look at it'. Many other former Stanford graduates still practise techniques they learned on Ray's course twenty years ago.

In contrast to corporate experiments such as Skandia's and Andersen's designer think-tanks, Professor Ray takes the approach that creativity is more individual than organisational. 'Some people live creatively in smokestack industries in the American MidWest,' he wrote in his 1986 book *Creativity in Business*. 'Others stagnate in Silicon Valley. It's easier to be creative in a company whose policies invite it, of course, but corporate policy is not a requirement for individual creative expression.' Creativity, in his definition, differs from problem-solving in being heuristic – an open, incomplete process that can lead to discovery – as opposed to algorithmic, which offers a mechanical rule for finding a solution.

Everyone, he teaches, has an inner resource – he calls it 'the Essence' – to which they need to surrender in order to tap creative thinking. 'The secret of creative decision-making is in deciding from your Essence, particularly from your intuition.' If you do this, he says, your intuition enables you to use a powerful little tool for simplifying decision-making – asking yourself if it's a yes or a no. Heidi Roizen, managing director of a Silicon Valley venture capital firm, still remembers that lesson from Ray's course in 1983. 'There have been so many times in my life when I've found myself over-analysing an issue, and I've stepped back and said, "Is it a yes or a no?" I rely on that technique a lot.'[17]

Ray also asks his students to think about a time when they had a great idea and to analyse the circumstances. The genesis of ideas is a subdivision of the creativity boom which is attracting research in the UK. Some years ago, an entrepreneur called Harry Alder published a book in which he asked 150 captains of industry how and where they got their best ideas; and more recently, two British consultants, Jean Lammiman and Michel Syrett, conducted a survey for Roffey Park Management Institute on where board directors get their ideas and inspirations from and what influences shape them – books read, plays seen, travel experiences, mentors. A sixth of the 120 CEOs, main board directors and senior managers they polled had found business inspiration through a specific fictional character in a novel and a fifth through an historical personality such as Winston Churchill, while the majority of their best ideas had come while they were on their own, away from the workplace, in relaxed settings such as a long train or plane journey, while walking the dog or listening to music.

For a subsequent report, Lammiman and Syrett studied the development of ideas in four organisations: a major international airline, a joint military headquarters overseeing peace missions, a dotcom start-up and an international aid charity. They identified five roles played by individuals in organisations whenever ideas are picked up and taken through to exploitation, and described them as sparks, shapers, sponsors, sounding boards and specialists. Sparks are those who create the idea or vision; sponsors, those who promote the idea or project and sustain interest in it; shapers, those who make it a practical feasibility for the organisation; sounding boards, those outside the organisation whose influence or knowledge helps push the idea forward; and specialists, those who draw on their own knowledge or skills to shape the idea in a specific direction. Without this chain of activity, the authors suggest, many ideas remain unexploited 'diamonds in the dust' because no one is mandated to recognise their value or to authorise their further refinement. More often than not, it is a process of pure happenstance, with no organisational system behind it.[18]

Testing ideas on the market

Two interesting management thinkers working at INSEAD, the international business school outside Paris, have also been researching the secrets of identifying winning ideas. W. Chan Kim and Renée Mauborgne, professors of international management and strategy, have devised six 'utility levers' to test the market viability of new ideas:

(1) **Customer productivity** What is the biggest block to customer productivity? How does the innovative product or service eliminate it? Example: Dyson's bagless vacuum cleaner made the job quicker and easier.

(2) **Simplicity** What is the greatest source of complexity for customers? How does the innovation dramatically simplify this? Example: Intuit's 'Quicken' software eliminated accounting jargon.

(3) **Convenience** What is the greatest inconvenience for customers? How does the innovation remove it? Example: Virgin's limousine service for business-class travellers helped ease the hassle of getting to and from the airport.

(4) **Risk** What are the greatest uncertainties customers face? How does the innovation eliminate these risks? Example: Enron took the volatility out of gas prices with its commodity swaps and futures contracts.

(5) **Fun and image** What are the biggest blocks to enjoyment and image? How does the innovation add emotion and cachet? Example: Starbucks coffee bars offer more than simply a place to drink coffee.

(6) **Environmental friendliness** What causes the

greatest harm to the environment? How does the innovation reduce or eliminate this? Example: Philips's Alto light-bulb, using less mercury, allowed fluorescent office lighting to be disposed of without special dumps.

One or more of these six criteria have to be met before the idea goes on to be tested for price and cost economics and other potential barriers to development.[19]

The British consultants Syrett and Lammiman differentiate between ideas that lead to a specific decision or solution and those which are more truly creative inspirations. Given that creativity is not another word for problem-solving, it is only worth nurturing within an organisation if it is going to lead to innovation for the business – and innovation, says the strategy guru Gary Hamel, is going to be as critical to business success in the next fifty years as the quality movement was in the last fifty. It will be even bigger in impact than quality management, Hamel argues, because it affects more than the products or services a firm provides. In the Internet economy, ruled by low entry barriers, the free circulation of ideas on the Web and competitors just 'one click away', innovation has to apply to entire business models.

Some of the most successful newcomers of the last decade have been doing this instinctively, and not necessarily in the digital economy. Virgin, for example, is not so much a new kind of business model as a maker of new businesses: it has created nearly two hundred of them, linked only by the powerful Virgin brand. So far the model has worked, thanks to the powerful brand factor of Richard Branson and the non-hierarchical 'speak-up' culture and mechanisms of business development which ensure that good ideas get considered and properly evaluated. The evaluations are led by Virgin Management, a small team that helps to launch new businesses in much the same way as a venture capital board. Virgin basically asks four questions before deciding to go for an investment decision: What is the potential for changing the market and benefiting consumers? Is the venture radical enough to fit the Virgin brand? What can Virgin's experience bring to the party? Is the risk manageable? The answers to all four have to be positive.

Forget foresight, invent a new business model

Gary Hamel made his now formidable reputation in 1994 with a co-authored book (with C.K. Prahalad) called *Competing for the Future*, which introduced the influential concepts of core competencies – the capabilities special to a company – and 'industry foresight' – the art of anticipating markets and customers five or ten years ahead. Six years on, Hamel's latest book *Leading the Revolution* and its associated seminars place far less emphasis on foresight because e-commerce has so dramatically foreshortened planning cycles that it's no longer a useful exercise. Instead, he advises adopting 'non-linear strategies' to create entirely new business models. No one ten years ago, for example, could have foreseen the sudden emergence of Amazon.com or the growth of online selling in areas such as books, CDs and travel. This was an entirely new business concept, and there are dozens of other examples on every high street, from Starbucks coffee shops to Wal-Mart discount supermarkets. In the digital age, companies now reinvent their strategies in opportunistic ways: AOL, the Internet upstart which stunned the media industry by taking over Time-Warner, has changed its underlying business model more often in its short life, says Hamel, 'than most companies change their product literature'.

Like Starbucks and Wal-Mart, not all new business

models are Internet-related. A French cosmetics chain called Sephora snatched 20% of its domestic market in its first year of operation. Its revolutionary idea was to sell all cosmetics brands together in one area, thus enabling shoppers to make comparisons on the spot. In every department store the entrenched custom had been (and still is) for each manufacturer to have a separate counter. Sephora has since been taken over by the luxury goods conglomerate LVMH, which owns such brands as Louis Vuitton, Moët and Hennessy. Another pioneering example of old-economy reinvention is GE Capital, originally an in-house department of General Electric for financing customers' purchases of dishwashers and washing machines, but now one of the world's most innovative financial services companies, managing products as wide-ranging as global insurance and department store customer accounts. It is also the biggest cash-generating engine within the massive GE group.

Hamel, who lives on Palo Alto's Sand Hills Road among the e-billionaires (next to Oracle's Larry Ellison) and runs his own strategic consultancy, Strategos, in the heart of Silicon Valley, has cornered a lucrative market in advising old-economy companies on how to 'bring Silicon Valley inside' (see Chapter 9). Large companies, says Hamel, have advantages that in many ways offset those of the Valley. They have resources, a ready source of capital, and brand and distribution strengths that the Valley lacks. Moreover, anyone in large 'legacy' companies can learn to 'blow up old models' and design new ones. Hamel offers these ten 'deep rules' or 'i-genes' for creating and sustaining a culture for continuous innovation, based on the fashionable principle of complexity science that small simple things lead to large, complex consequences (see Chapter 5):

(1) **Unreasonable expectations** GE Capital expects

to grow its earnings by 20% every year. The company says: 'When you have objectives that are outlandish, it forces you to think very differently about the opportunities.' Charles Schwab, the fast-growing online discount broker, has a similar 20% target every year, starting from zero. There are no mature industries, says Hamel, 'only mature managers who unthinkingly accept someone else's definition of what's possible. Be unreasonable!' Lettuce-growing, he points out, was considered a pretty mature business until someone thought up the idea of bagging lettuces as pre-washed salad leaves at a premium price. Result: a business that zoomed from zero in the late 1980s to $1.4bn in 1999.

(2) **Elastic business definition** 'Too many companies define themselves by what they do, rather than by what they know,' says Hamel. He quotes Virgin's head of business development, Gordon McCallum: 'There is no assumption about what business Virgin should or shouldn't be in . . . the culture is one of why not, rather than why.'

(3) **A cause, not a business** Charles Schwab has a saying: 'Around here, we think we're curing cancer.' David Pottruck, Schwab's CEO, expresses it more lyrically: 'We are the guardians of our customers' financial dreams.' Schwab lists 'empathy' with its customers as one of its core values.

(4) **New voices** Seek out young people – 'they are living closer to the future', says Hamel. CEO Gerhard Schulmeyer at Siemens Nixdorf appointed 'reverse mentors' in their twenties to give senior executives an understanding of the next generation. Procter and Gamble have instituted a similar scheme. Anheuser Busch, the US brewing giant, has a young 'shadow executive committee' reporting directly to the board. GE Capital put together a research team of under-thirties 'to come back and tell us where the opportunities were'.

(5) **An open market for ideas** Enron, the once-iconic US energy group, used to cover walls with whiteboard and tell its staff, 'any time you have an idea, put it on the whiteboard'. Virgin Group claims that everyone has the phone number of chairman Sir Richard Branson, 'and he probably gets three calls a day from employees wanting to try something new'.

(6) **An open market for capital** Shell's 'Game Changer' project has a panel of six empowered to spend a budget of $20m on any business ideas they rate highly enough. Anyone in the company can submit an idea, and four of the group's five best recent growth businesses have started this way, leading among other results to a $30m new oil exploration operation in Gabon.

(7) **An open market for talent** The Disney Corporation, which has colonised whole territories of the global leisure market, believes that 'people want to be able to work on interesting projects. That's why we took the best people we had in theme parks and let them help launch the cruise ship business.' Hamel tells his seminars: 'Every individual in the organisation should have the same opportunity to change the destiny of the corporation as the CEO.'

(8) **Low-risk experimentation** Launch a new business concept by starting it small and inexpensive. GE Capital explains: 'We go for things where the barriers to entry are small. We always start by buying a "popcorn stand" – a little business we can use as a beta-test.'

(9) **Cellular division** Virgin says: 'We don't run an empire, we run a lot of small companies . . . We want to be a substantial business with a small company feel, so people can see the results of their own efforts.'

(10) **Personal wealth accumulation** In 1999, says Hamel, a quarter of Harvard and Stanford MBA graduates went to work for companies with fewer than

fifty people because 'they know their best chance of accumulating wealth is to go work for entrepreneurial companies that reward people for wealth creation'.

De-tox the organisation

There are other components to the innovation agenda, and the majority involve redesigning management processes – most of which, Hamel says, are 'controlled by defenders of the past'. A company risks being 'toxic to innovation' if its management processes are 'calendar-driven, conservative, biased towards its existing business model, focused on its existing customers and markets'. Organisations need to train people at all levels to become innovators and to make themselves receptive to change by encouraging rule-busting 'activists' with good ideas. 'Change almost never starts at the top,' he points out wryly. 'How often does a revolution start with the monarchy?'[20]

Since the springs of innovation and ideas themselves are the fuel of the new economy, it's not surprising that a number of would-be Big Ideas centre on cognitive theory, from the workings of neural networks to emotional intelligence or EQ and 'spiritual intelligence' or SQ. There is also an upsurge of interest in the age-old techniques of meditation and religious retreats as a channel to better self-development and the management of others (see Chapter 6). EQ, which has been hailed as a major breakthrough in business thinking, is the brainchild of former *Wall Street Journal* writer Daniel Goleman who, in the way of those who hit the jackpot with a book that turns into a new management fad, has become a mini-guru in demand at conferences on both sides of the Atlantic.

Inspired, as he freely admits, by the work of Harvard professor Howard Gardner in the field of multiple intelligences and how great leaders rouse impassioned responses in untutored minds, Goleman has spun several books (starting in 1995 with the bestseller *Emotional Intelligence*) out of his central argument that competencies such as self-awareness, self-discipline, persistence and empathy with others are of greater consequence than IQ in much of life. It may be IQ that gets individuals into their chosen career in the first place, but after that it becomes irrelevant by comparison with the ability to manage one's own emotions and those of others – the key to drawing out the best performance in people. In his later *Working With Emotional Intelligence* (1998), Goleman finds the principle even more important in today's 'virtual organisations' that increasingly depend on the talents, creativity and motivation of independent agents (see Chapter 6).

Rewiring the brain

In neural studies, a new figure on the management conference circuit is the American-born physicist and psychiatrist Danah Zohar, based in Oxford. Her dual speciality is how we can use our brains to much greater effect and at the same time develop something she calls 'spiritual intelligence', the cognitive dimension that addresses the big meaning-of-life questions. In a master-class given at the 1999 National Conference of Britain's Institute of Personnel and Development (IPD), Zohar put forward her theories about 'rewiring the corporate brain' using the new physics of the twentieth century, particularly quantum and chaos physics, as a model for overturning the Newtonian training that has led us to develop our brains in a linear way.

We are not using our whole brain, Zohar contends. We come into the world with our brains almost completely unwired, unlike every other species with the exception of chimpanzees (who share 98% of human DNA). This is what makes humans creative. But by the age of 18 or earlier, we are all wired to believe certain things, think in certain ways, see the world as we learned to see it. People who see things through the filter of deeply held assumptions are prevented from thinking about other possibilities that exist in every situation. However, 18 is no longer, as was once thought, the peak of intellectual ability: everyone can rewire his or her brain until the day he or she dies. We can 'blow up the brain' and escape from ingrained assumptions. Recent advances in the understanding of how the brain works have discovered that its neurons 'oscillate coherently in unison', moving from the front to the back of the skull at 40 cycles per second. So although different parts of the brain are involved in transmitting images and information, a holistic process is at work which Zohar calls 'spiritual intelligence' or 'spiritual quotient' (SQ). It is this, she argues, that gives us our creativity, the ability to think at the edge. 'This has nothing to do with religion; it comes from spiritus, the vitalising principle, our quest for meaning as humans. SQ is our "asking why" intelligence – all those niggling questions we ask at 3am when we can't sleep. If we want to use the whole brain we have to do so in terms of meaning, purposes, vision and values.'[21]

In a recent online interview, Zohar explained further: 'It takes a hell of a lot of energy to change the wiring in the brain, but I've concluded that only by tearing out the corporate mindset and putting in new neural pathways will we ever see the kind of change demanded by the twenty-first century. Corporate management must start talking about the spiritual and philosophical questions of our time. A lot of companies have been restructured lately; isn't it time we started talking about how to restructure ourselves? Our communities? Our society? If I had my way, I'd send a lot of corporate chiefs off to reflect for a year on a few deep, existential questions. And I'd have them read some of the great books.'

In her own latest book, *SQ – The Ultimate Intelligence*, co-authored with her psychiatrist husband Ian Marshall, Zohar claims that 'the search for meaning, vision and value is the most important aspect of being human. If you have a high SQ, you will become much more productive.' She would turn on its head Abraham Maslow's famous 'hierarchy of needs', that pyramid rising from the basic requirements of food, shelter and security to the desire for inner fulfilment. 'Meaning is the basic stuff of human existence,' she argues.

The principle of SQ draws on that of quantum physics and its modern offshoots, chaos and complexity science, which contend that things are not predictable and ultimately controllable, that living systems are complex, not simple, and that the whole is greater than the sum of the tiny parts which Newtonian physics advocated studying and understanding. Quantum physics, explains Zohar, tells us that the world does not consist of separate pieces, that every part of the universe is implicated in every other part and it is all about relationships between them. Fuzzy logic (now so accepted as to be a computerised feature of the latest washing-machines, enabling the machine to sense how to deal with different types of fabric and degrees of soiling) is the outcome of quantum thinking, as is scenario planning. Systems need to be unstable to be receptive to information. In Zohar's words, 'It's scary at the edge of chaos, but that's where creativity happens.'[22]

In basing her SQ theories on the quantum view of the universe with its creative swirl of chaos and complexity, Zohar is one of many management thinkers and visionary corporate leaders tapping into a rich new vein of research, that of living systems and ecological principles. The mother lode of this research is to be found, ironically, just 25 miles from Los Alamos in New Mexico, where atomic science reached its destructive apogee during World War Two. At the Santa Fe

Institute, however, the science is all about life as well as death in nature, and has as good a claim as any to be the next Big Idea.

Powerpoints

- The biggest idea of all in a business world now run on the power of ideas would be to get more of them out of the people you work with.
- Ideas are best generated by a readiness to risk failure, by encouraging cross-pollination among creative people and by using old ideas in new ways. Creativity comes out of conversation: have plenty of informal meeting places at work.
- Innovation may be encouraged by a conducive environment but it has also famously flourished in garages. 'Great' or 'hot' groups can work miracles anywhere if they believe in the worth of what they are doing.
- Technology enables the exchange of information and ideas but can never substitute for face-to-face brainstorming.
- Creativity by itself is not enough. There must be mechanisms in the company for identifying winning ideas.
- Innovation will be as critical to business as the quality revolution was fifty years ago. But innovation is now about more than inventing new products; it is about inventing whole new business models.
- We can change the wiring in our brains for better performance, better self-development and the exercise of emotional and spiritual intelligence in order to understand others and ourselves better.

NOTES

[1] *Harvard Business Review*, May/June 2000

[2] Skyrme, David and Amidon, Debra: *Creating the Knowledge-Based Business*, Business Intelligence, 1997

[3] Baghai, Mehrdad; Coley, Stephen and White, David: *The Alchemy of Growth*, Orion 1999; author interview

[4] *FT*, 30/31 December 1999

[5] H-P Web site: www.hp.com/ghp/features/invent/rules.html

[6] Lipman-Blumen, J. and Leavitt, H.J.: *Hot Groups*, OUP, 1999

[7] Bennis, W. and Biederman, P. W.: *Organizing Genius*, Nicholas Brealey, 1997

[8] author interview, September 2000

[9] Leonard, Dorothy and Swap, Walter: *When Sparks Fly*, Harvard Business School Press, 1999

[10] Kelley, Tom: *The Art of Innovation*, Currency Doubleday, 2001

[11] Scase, Richard: 'The net won't kill the office', *Observer*, 15.10.00

[12] Syrett, M. and Lammiman, J.: *Entering Tiger Country: How Ideas are Shaped in Organisations*, Roffey Park Management Institute, 2000

[13] Scase, Richard: *Britain in 2010*, Capstone, 2000

[14] Graduate School of Business, Stanford University, Case No. EC-16, May 2000

[15] Kelley, Tom: *The Art of Innovation*

[16] *The Economist*, 17.8.96

[17] author interview, Stanford, September 2000; *Fast Company*, June 2000

[18] Lammiman, J. and Syrett, M.: *Innovation at the Top: Where Do Directors Get Their Ideas From?*, Roffey Park Management Institute, 1998; *Entering Tiger Country: How Ideas are Shaped in Organizations*, Roffey Park, 2000

[19] Kim, W. Chan and Mauborgne, Renée: summarised from 'Knowing a Winning Business Idea When You See One', *Harvard Business Review*, Sept/Oct 2000

[20] author interview, February 2000; IIR seminar, London, March 2000; Hamel, Gary: *Leading the Revolution*, Harvard Business School, November 2000

[21] IPD conference papers, November 1999

[22] Zohar, Danah and Marshall, Ian: *SQ – The Ultimate Intelligence*, Bloomsbury, 2000

CHAPTER FIVE

BIRDS, BEES AND BUSINESS

The Santa Fe Institute, a collection of low, landscaped buildings on the outskirts of the New Mexico state capital, is the intellectual powerhouse at the heart of the new economy, and it is rewriting the rules economists have followed for two centuries. What is sometimes known as the Santa Fe school of economics has shifted the entire Newtonian model of historic economic theory to the complex adaptive systems found in quantum physics and the natural world. Its principles have been influencing business corporations of the stature of Royal Dutch/Shell, BP and Hewlett-Packard, as consultants and management thinkers such as Richard Pascale disseminate Santa Fe's work among industry.

The institute itself does not develop business applications out of its research into living systems, but maintains a Business Network to spread the fruits of its research and harvest revenue through corporate subscriptions of $30,000 a year. This diaspora of ideas, along with a stream of books on the science of complexity – what Pascale describes as 'a broad-based inquiry into the common properties of all living things' – has uncovered a huge potential for fresh thinking about the art of managing business enterprises. In Pascale's words it has 'begun to challenge the machine model as a suitable management platform for the information age'.

Unravelling complexity

Complexity science, the basis of the new management thinking, is well named and is often confused with its two major sub-studies, chaos theory and complex adaptive systems. Essentially, complexity is about finding patterns in a variety of apparently haphazard phenomena in the universe, whether from the natural, biological world or the technological and economic world, and establishing how order in these 'complex adaptive systems' emerges from chaos through the interplay of relationships. In business applications it attempts to identify the underlying processes and relationships in companies to help them become as adaptive and creative as possible. Its study was only made possible by the advent of powerful computation technology, and it was spearheaded in the early 1960s by the chaos theory work of Edward Lorenz, a scientist modelling weather systems on a primitive computer at the Massachusetts Institute of Technology. The one axiom everyone remembers about chaos theory is that small changes can lead to large results, exemplified by Lorenz's 'butterfly effect', the proposition that a butterfly flapping its wings in Brazil could set off a tornado in Texas.

Chaos theory was the first aspect of complexity science to become fashionable, mainly as a result of a best-selling book by James Gleick in 1987, but while it spawned learned journals and conferences by the score, it did not seem to have particular relevance to the world of business – apart from the small changes/large results effect, which is now a recognised feature of successful change management. The behaviour of complex adaptive systems, on the other hand, offered tempting parallels. Pascale explains the difference thus: 'The world is not chaotic, it is complex . . . A swarm of bees or the ants that overrun a picnic blanket may seem chaotic but they are actually only behaving as complex adaptive systems.' The new economics teaches that economic structures such as financial markets do not merely imitate biological or eco-systems, they actually obey the same universal natural laws and therefore *are* biological in essence.

'Complex adaptive systems' are found everywhere in nature from the cosmos to the garden pond, and in the instinctive intricacies exhibited by termite communities. They are also, the theory runs, the driving force behind such human endeavours as business organisations and the movements of stock and futures markets. They are made up of independent but dynamically interacting agents, whether ants, cities, molecules, galaxies or the Internet, that evolve their optimum performance by constant learning, changing and adapting to their environments. However chaotic the process looks at any point, it always evolves to a state of creative order, a state famously defined by the Santa Fe scientist Norman Packard as 'the edge of chaos'. Because it is a bottom-up process, not directed by any individual or group of individuals at the top, these dynamic interactions are said to be self-organising – and ever since Douglas McGregor invented Theory Y in the 1950s, the ideal for enlightened business enterprises has been the self-organising, non-hierarchical team, so the idea of studying complex adaptive systems in a business context has obvious attractions. The constantly turbulent sea of change in which businesses now operate is another persuasive reason for looking at how adaptive systems work.

In this context, the Internet is often put forward as a perfect example of a complex adaptive system, resembling a beehive in the way information moves horizontally and is shared rather than being first channelled up to the CEO and then down again through the organisation in decision form. Nobody is in charge of the Internet, so decisions can be made immediately by the people most intimately involved. Warren Bennis, the leadership guru and co-author of *Organizing Genius*, a study of phenomenally productive project groups in history, observes that most urgent projects require 'the co-ordinated contributions of many talented people working together. Whether the task is building a global business or discovering the mysteries of the human brain, it does not happen at the top.'

Pascale, a one-time McKinsey researcher who made his name in 1981 with a co-authored study of Japanese industrial success, *The Art of Japanese Management*, is the leading international figure in this new management approach to natural science. He is the former Stanford and London Business School professor who in his influential 1990 book *Managing on the Edge* warned successful companies that they carried the seeds of their own failure within them if they failed to break and reshape their locked-in ways of thinking by fostering creative dissension in their management. From here it was a natural progression to studying how eco-systems deal with the stagnating state of equilibrium. 'For any company, equilibrium is death,' says Pascale. 'Jack Welch (General Electric's chairman) is a master of the theatre of disequilibrium. He knows on a very large scale how to cause an organisation to question itself.'

Pascale spent much of the 1990s working as a visiting scholar at Santa Fe and adapting the lessons of natural processes and evolution to business organisations. He is convinced that here is the seedbed for a dominant Big Idea of the twenty-first century. 'This will be the century of the living sciences,' he said in mid-2000. As a management theory, he thinks it will last 'at least thirty years and maybe a hundred. We are experiencing a profound shift and entering a new scientific renaissance.' Living systems, he believes, are particularly suited to the way the digital economy works –

computer networks behave in similar ways – and learning from them is an idea whose time has come. The catalyst, he thinks, is the convergence of life sciences with the power of information technology and the constantly expanding breakthroughs common to both. 'It's usually the convergence of several things that causes an idea to have staying power. We're talking about everything from beehives to bond traders, ant colonies to amoebae; we're talking about microbiology, ecology, the way markets behave. It's about independent agents acting in parallel, bound by simple rules creating larger and much more complicated structures.'[1]

Eric Beinhocker, a formidably bright young McKinsey consultant and a member of the advisory committee to Santa Fe's Business Network who has been working on similar lines to Pascale, says the Santa Fe biological hypothesis is very much a 'work in progress', but thinks that the results already 'suggest ways in which complexity thinking may confirm, build on or overturn many traditional ideas in management'. Complexity, he explains, arises from the effect of each agent's actions in the system on one or more other agents. If the rules by which they interact are fixed, such as laws of physics or economic diktats such as cutting your price when your competitor does, this is known as a complex system. If the rules are still evolving, 'as with genes encoded in DNA or the strategies pursued by players in a game, the result is a complex adaptive system'.[2]

Strategy based on complexity thinking, he argues, is more likely than one based on traditional frameworks to be of use to a CEO operating in industries facing deregulation, convergence, globalisation and bewildering technological change. 'What this CEO needs is a model of a world where innovation, change and uncertainty, rather than equilibrium, are the natural state of things.' Closed equilibrium systems, developed by nineteenth-century physicists, were at the heart of traditional economics and retain their hold on management thinking. Nature, however, offers abundant evidence of the creative/destructive power of 'punctuated equilibrium', which is more in tune with the way businesses need to be run in the new economy.

Punctuated equilibrium, edge of chaos and 'robust strategies'

Punctuated equilibrium is a much-used metaphor in the new economics. In nature it occurs when periods of relative calm and stability are interrupted by violent, stormy interludes. These often result in a dramatic restructuring and change – even, periodically, in the destruction and replacement of plant or animal species. Stephen Jay Gould, the writer of popular paleontological history, has illustrated from his studies of fossils how evolution came about largely through such big, traumatic events, rather than by the Darwinian interpretation of gradual incremental adaptation.

What such traumatic events do is move the patterns of growth closer to the 'edge of chaos', a term originally coined to describe the arena in nature where revitalisation takes place, caught between equilibrium and chaos. Hurricanes, typhoons and catastrophic forest fires are simple examples of traumatic events that operate on the edge of chaos; violent weather changes disturb the oceans and the atmosphere, cleaning and replenishing them with oxygen, carbon dioxide and other nutrients, as well as clearing out dead or insecure plant life. 'Major environmental disturbances such as asteroid impacts or radical shifts in weather can trigger the proliferation of new species and accelerate adaptation within species,' writes Pascale in his latest book, *Surfing the Edge of Chaos*, based on his Santa Fe work. Fires, as ecologists find when they try to replicate a stretch of prairie or savannah, are essential for the regeneration of biodiversity. Some plants typical of the habitat simply do not reappear in the controlled regrowth, and the reason has proved to be the absence of fire.

Relating these findings to business activities offers some obvious parallels: booms and busts in the stock market, or massive technology shifts that put old-economy models under severe strain and soon break them and reinvent them, or render them obsolete. Not surprisingly, the edge of chaos has become a phrase beloved of the business guru industry, though it is often just another way of describing the forces that periodically unnerve old, complacent industries. Not long ago, market hurricanes in the shape of 'category killer' entrants such as Wal-Mart and Toys 'Я' Us sent traditional retailers into a tailspin from which many had barely started to recover before they were hit again by the Force 12 arrival of e-commerce. Apple's personal computer was a business earthquake that erupted under the mighty market leader IBM, forcing radical change in an organisation that had been accustomed to decades of dominant equilibrium.

Every standard text on change advocates radical, in the sense of root-and-branch, treatment, rather than allowing resistance to build and undermine the process. Niccolò Machiavelli, the Renaissance master of manipulative diplomacy, understood this when he advised the new rulers of a captured state to take the most difficult, ruthless decisions first.

Historically, says Eric Beinhocker, 'the equilibrium view of strategy has focused on how to be a good competitor, not a good evolver. There are tensions and tradeoffs between the two. Yet the most successful companies do not simply strike a middle ground, but manage to excel at competing and evolving simultaneously, despite the tensions.' Among the essentials of successful evolution is what Beinhocker describes as 'being both focused and robust', or, in another academic paper, as 'populations of robust strategies'.[3]

This phrase relates to nature's tendency to foster a flock of alternative survival plans in order to test the fittest for any future environment. In business terms, the Californian venture capital enterprise Idealab does it by backing hosts of potential start-ups. It can tolerate those that fail to make the grade because it is more than compensated by the few that make it big. Capital One, the credit card-issuing virtual bank, follows a similar strategy in its scatter-gun marketing, offering low entry borrowing terms to huge numbers of people, only a fraction of whom will prove profitable customers for the bank. Bill Gates flummoxed both customers and competitors by simultaneously investing in Windows and in its principal rival technologies, but he was effectively hedging his bets by fostering a population of alternative strategies.

Robust strategies, says Beinhocker, differ from scenario analysis because they do not attempt to identify the most or least likely future. Instead, to quote Francis Crick, the co-discoverer of DNA, they accept that 'evolution is cleverer than you are'. In effect, the concept 'makes a company more like a market, with a population of strategies that cover a broad array of possibilities and evolve over time, some succeeding and some failing'.[4]

Living systems as a business model

In *Surfing the Edge of Chaos*, Richard Pascale sets out to distil a whole new management model from complex living systems. He offers four 'bedrock principles that are inherently and powerfully applicable to the living system called a business':

(1) 'Equilibrium is the precursor to death.' Living systems are less responsive to external change pressures when in a state of equilibrium and are therefore at maximum risk.

(2) 'In the face of threat, or when galvanised by a compelling opportunity, living things move towards the edge of chaos' – a condition which brings new solutions and 'the sweet spot for productive change'.

(3) When this happens, living systems 'self-organise' to enable new entities to evolve.

(4) 'Living systems cannot be directed along a linear path' – they need to be disturbed to provoke the desired outcome.

Silicon Valley itself, says Pascale, is an example of a living system obeying all these rules. It is a 'design for diversity', with the whole community behaving like a super-organism: 'ideas, employees, capital and technology flow rapidly within the system . . . the turmoil contributes to the region's intellectual and economic vibrancy'. It displays self-organisation in the way scientists from the universities, entrepreneurs and investors come together in a continuously changing stream to form start-ups, and in the way businesses, academic institutions and venture capitalists form and re-form strategic alliances, partnerships or project teams. It combines the ingredients necessary for the emergence of new life in the shape of technologies or business platforms such as e-commerce: innovation, technology infrastructure, capital, intellectual and ethnic diversity (many leading Valley software engineers and designers are Asian) and atmospheric stimulation, both physically (from the climate) and intellectually. 'In Silicon Valley . . . species gain resilience by banding together, sharing resources and working in tandem. If one leg of a network buckles, others can keep it intact,' writes Pascale. 'This web of self-organising relationships has become a conscious operating model for the Valley.' There is a rich supply of independent programmers feeding talent into such projects as Sun Microsystems' applications programme for Java, while the ever-churning turnover of employed staff means that a further wave of talent is kept on the move among competitor firms. On average, says Pascale, each of 20 Valley firms whose connections were charted in a *Fortune* magazine article turned out to have 10 shared connections, and some had more than that.[5]

Companies with adaptive strategies

Several major companies are said to be absorbing lessons from living systems into their organisations, among them Royal Dutch/Shell, Hewlett-Packard Laboratories, Monsanto and BP-Amoco. Sir John (now Lord) Browne, the widely admired chief executive of BP-Amoco, has been convinced of the value of adaptive strategies since he was appointed managing director of the oil group's exploration division in 1989, at a critically competitive time for the industry. Browne had to distil a bloated and wastefully competing array of regional baronies into an organisation more capable of focusing on the competition, and there was only so much he could do through operational decisions. The turning point, as recounted by Pascale (a consultant to BP) in *Surfing the Edge of Chaos*, was his public admission to BP's top one hundred managers that he needed their help in 'how to do this together'.

Browne invited them to divide into teams and conduct an organisational audit, based on the McKinsey 'seven-S' framework, with each team taking one 'S' – structure, systems, strategy and so on – and analysing BPX in that context. This process resulted in what Browne called a 'real-time case study of the business', and was further analysed down to 'nine big problems'. Nine teams were then set up and a three-day offsite workshop scheduled for six weeks ahead, to draw up a course of action for each problem. The announcement produced uproar among executives who were already entering one of the busiest periods of the year and felt overloaded to begin with; in Pascale's reading, Browne had created the equivalent of violent natural disequilibrium, pushing people and problems onto the 'edge of chaos'.

Amazingly, on the third day of the workshop, with time running out, each team managed to come up with a proposal for tackling its 'big problem', and delivered it publicly in a quarter of an hour. Browne kept the sense of disequilibrium going by requiring each team to produce a 'green paper' in 90 days. The work already done had to be backed up by benchmarking, fieldwork, pilot projects and intensive consultation. Calendars were ripped up and a sense of near-panic took over, but six weeks later the green papers were ready for active participative debate at a big meeting in Phoenix, Arizona. The true nature of the 'big problems' unravelled and became understandable. Solutions emerged, the organisation came out of its edge-of-chaos zone energised, optimistic and adaptive, and BPX's competitive position in the market was revitalised. The turnaround became the stuff of admiring case studies, and Browne was soon moving upward to become chief executive of the group.[6]

Shell followed a similar deliberate strategy to disturb its human ecology, after an earlier attempt at corporate culture transformation had failed. Like BP, the Anglo-Dutch oil group had suffered from hardened arteries over a long period of market ascendancy; bureaucracies and baronies abounded, people and processes were frozen in a status quo that had performed satisfactorily for decades until the competitive pressures of the 1990s. Cor Herkstroter, the Dutch chairman, tried a consultancy-driven change programme based on downsizing, streamlining and restructuring the over-independent operating companies in a quid-pro-quo deal to give more focus and power to the centre. The operating companies soon saw through this, however, and resisted it.

The person who finally achieved breakthrough was Steven Miller, head of the oil products business and a member of Shell's five-strong committee of managing directors – the entity that really ran Shell. The process by which he eventually broke down the fossilised structure and released dynamic living energies is fascinatingly detailed by Pascale, who sees Miller's work as transformative. Miller took a view of Shell as a living organism that needed to evolve into change rather than be driven into it like a machine. Disturbing the equilibrium was an early priority, achieved by going public with Shell's problems – a shocking procedure for a company accustomed to keeping its public image polished and impregnable. After that, the process of getting senior management more in touch with the frontline people, of workshops and deadlines and fieldwork, was more complex than at BPX, given the scale of the organisation and its challenges, but the results were similarly energising.

At the heart of Shell becoming an adaptive organisation was the 'fishbowl', the term for its system by which members of the top management team sit in a room with a regional team – all under scrutiny by other teams sitting on the perimeter – while the regional people set out what they plan to do and what they require from the centre. In the culture of old Shell such direct conversation between field executives and senior management had rarely happened. The process, in Miller's words, created 'complete transparency between the people at the coal-face and me and my top management team . . . It creates a personal connection, and it changes how we talk with each other and work with each other . . . After that, I can call up those folks anywhere in the world and talk in a very direct way because of this personal connectedness. It has completely changed the dynamics of our operations.'

Bottom-line results from the adaptive approach to change, as opposed to the planned top-down approach that had failed, were almost immediate. Miller's initiatives were in full swing in 1996, and in assessing Shell's performance for 1997, auditors were attributing a $300m net profit gain directly to these initiatives, while market share was increasing through the European operating companies. The release of new energies threw up other innovations. The group's research and technical services organisation, previously costing £2bn a year, metamorphosed into Shell Global Solutions, now the world's eleventh largest technical services consultancy and a modest profit centre for Shell instead of a mammoth cost. However, the forces of resistance should never be under-estimated, sometimes from shareholders as much as from middle management, and Shell's current strategy has backtracked from Miller's vision of living growth to a much more conservative model, governed by restrictions on capital investment. Once again, says Pascale, it 'teeters on the brink of equilibrium'.

At Hewlett-Packard, however, the initiative at H-P Laboratories to introduce the ideas of living systems not only succeeded in its own arena but has spread to other parts of the group as its CEO Carly Fiorina, appointed in 1999, pursues her strategy to reinvent H-P and take it back to its innovatory roots. Here, the transformation was led by Joel Birnbaum, then director of H-P Labs and now the group's chief scientist, and Barbara Waugh, whom he co-opted as Worldwide Change Manager. The objective was to harness a commitment to become 'the world's best industrial research lab'; it was pursued through a host of bottom-up initiatives and cross-pollinations, to galvanise ideas and encourage young talent to promote itself more. Four years into the programme, H-P Labs have become a living web of emergent activities instead of a somewhat compartmentalised set of scientists who often felt their role was being sidelined. New business platforms have been created for H-P that have cumulatively contributed more than $1bn of extra revenues.[7]

A new ideas industry?

Some time before Pascale published *Surfing the Edge of Chaos*, other writers were exploring Santa Fe territory, tapping into a growing acceptance among business thinkers that companies, to be sustainable, should be regarded as social systems, living organisms in themselves and not mere money machines for shareholders. In Britain, the move towards this humanistic view, though not specifically linked to living systems theory, has been led by the business and social philosopher Charles Handy and the 'Tomorrow's Company' project, a study of best practice management for the twenty-first century set up by the 247-year-old Royal Society for the Arts, Manufactures and Commerce, commonly known as the RSA.

Launched in 1995, the RSA project has now progressed to a stand-alone charity supported by some fifty blue-chip companies which subscribe to its core principle, that a company 'clearly defines its purpose and values and communicates them in a consistent manner to all those important to the company's success'. The latter include corporate leaders, investors, people and society at large, recognising that 'the centre of gravity in business success is already shifting from the exploitation of a company's physical assets to the realisation of the creativity and learning potential of all the people with whom it has contact, not just its employees'.[8] Elsewhere, the ubiquitous Arie de Geus, a sought-after conference speaker, continues to spread the gospel of his book *The Living Company*, which argues that organisations can ensure longevity by good stewardship and care for their human assets.

Complexity science emerged as a coming Big Idea for business in a number of books and newspaper articles in 1998, and has since spawned a burgeoning genre of publishing in which science, or pseudo-science, is invoked as an aid to better management. A much-praised book called *Competing on the Edge*, by McKinsey consultant Shona L. Brown and Stanford professor Kathleen Eisenhardt, was one of the first to advocate the business/science convergence in order to create an organisation capable of continuous dynamic change and adaptation. Around the same time a science writer named Roger Lewin, author of an early book on complexity, teamed up with Birute Regine, a Harvard-educated psychologist, to produce *The Soul At Work*, looking at business case studies in terms of complex adaptive systems. Taking its examples mainly from companies in the new economy, the book asserted that complexity science provides a model for management practice 'likely to nurture underlying processes in companies so that they will naturally be as adaptive and creative as they can be'. Since complex adaptive systems operate through interacting agents, and in companies those agents are human individuals, this suggested to the authors a new synthesis of the human and scientific management approaches, one more suited to the fast-changing, unpredictable, computer-driven age than the linear, mechanistic model of the past.

The book's somewhat fey title refers to the value that a complexity model of business places on workplace relationships and mutual respect. One of its exemplars is the fashionable London advertising agency St Luke's, which has become an icon for new-age thinkers because of its maverick resistance to structure (it is arranged in cells of an optimum 35 people and its employees work as and where they can find a desk, not in offices) and its corporate bonding sessions where everyone is encouraged to speak publicly about themselves and their favourite things. St Luke's had a solid corporate background to seed its new culture, being the former London branch of the New York agency Chiat-Day, and it has been undeniably successful in attracting plum accounts. It also has a pragmatically innovative way of operating: everyone connected with a client, from the account-handlers and planners to the creative side, works together in one space, the 'project room', rather than in the linear fashion of a traditionally compartmented business.

The fast-growing popularity of living systems theory among consultants and academics writing about management can lead to a suspicion that some of the case studies are being presented in a contrived way as *post hoc* proof of this superior way of running a business. The reader is left uncertain whether the companies have consciously set out to model their systems on natural principles or whether the observers have imposed this pattern with convenient hindsight. In *Profit Beyond Measure*, for instance, a study of Toyota and Scania published in 2000 by H. Thomas Johnson and Anders Broms, an American professor of quality management and a Swedish management consultant respectively, no one seems to have asked the two profitable vehicle manufacturers whether they planned their respective production and design innovations around the principles of living systems or whether the results just happened to fit the authors' theory.[9]

The basic argument advanced is that human work is more effective when organised according to the principles of nature's living systems (self-organisation,

interdependence, diversity) rather than driven mechanistically by management accounting targets. Johnson
and Broms compare the goal-oriented management of
the 'Big Three' US auto-makers in the decades after
World War Two with the 'more systemic thinking' of
Toyota, which linked everyone involved in the
production process in a web of relationships. Each car
worker co-operated with his or her next internal
'customer', gaining information and feedback and thus
filling the external customer's order more efficiently.

This system, they claim, enabled Toyota to operate
for decades at much lower cost and with more stable
earnings than any other car-maker in the world. Toyota
had learned from studying Ford's River Rouge plant
how to marry mass-production benefits to variety of
product by managing the changeover between products
without interrupting the balanced flow off the line. Each
step was designed 'to carry small loads and make
frequent trips' like the water-beetle of Japanese fable,
and each trip had to count, hence the application of the
'right first time' approach that Japanese manufacturers
had learned from W. Edwards Deming in his seminal
teachings in the war-devastated country in 1950.

The authors acknowledge their *post hoc* approach
quite early in the book when describing Toyota's new
thinking on mass-production techniques. 'Significantly,
that thinking caused Toyota to create a production
system with features that resemble those commonly
found in living systems ... Whether or not Toyota
consciously designed its system in the light of living-
system principles, its pervasive similarities to a natural
organic system undoubtedly contribute to the
company's legendary prosperity.' But they acknowledge
that the only public statement by Toyota's chief
engineer, Taiichi Ohno, who was responsible for
evolving the just-in-time system (after observing how US
supermarket shelves were restocked as required), was

that Toyota aimed 'to produce what can be sold at the lowest possible cost'.

With their talk of Toyota's production flow-line resembling the metabolic structure of a tree, Johnson and Broms are probably only the first of many ideas merchants attempting to graft natural-systems theory onto industrial practices that would have grown out of quite different ideas. What such practices do share, however, is a respect for human ability to act responsibly, co-operatively and with initiative, unlike the industrial practices of half a century ago.

Apes and insects

There is, of course, nothing particularly new or revolutionary about drawing lessons from natural science and applying them to the management of organisations. Thirty years ago, Desmond Morris popularised the study of parallels between animal and human rituals, while the behaviour of primate societies and pack animals has been the stuff of leadership seminars for years. The US cognitive anthropologist Robin Dunbar has demonstrated that the optimal number of the human tribe working effectively together is around 150. Hewlett-Packard and 3M find that their most productive work groups rarely exceed 200 people, and other companies report similar results. Karen Stephenson, an anthropologist working at UCLA on new theories of corporate networking, finds a similar optimum size for an effective team or work unit, based on the limit to the number of simultaneous links the human brain can handle – these links being basically 'you scratch my back and I'll scratch yours' equivalents of mutual grooming among primates.

In the 1990s, Meredith Belbin, the guru of team-role selection who gave his name to a widely used recruitment technique, extended his studies of organisations to the world of ants, termites and bees, concluding that much could be learned from the collective way in which insect societies maximise their intelligence for the benefit of the community. What we learn from the 'higher social insects', according to Belbin, is primarily the value of networking and communication in decision-making. 'The social insects are able to utilise a much larger network of information in reaching decisions about what to do in any given situation. This is highly relevant to us now that our lives are being transformed by information technology and the new tools at our disposal. Ants operate in a multimedia way using several sensory channels, whereas we tend to rely on a single one. They have extraordinarily big brains in relation to their body weight and can process larger amounts of information than we can, very much like a computer.'[10] If a crisis strikes the anthill community, information is exchanged in concert, cross-linked and grounded, in contrast to the hierarchical nature of human organisations, where 'a limited amount of information is fed upwards and away from the practitioners; a decision is then eventually made, often by a single person, which is then binding on everyone else'. The information flow in human organisations, Belbin argues, leaves a large margin for error in comparison to the massive, simultaneous absorption of information possible in ant societies.

Belbin's intense late-life fascination with insect societies was sparked by his discovery of the complex termite mounds of northern Australia. He was astonished by the sophistication of functions in these communities, including control of the 'labour market' in the anthill and of the 'career development' of young termites, accomplished by chemical management of the larvae to produce more of one skill base than another, as needed. 'They have highly differentiated roles and can assemble the appropriate skills to handle specific problems, with none of the protracted planning or referral procedures of human organisations,' says Belbin. 'Nearly all human systems are designed for inbuilt delays and the overriding of decisions. Most large human organisations are cumbersome and slow-moving. The bigger the group, the more foolishly it behaves.' Without the restrictions of a command or reporting chain, ants can implement decisions rapidly. 'The basis of their superior organisation lies, first, in the availability of on-the-spot specialists who work together to formulate the shape and nature of group effort in their respective spheres and, secondly, the existence of a system geared for concurrent activities. For humans, life is far more complicated; they have to take one step at a time. In the case of bees and ants, it can all happen together.'

Belbin considers ants and termites far more advanced in their organisational abilities than bees, which have a much larger literature devoted to them. In view of the current management fascination with collective leader-ship, he has suggested that they could form models for large human organisations to reinvent themselves as a series of small teams: 'Small interacting teams act without interference and rely on their superior capacity for generating and acting on complex information ... Concurrent teams, comprising small competing teams, produce better results in tackling complex problems than one large conferring group headed by a leader.'

The workings of termite communities are significant to students of organisational theory because of the disciplined results of their unplanned, undirected actions. Belbin says that some of their mound com-munities are the equivalent in organisation and complexity of human cities the size of New York, complete with efficient waste recycling and climate control. The 12-foot-high mound built by the African termite has opening and closing vents that keep the internal temperature of the mound to within one degree of a consistent 31°C, regardless of weather extremes on the outside that can range between 3°C and 40°C. No single termite has the capacity to initiate the building of an anthill; ants are programmed by their DNA to obey pheromones, chemical signals that pass information between insects in proximity to each other. All they know instinctively is that each ant has to place itself between two others and pass on the chemical communication received.

Clearly, there are limits to what human organisations can learn from the higher insects, but Belbin's work suggests two main strands:

- 'There are better ways of managing a complex organisation than by making it the responsibility of a single boss. If a major decision-making function is needed, it should be based on the concept of a co-operating "caste". Members of that "caste" should be selected and trained for the position in the same way as larvae are nurtured by a nurse . . . in human terms, the emerging adult contributor needs to be prepared for the position by a personal development coach.' But relying solely on that approach, says Belbin, would restrict biological adaptability, so the 'caste' should have two sources of entry: one trained from the outset and the other recruited at shorter notice.
- A collection of individual castes functions best when their complementary activities operate 'simultaneously, in unison and free from the delays associated with relationships of rank'. Most of Belbin's book, *The Coming Shape of Organizations*, is devoted to practical explorations of how human organisations could be built around concurrent systems, differentiated in function and scope but interlinked.

If you dispense with the traditional hierarchical

career ladder, however, you need a radical change in organisational design. Belbin has evolved a 'progression helix' concept, a system of interacting circles continuously spiralling upward in which recruits enter at different points and in different positions, moving ahead to seniority as they prove their contribution to the team in strategic, professional or operational roles. Membership of teams can overlap and interact as in the hive or anthill, with the advantage that the human capacity for strategic thought and managing change – not, thankfully, a termite ability – can also work concurrently. Teams working like this, says Belbin, would offer a number of advantages. They could:

- generate a wider range of ideas and innovations than a single group;
- shorten decision times; and
- expose problems that might be kept hidden by traditional managers for their own career advantage.[11]

Leading in a leaderless world

It is far too early to guess whether living systems theory and all its ramifications are going to develop into the Big Idea of the twenty-first century, as Pascale suggests. It would be easy to dismiss it all as intellectual games-playing, part of the turn-of-the-century fascination with popular science and the mysteries of the universe, and the eminent scientist and author Richard Dawkins has warned against too facile a use of science/business comparisons (see Chapter 2). But a great many serious scholars are using parts of the discipline to enlarge and enrich traditional ways of looking at organisations and how they are led. Living systems and the biology behind them are, for example, framing much of the latest thinking on adaptive leadership, the particular field of

Professor Ronald A. Heifetz, a psychiatrist by training and the director of the Leadership Education Project at Harvard University's John F. Kennedy School of Government.

Adaptive leadership, as Pascale pays tribute to it in Heifetz's work, is the art of managing disequilibrium by releasing the intelligence distributed throughout an organisation, instead of restoring it to a state of stability, which would be the reaction of traditional leadership. Adaptive leadership does not rely on traditional authority figures, nor does it draw much inspiration from the animal or insect world, although Heifetz's book *Leadership Without Easy Answers* contains a chapter analysing the role of authority in primate societies. In his small, book-lined office by Boston's Charles River, the professor explained: 'Animal studies are very rich and helpful in dissecting the nature of authority systems and how they function and co-ordinate behaviour, and how vital those functions are, but I don't think that when you begin to distinguish leadership from authority they tell us what we need to know.' Animals, as he pointed out, merely 'tap into their repertoire' – with primates it's a learned programme, and with ants a genetic one. 'I think the lessons from animal societies are more about the nature of authority and dominance, and the role of authority structures. Those in ant communities are more about structures of co-ordination. I wouldn't call either of those leadership because the learning it takes to do adaptation in a biological system does not take place within a generation, it takes place over evolutionary time through trial and error. The kind of adaptation I'm interested in is where human systems can do adaptive work within a generation, or within a year.'[12]

The centrepiece of Heifetz's work is understanding how leadership can operate without authority, though he doubts that society can ever do away completely with authority relationships. In a knowledge-based economy where, for a variety of social, educational and technological reasons, people are increasingly unwilling to be directed in traditional ways, this will assume ever-greater importance. The next Big Idea is almost certainly going to be connected with the new economy's intensified demands on people management.

Powerpoints

- Learning from nature's 'complex adaptive systems' could prove a Big Idea for much of the twenty-first century. Advocates believe it helps businesses respond dynamically to change.
- Complex adaptive systems work through self-organisation, already a powerful business principle. The optimal number of the old human tribe – around 150 – is still the best for effective working groups.
- Beyond individual companies, the whole Internet economy is becoming a web of self-organising relationships, epitomised by Silicon Valley itself.
- Adaptive principles simulating sudden disequilibrium and edge-of-chaos conditions have been successfully introduced into major corporations such as Shell, BP-Amoco and Hewlett-Packard.
- Other natural models for new types of self-organising business structures can be found in Meredith Belbin's studies of insect communities.
- Living systems are also producing new thinking on 'adaptive leadership', which does not rely on traditional authority figures.

NOTES

[1] author interview, July 2000

[2] Beinhocker, Eric D.: 'Strategy at the edge of chaos', *The McKinsey Quarterly*, 1997, No. 1

[3] Beinhocker, Eric D.: 'Robust adaptive strategies', *Sloan Management Review*, Spring 1999, Vol. 40, No. 3

[4] Beinhocker: 'Strategy at the edge of chaos'

[5] Pascale, Richard: *Surfing the Edge of Chaos*, Texere, 2000

[6] ibid.

[7] ibid.

[8] The Centre for Tomorrow's Company, RSA

[9] Johnson, H.T. and Broms, A.: *Profit Beyond Measure*, Nicholas Brealey, 2000

[10] author interview and article in *MBA* magazine, April 1998; Belbin, Meredith: *The Coming Shape of Organizations*, Butterworth, 1996

[11] Belbin: *The Coming Shape of Organizations*

[12] author interview, Harvard, September 2000; Heifetz, Ronald A.: *Leadership Without Easy Answers*, Belknap Press of Harvard University, 1994

CHAPTER SIX

NEW WAYS TO MANAGE THE HUMAN ANIMAL

If living systems are to provide the next Big Idea in business organisations, managing the people who work in them will undergo a profound change. A living systems model with its self-determination through interaction would certainly fit the new knowledge-based economy with its army of independent, roving talents more easily than the traditional mechanistic business organisation based on linear reporting structures, control and predictability. If, as Richard Pascale observes, people now need to be managed with 'a combination of freedom and discipline', the ideal environment must be one of self-organisation, where individuals work instinctively towards common goals through a deep understanding of the business, their function within it and how their actions affect it.

The trend towards more open working structures of independent or semi-independent agents has been developing for some 10 to 15 years, with a variety of flatter, team-oriented organisational models emerging over this period. Peter Drucker, the grand old man of management thinking who has furnished two generations of gurus with ideas he pioneered in the 1950s and 1960s, was the first to suggest the concept of the company as an orchestra of talents with the CEO as conductor/coach. From here it was natural to go on to explore ways in which individuals within an organisation could be enabled to develop their skills, knowledge and competencies for mutual and collective benefit.

'The learning organisation', the Big Idea which took flight in the early 1990s, advocated workers and managers learning from each other, from customers, competitors, suppliers and the outside community, and sharing that knowledge in pursuit of a more competitive corporate effort. If no one has yet managed to find a real-life example of a true learning organisation, that naturally does not prevent the search for the grail continuing, nor the stream of related books and seminars purporting to tell companies how to achieve it.

The idea had a number of godfathers, though it did not become a full-blown management trend until Peter Senge, director of the Center for Organizational Learning at the Massachusetts Institute of Technology, published *The Fifth Discipline* in 1990. Back in 1978 there was Chris Argyris, the formidably cerebral Harvard academic who evolved the theory of single-loop and double-loop learning along with Donald Schon of MIT. Probably few managers understood this heavily academic cognitive research into how executives subconsciously defend the status quo to protect themselves while imposing change on others, but *Organizational Learning* was a highly influential work among management theorists. In 1987 and 1990 the British management consultant Bob Garratt published two books with 'learning organisation' in the title, but though more readable than Senge's, they were unfairly overshadowed by the MIT heavy hitter.

There was also Arie de Geus, credited by Senge with the original concept of the learning organisation. De Geus, a former head of planning at Royal Dutch/Shell, famously said 'the ability to learn faster than your competitor may be the only sustainable competitive advantage' – a quote that duly turns up in almost everything written about the learning organisation. His development of scenario planning at Shell is generally supposed to have helped the company cope better than its competitors with the OPEC oil producers' price shocks of the early 1970s. De Geus is now an international lecturer and adviser to governments and private institutions and still a key figure in new-age thinking about business organisations. His principal theme now is for companies to survive and flourish by looking upon themselves as living organisms or human communities rather than as machines for making money and returning profits to investors.

The company as a living organism

De Geus was also an early advocate of adapting nature to business practice. His book *The Living Company* (1997), and the numerous spin-off lectures and seminars it has generated, presents a gardener's organic view of business enterprises dedicated to 'stewardship' and sustainability, rooted in care for their employees as much as for their customers and shareholders. It draws on parallels from biology, anthropology and psychology to reveal how companies can learn, grow, adapt and survive to be long-lived instead of dying prematurely as so many businesses do. If they run into trouble, the first priority should be 'to mobilise human potential, to restore or maintain trust and civic behaviour and to increase professionalism and good citizenship'.

Britain's social philosopher Charles Handy, who made his reputation as a management guru writing about the differing characteristics of organisations, is another leading proponent of the idea that companies should be conceived as living organisms of mutual benefit to their employees, customers and the wider community. Both he and de Geus are influential figures in the Royal Society of Arts project to define 'Tomorrow's Company', but the reality, as Bob Waterman once glumly observed (corroborated by some hard-nosed audience reaction at one RSA presentation by Handy), is that most managers remain profit-oriented, unreconstructed Taylorists at heart.

Frederick W. Taylor, the original machine-age management consultant, was already 35 years in his grave when the industrial psychologist Douglas McGregor defined the Theory X and Theory Y of management in the mid-1950s. Theory X was pure Taylorism as the world perceived it – authoritarian, believing that employees had to be constantly coerced and directed. Theory Y was participative, collegiate, believing in people's innate desire for responsibility. McGregor said it challenged management 'to innovate, to discover new ways of organising and directing human effort, even though we recognise that the perfect organisation, like the perfect vacuum, is practically out of reach'. McGregor, who died in 1964 aged only 58, remains the most underrated business thinker of the last half-century, probably because his single book, the *Human Side of Enterprise*, ranks among the most unreadable of the century, with only a few of its pages devoted to the famous theories.

Until a few years ago it was thought that Theory Y had never been fully tested in McGregor's lifetime, but in 1994 Robert Waterman, the co-author with Tom Peters of *In Search of Excellence*, revealed that in 1954 McGregor had indeed designed a detergent plant in Atlanta, Georgia, for Procter and Gamble run on Theory Y self-management lines. It proved the most productive of all P&G factories – so much so that the firm kept it a trade secret for forty years. The Santa Fe work on complexity and chaos in nature takes McGregor's work a step

further and puts a scientific ecological spin on the
concept of employees as free agents interacting with one
another to a common purpose.

Close on the heels of the learning organisation craze
in the 1990s came the concepts of intellectual capital
and knowledge management. These were not quite
visionary enough to catch on as a wildfire Big Idea and
depended heavily on effective technology to make them
work, but they were thoroughly sensible concepts based
on quantifying the knowledge within a company – not
least the implicit knowledge held in its employees' heads
– and locating, collating and sharing it. As every
company that rashly downsized in the 1990s recessions
discovered to its cost, priceless knowledge about
products, customers, competitors and previous experience can be lost for ever when employees leave or are
'let go'. Since then, knowledge management has
become a big consultancy sub-industry on its own.

All this concentration on human and intellectual
capital as the key value resource of the company should
at last put some real meaning into that usually vacuous
annual-report mantra, 'our people are our greatest
asset'. The displacement of the old manufacturing
economy by the knowledge economy and Peter
Drucker's 'knowledge workers' has brought greater
corporate valuation and respect for employees' talents
and brainpower, the 'assets that go home every night'.
While intellectual capital is still hard to measure, some
companies – such as Skandia, the Swedish financial
services group which was the first company to appoint a
chief knowledge officer – are experimenting with
putting real asset value on it.

A world of freelance brains

The Internet economy is redrawing the map of
management in this as in other ways. 'The way we think

of human capital and the way we manage people is changing,' says Don Tapscott, a Canadian management consultant and authority on information technology who has been described by former US Vice-President Al Gore as 'one of the world's leading cyber-gurus'. Tapscott has spotted one of the key shifts the Internet has imposed on business structure and strategy: companies now have access to the skills of people without having to own those skills on their payroll.

Knowledge-management theory makes much of the term 'human capital', meaning the sum of the capabilities of individuals within enterprises, or the intellectual assets they represent. Tapscott claims that such corporate human capital now extends to people across the 'b-webs' (inter-networked, Web-based businesses). It also extends to freelance brains, so that authors, reviewers and readers, for example, may be viewed as part of the human capital of Amazon.com, the Internet bookseller which runs book reviews and readers' opinions on its Web site. When human capital becomes inter-networked in this way, all b-web stakeholders, both organisational and non-organisational, can together accomplish infinitely more than was possible in the old economy.

In his book *Digital Capital*, Tapscott and his co-authors David Ticoll and Alex Lowy formulate nine imperatives for managers to foster value creation and a high-performance culture in a global environment, among them information transparency, managing knowledge across the b-web, quick decision-making and problem-solving at all points in the b-web. It is also vital, they argue, to embrace and understand the Net generation – young, technologically adept people who can simultaneously surf the Net, respond to email, talk on the phone, watch TV and read a magazine, because this is the generation that will create a push for innovation and radical change. It is also the first generation to find it natural to share knowledge – the only resource, it has been said, that increases by being used. Earlier generations, certainly in corporate life, guarded knowledge for career reasons, seeing it as power and territory, but b-web development works in the opposite way: success depends on opening up management systems and valuing the global scope of human capital.

The universal accessibility of information technology has stood hierarchical, command-control cultures and scientific management on their heads, says Tapscott, and is radically changing the basic corporation model developed over the last century. The vertically integrated corporation made sense in its time, he explains, because of the heavy transaction costs of those days, but 'now there are Xchanges and auction devices, even for finding people. This is the biggest thing in management since Henry Ford built the Ford Motor Co.'[1]

The big international accountancy and management consultancies have not been slow to perceive the tradeable potential of human capital that can now be said to be owned by individuals as well as corporations. Stan Davis and Christopher Meyer of the Ernst & Young Center for Business Innovation sketch out a financial world in the not-too-distant future where everything of value will be traded in efficient virtual markets, including talent. This in fact began to happen before the 1990s were out. On 28 April 1999, a team of 16 employees from a major Internet service provider put themselves up for auction on eBay. They were willing to leave as a group and they set their minimum price at $3.14m.

No one bid, but the idea of marketing a package of human brains and skills had been publicly displayed. Sites such as bid4geeks.com and talentmarket.Monster.com followed, as did others for the global trading of knowledge. A Canadian venture, www.knexa.com, claimed to be the world's first knowledge exchange for the auctioning of knowledge and experience. The market analysis company Datamonitor has estimated that 'information exchanges' on the Internet will have revenues of $6bn by 2005. In their book *Future Wealth*, Davis and Meyer also foresee companies investing directly in their employees, not just through training and development, and treating business units as units of financial risk whose worth equals the quality of their intellectual capital. Individual employees, they believe, will think less about jobs and more about investing in their own human capital. And the more that individuals gain investment knowledge, the more prepared they will be to accept higher risks for potentially higher rewards. Davis and Meyer argue that the trading of risks benefits both parties. 'And in truth it is only a small leap from investing in such ideas to investing directly in the people who have them. You have two investment opportunities: (1) the idea in the intellectual property and (2) the person (human capital) who created it. Separate the risks and invest in both.'[2]

The age of 'humanagement'

With the term 'human resources' taking on new implications, it was never going to be long before some would-be guru coined a new buzzword like 'humanagement'. Enter two Swedish assistant professors at the Stockholm School of Economics, Jonas Ridderstråle and Kjell Nordström, authors of a millennium bestseller called *Funky Business*. Their theory is that employees' ideas and brainpower *are* the corporation, that the emergence of the e-economy has made consumers and employees the masters of capital. What does this imply for business and society? the pair were asked by an interviewer on the London *Financial Times* supplement *The Business*. 'In general,' they replied, 'it means employers must become much better at transforming their core competents – those human knowledge monopolies that actually embody the critical skills – into core competencies. If human capital cannot be transformed into structural capital, these core competents will be irreplaceable, and they will demand a share – in cash or stock options.' Companies must manage this transformation through communication, a high tolerance for failure, continuous development of management and employees, recognition that people differ, a philosophy of 'hire for attitude and train for skills', and definitions of the kind of motivation they want employees to have, rather than job descriptions.[3]

The Nordström–Ridderstråle approach chimes neatly with Don Tapscott's view of the Net Generation and that great undirectable force in people management known as the Generation X factor – those young, freewheeling spirits born after the mid-1960s who will not choose their jobs for security and are essentially looking more for values than for monetary value. All technology-related businesses know the problem of attracting and retaining talented Generation X-ers who see themselves as economic units in their own right rather than players in a corporate team, and who crave the freedom to move their skills around. But Sumantra Ghoshal, the British-based strategy guru who is helping to develop a new institute of management in his native India, thinks something more fundamental is going on that will force big companies to rethink the whole nature of their relationship with key employees.

A new 'moral contract'

Ghoshal, professor of strategic and international management at London Business School and co-author with Christopher Bartlett of the influential *Managing Across Borders* (1989), an early study of transnational management skills, has lately been developing with his colleague a theory they floated in their second book, *The Individualized Corporation* (1998). This is the idea that sustainably successful companies – those which create value organically rather than acquire it by takeover – exercise a new kind of 'moral contract' with their key people. It revolves around respect for the individual as a value creator for the company and carries a responsibility for helping employees to fulfil their best potential.

Ghoshal is deeply concerned about the failure to engage the Net generation in corporate work. Out of 140 students on a management course he taught at LBS in 1998, only six wanted anything to do with careers in large companies. It was as much to do with quality of life and relationships as with the work itself, he found. 'Most of their parents had worked for big companies – quite a few had reached senior management level – and these guys had seen what their life was like from inside the home,' Ghoshal told the author in 1999. 'Their answer was: not us, no way.'

One clue to the declining interest in corporate careers, Ghoshal thinks, may lie in what Richard Pascale has dubbed 'the third place'. Historically, a person's waking life could be divided into three: there was work, there was the family, and there was 'the third place', somewhere that did not carry the pressures and obligations of the other two; somewhere, as Ghoshal says, 'where you could be what you are, where you found your social identity'. In Britain's more stratified society this might have been either the pub or the gentleman's club; in America, the Elks or some other form of community participation.

'Third place' enjoyment is part of what Generation X-ers seek, Ghoshal believes. Perhaps, he ruminates, the global manager of the future will be like his own adult children – 'born in India, brought up in America, their identity-defining phase spent in France. They speak French as their first language, English as their second, German as their third, Hindi as their fourth. They don't care whether they are in India, Germany or Japan. They want the most exciting assignment, where they can grow, where they can have fun.'[4]

Charles Handy has also studied some of the drives behind this autonomous, innovative and diverse group of talent and sees them as a source of entrepreneurs, individuals he calls the 'new alchemists' who 'create something out of nothing'. Handy, ever the social optimist, believes that 'the exciting thing about the future is that you can shape it' and that part of inventing the future is inventing a new way of organising ourselves. 'The interesting thing about what I have called the "new alchemists" is that they are passionate, they persevere through failures, difficulties and doubt, and they dare to be different,' he said in an interview in 1999. 'They really are inventing the future. I would love to see the word *alchemy* becoming more popular in organisations; by that I mean a bit of magic, a bit of imagination, a bit of wild free-thinking that will put fire in the belly. As I wander round the corridors of many large organisations, I don't sense passion. And if you don't have passion, people are not going to work as hard, or learn as much, as they could. They are not going to take risks with their ideas. One problem is that corporations develop a sort of corporate mindset and it's very difficult to break loose, so that most creative ideas come from outside or from people on the fringes, which is a pity, because in every organisation there is a lot of hidden wisdom and hidden knowledge, and it is often not where you think it is.'

So how do we get passion into corporations? Handy thinks the only way is by giving people space, by enthusing them with the mission of the organisation, so they feel they have a chance to shape the future, to make a difference to the world, using the resources of the corporation. It is only then, he believes, that 'all sorts of magical things will start to happen'. Handy recommends looking to models outside business where the 'e-factors of energy, excitement and enthusiasm' are at work. 'We keep saying that corporations should have a vision and a mission which should be about more than creating shareholder value – that isn't the kind of thing that gets people leaping out of bed in the mornings, you need something grander. What organisations have grander visions? The voluntary organisations, the charities. Wouldn't it be interesting if the top managers in a business went to talk to the top managers in charities to see what it's like to run an organisation where the vision is much more than the money, and see if that motivates people in a different way?'

Handy, whose son Scott is an actor, is also fascinated by the theatre as an organisational model. 'What it does is pull in individuals and put them together for a project – a production – and this project has a changing pattern of leadership, from the producer and director to the actors on the stage. And everyone connected with that production is mentioned by name in the programme – that's real recognition of an individual as an important asset. Furthermore, all these individuals have agents. It wouldn't surprise me in the next 10 to 15 years if we find that the key people in a corporation have agents, because they will be walking bodies of knowledge and wisdom who will be purchased for other projects in other companies.'

Big corporations, Handy acknowledges, have a problem in juggling efficiency and creativity. 'In order for things to be efficient, they want to control them, to make people accountable for targets and performance, and that's all very right and proper. But if you want to encourage creativity, you inevitably have to accept some failures, and you have to give people space. You won't always know exactly what they are doing, and that's very annoying to people who are in a sense control freaks at the top of large corporations. The BBC was always the most wonderful organisation for young people, and although it has something of a bad managerial image now, it is still the preferred organisation for graduates, who queue to get into its training courses. This is because by the nature of its technology and its product it had to practise subsidiarity, to allow people to go out and make a programme without being able to watch every step or tell them in advance what to film. That means that at a very young age people have a lot of responsibility, which is very exciting. Other kinds of organisation should allow people to take big responsibilities and only check them after the event. That creates commitment and loyalty.'[5]

People management is clearly going to become even more challenging for big companies, made tougher by the e-economy because the competition for talent is becoming phenomenal. In most companies, human resource departments are still not fully equipped or given sufficient clout on the board to help them tackle the problem. Talent wars are already one of the biggest issues facing business today. Even big, powerful consultancies like McKinsey and Bain, which not long ago could pick the cream of business school graduates, are having difficulty competing with the lure of the digital economy, and it is not solely to do with fortune-hunting. What is going on?

Interview the company, not the other way round

Alec Reed, founder and chairman of the temping agency Reed Executive, says simply that the world has changed. And it is not just about the e-business boom.

The incentives offered by the traditional big company – whether prospective partnerships, money, perks, stock options or influence – have lost their lustre. Organisations are facing a different world, with different economic and ideological ground rules. They are operating in a new economic state where brainpower becomes the most important factor of production – a phenomenon Reed calls 'peoplism'.

To explore its full implications, Reed has set up a think-tank, the Academy of Enterprise, with work sub-contracted to Demos, the Adam Smith Institute and the Employment Policy Institute in the UK. One of the issues they are working on is how managers and investors can keep score when traditional accountancy is disintegrating around them. Another is the need to develop individuals for social as well as economic entrepreneurship, so that 'peoplism' doesn't degenerate into rampant individualism. Meanwhile, Alec Reed has taken action within his own organisation. The company now manages by business plan, not by budget, and switches between the two when necessary. It invites bright young graduates to interview the company, rather than the company interviewing them. Individuals decide their own pay increases, within limits, the company provides interest-free loans of up to £1,000, and it pays for all vocational training and 50% of non-vocational training.

Many of Reed's preoccupations were reflected in the findings of the Futures Observatory, run by Britain's Open University, the Strategic Planning Society and others, when it debated the trends most likely to shape working lives over the next 25 years at a millennium conference in 2000. Leading the debate was David Mercer, senior lecturer in the Open University Business School and author of a book called *Future Revolutions*. Mercer believes that 'if you analyse people's expectations and the trends they display then you can predict the future'. For the past five years he has run focus groups with thousands of people about their thoughts on the future. 'Social trends are the most important indicators – what decisions people are going to make based on the new technology and the ability they have available to them.'

From these findings, Mercer identifies six main drivers that he thinks will shape future business:

- individualism or individual empowerment, resulting in greater power for women and a desire for 'new values and a search for meaning';
- technological communication will realise the global village and homeworking will become a reality, as will computer implants in the human brain;
- health education and medicine, contributing to longevity and more than one career;
- lifelong learning, expanding the notion of continuous professional development;
- a new economics based on 'a knowledge society';
- Europe taking over global leadership from the United States.[6]

Bruce Tulgan, the American writer who first popularised the term 'Generation X', says in his latest book *Winning the Talent Wars* that employers need to stand many old reactions on their heads in order to keep their best people. Instead of asking them 'what can we do to keep you?' on the day they resign, they should be asking this on the day they join the company.[7]

New leadership models needed

What sort of leadership qualities will be needed for this volatile new market of self-organising talent and shifting economic structures? Professor Ronald A. Heifetz, director of the Leadership Education Project at Harvard's John F. Kennedy School of Government, has evolved a theory of adaptive leadership that looks more suited to the twenty-first century than traditional models. In his book *Leadership Without Easy Answers*, Heifetz makes the distinction between *operational* and *adaptive* leadership. Operational leadership entails the exercise of authority and a solution rolled out from above through the ranks, which is not in tune with the way people are managed in the new organisation, nor with the autonomy of the new employee. Adaptive leadership is frequently also equated with authority and 'makes happen what isn't going to happen otherwise', but Heifetz observes that the notion of authority is misleading in this context since many people occupy positions of authority but do not provide leadership.

While authority generally includes power to manage the adaptive challenge, Heifetz identifies definite advantages in leading without authority, which he claims is the type of leadership that fits the e-enterprise age. A leader without formal authority, he argues, has more latitude for creative deviance, can focus better on issues and work more closely with the stakeholders, thus gaining direct, frontline information. History, as he points out, is studded with examples of individuals with little formal authority who have changed the world, beginning with Jesus Christ, the Buddha and the prophet Mohammed, and in the twentieth century Gandhi, Martin Luther King and Nelson Mandela.

Heifetz sets out five 'principles of leadership' which focus on managing the social environment. These apply to leaders with or without authority:

- identifying the adaptive challenge;
- keeping distress within a productive range;
- directing attention to ripening issues and not diversions;
- giving the work back to the people; and
- protecting voices of community leaders.

For Heifetz, a physician and psychiatrist by training, leaders are to a social system what a properly shaped lens is to light – they focus intention and may do so for better or worse. An adaptive intention requires the social system to be disturbed in a profound and prolonged fashion. The adaptive leader, with or without authority, doesn't move on an issue too quickly or reach for a quick fix. Instead, emphasis is given to mobilising followers deep within the ranks to help find the way forward. In the Heifetz model of leadership, it is the leader's role 'to engage people in facing the challenge, adjusting their values, changing perspectives, and developing new habits of behaviour'. Above all, it requires the exercise of trust, which Heifetz sees as sadly lacking in his own political society.

'There are more options now for exercising leadership without authority than when I started teaching here 17 years ago,' Heifetz reflected in his small Harvard office in the autumn of 2000. A combination of natural trends with changing technology, he added, was making such ideas more accessible to people, but in US society there had been such a loss of trust in authority that it had brought a host of new problems, such as the misuse of teams. 'Part of the leadership challenge is to find ways of recovering people's capacity to trust,' he said. 'I don't think you can ever move to a complete elimination of authority structures because what that would truly mean is that you have no differentiation of roles. Every role is an authorisation. A job description is an authorisation. Doing away with authority relationships would be like saying I'll never need to trust a car mechanic to fix my car. One couldn't have civilisation without that. The human capacity to construct authority relationships is critical to the development of any civilisation. To get beyond face-to-face groups, you've got to be able to entrust someone with power to make decisions for you, expecting them to operate in a trustworthy fashion.'[8]

Trust in decision-making is a key component in the new 'psychological' or 'moral' contracts that employers are having to think about to replace the old career anchors, and it is an issue that W. Chan Kim, a Korean-born academic, and his American colleague Renée Mauborgne, both professors of strategy and management at INSEAD, the international business school outside Paris, have addressed while researching into manufacturing industry in the US. They studied over 35 companies in which a culture of trust had been built up and concluded that this increased both productivity and the genesis of ideas.

The places other ideas don't reach

Kim and Mauborgne have named their discovery of how this happens 'fair process' and claim that it reaches into areas of human psychology that are little explored in conventional management theory. Their argument is that people in an organisation choose to release their fullest creative abilities only when they completely trust the processes by which corporate decisions are made and carried out in the organisation. This involves extensive consultation and frank explanation by the decision makers: it does not mean that the employees agree with the decisions, but it does mean that they are enabled to understand that the decisions were fairly made.

The INSEAD professors owe the germ of their theory to two social scientists in the 1970s, John W. Thibault and Laurens Walker, whose big discovery was that people involved in a generally much trusted public institution like the legal system care as much about the fairness of the process itself as about the outcome. Researching in industry over some ten years, Kim and Mauborgne concluded that a direct connection existed between the process, fair or otherwise, and the attitudes and behaviour of people in the organisation. 'Fair process will be a powerful management tool as industry moves out of the production economy into the knowledge economy,' says Kim. It 'profoundly influences attitudes and behaviours critical to high performance. It builds trust and unlocks ideas. With it, managers can achieve even the most painful and difficult goals while at the same time gaining the voluntary co-operation of the employees affected.'[9] The pair identify three planks underpinning fair process which they call the 'three Es': engagement (participation and open debate), explanation and expectation clarity (clearly setting out targets and responsibilities).

The key to fair process is that an idea is accepted by the majority through understanding, not necessarily agreement, thereby differing from Japanese management's emphasis on consensus. One of the case studies offered by Kim and Mauborgne was the rapid cultural transformation wrought by CEO Gerhard Schulmeyer at Siemens Nixdorf Informationssysteme AG in Frankfurt. Schulmeyer, a former senior executive at ABB (Asea Brown Boveri) infused with the communication philosophy of the then ABB chairman/CEO Percy Barnevik, decided to put culture change ahead of process change and from the start involved thousands of staff in explanation and consultation about what the company was doing and the tough decisions that would have to be faced. Although the corporate change programme was designed by consultants, the dynamic of it came entirely from the employees. Schulmeyer invited key managers to recruit change agents at all levels of the company and within months had 10,000 people committed emotionally and intellectually to the change programme, cascading it throughout the organisation. It was fair process in action, and the transformation of an old-fashioned German manufacturing company (albeit one in a high-tech industry) was accomplished in months.[10]

Kim and Mauborgne take the view that although Frederick Herzberg's motivational definitions of employee satisfaction worked well enough in the old production economy, these are no longer enough. If trust and commitment are lacking, they argue, good ideas will not be shared and company performance will suffer. Nor do they suggest that this is only for the new economy: much of their fieldwork was done in old 'rustbelt' industries, and productivity and innovation still boomed.

The changing nature of the employer–employee 'contract' is an issue that deeply concerns Sumantra Ghoshal as he ponders what new kinds of working relationships are required to meet today's different needs of organisational and people management. 'The pattern of relationships in human lives has been fundamentally changing over a period of time – relationships of one individual to another, of the individual to the institution or organisation, and of the individual to society,' he says. 'I believe we have not explored in any richness the implications at the individual-organisational level. I think the need for loyalty and commitment to an organisation is very basic but, at the same time, a profound sense of autonomy is rising.'

This combination of autonomy and diversity presents a huge challenge for big corporations, yet Ghoshal is confident they will endure. 'Big companies play a very important role as the marshalling yard of society's resources; a profoundly important role in driving economic progress.' Even in Silicon Valley, shrine of the start-up, he claims, it is big companies like Intel (with 350 venture capital relationships within Silicon Valley alone) that provide the essential resources. Global corporations such as Shell, Unilever or ABB will, however, have to rethink the way they have traditionally recruited their managers. There used to be tough, spartan cadres of young, ambitious, mostly unmarried individuals who roved the world for the big multinationals, running their subsidiary businesses in primitive, even hostile environments before working their way up through different sections of the company to top management positions. Ghoshal thinks fewer will want to sign up for that sort of life in the future.[11]

Managers with ambitions to be leaders in this new and more demanding world of skills for sale need to develop some personal qualities that were not so critical in the days of the big structured corporation. Among them, currently bidding for Big Idea status (see Chapter 4), is 'emotional intelligence' or EQ, meaning competencies based on the ability to empathise with others. Daniel Goleman, the New York journalist turned guru who has spun a second career out of his theory, argues that EQ plays a more important role in star performance than either IQ or technical skills, and that the individual first needs to manage himself or herself (through self-awareness, self-regulation and motivation) before progressing to the social competencies that determine how we handle relationships with others.

EQ and SQ: the right brain takes over

In *Working With Emotional Intelligence* (1998), Goleman claims that both individuals and companies benefit in performance from cultivating workplace competencies based on emotional intelligence. His model framework divides into personal and social: personal competencies, which determine how we manage ourselves, comprise self-awareness, self-regulation and motivation; social competencies, which determine how we handle relationships, comprise empathy and social skills. Within the 'virtual organisation', Goleman argues, 'the premium on emotional intelligence can only rise as organisations become increasingly dependent on the talents and creativity of workers who are independent agents'. He says that about 77% of American 'knowledge workers' claim to operate as their own boss, deciding what to do on the job rather than being told by someone else. This autonomy can work only if it goes hand-in-hand with 'self-control, trustworthiness, and conscientiousness'. These comparatively 'free agents' form co-ordinated working groups with a specialised mix of talent and expertise to meet a specific need and then cease to exist once the task is accomplished. 'Virtual teams', in this context, 'can be especially agile because they are headed by whoever has the requisite skills, rather than by someone who happens to have the title "manager"'.[12]

Emotional intelligence and its godchild, spiritual intelligence, promoted by the psychiatrist Danah Zohar ('the search for meaning, vision and value is the most important aspect of being human'), are in step with a general trend towards right-brain (intuitive rather than logical) thinking in making management more effective with the managed. Much of this trend focuses first on improving the individual's own emotional wellbeing and balance. A survey of leadership qualities by the UK's Institute of Directors identified 'enthusiasm' as the most important. Other research has laboriously come up with findings that might be thought already well established – that happier workers are more effective workers, for example, and that people who pray regularly have greater wellbeing than those who don't. Every other manager, it seems, is searching for the answers to such self-development questions as how to harness your vision, control your career and expand your mental horizons – even, in one course linked to the Cranfield School of Management, how to develop intuitive powers, with contributions by professional psychics.

Within the last two years a whole cluster of practices

associated with philosophy, theology and 'getting a life'
has captured attention in the world of business.
Christian Schumacher, son of the late E.F. Schumacher
of *Small is Beautiful* fame, is a specialist in designing the
structure of work. He believes 'that many of the evils
apparent in our society are rooted in job design – the
loss of ownership, the task fragmentation, the de-
skilling, the rendering of work psychologically meaning-
less to the worker'. (Long ago, F.W. Taylor was held
responsible for just such a dehumanising of work.) The
inspiration for Schumacher's success in work
organisation – he runs a large consultancy and for six
years served on the Industrial Committee of the Board
of Social Responsibility of the Church of England – are
the texts of the medieval Church fathers, the theology of
which Schumacher considers 'very mainstream'. It is
the application of their principles, he believes, that is
radical, and in his book *God In Work* (1999) he says the
real source of his inspiration for the best way to organise
work came through 'a synthesis of theology and science'.

Theology is getting into management ideas in other
ways. Benedictine monks and managers regularly come
together in rural England in ways that are not far
removed from the age-old practice of going on retreat.
Weekend workshops at Ampleforth Abbey in Yorkshire
and Douai Abbey near Reading aim to explore the
application of St Benedict's teachings to contemporary
business issues, including problem-solving, decision-
making and leadership. The course content emphasises
that 'although written in the sixth century, the Rule of
St Benedict continues to have much to say that is
relevant and inspiring for leaders and managers'.
Participants have the opportunity to join the monks in
prayer and to take time for reflection before 'returning
to the workplace refreshed and inspired'.

The pursuit of happiness at work

The Douai seminars on Spirituality at Work, organised by Father Dermot Tredget, a former businessman and MBA turned Benedictine monk who aims to encourage more 'soul-friendly' working environments, are attracting growing numbers of executives seeking simplicity in their complex business lives. 'I would hope that in the end they feel their spirituality is not something they have to leave behind, but is also something that can improve the quality of the workplace, to make it more productive and less political, to make them feel more valued and part of the decision-making process,' he says. Those attending have been largely senior and middle managers and consultants in change management. Father Tredget says many are keen to tie spirituality in with current corporate notions of values, culture and change, and that people who seek to understand their spiritual nature have a greater chance of happiness, though the seminars are open to those both with and without faith. The Rule of St Benedict, by which the monks live, seeks to enhance the value of work by making it a dimension of prayer, as reflected in the order's motto: *orare et laborare* (pray and work).[13]

Pierre Winkler, a teacher of management, IT and business ethics in The Netherlands, points out that the theory of interrelated connectedness in the search for meaning to life and work is not new. 'Many, if not all, religions have carried this message for centuries. However, it has been given a new dimension by linking it directly to the economical wellbeing of organisations,' he says. 'The question of how to live a meaningful life, once the preserve of philosophers and theologians, has now found a place at the very heart of business economics.'[14] Strategy guru Gary Hamel and Professor John Kay, formerly of London Business School, have separately observed that employees are not likely to leap out of bed in the mornings all fired up by the idea of shareholder value, a 1990s corporate mantra.

Kay thinks the pursuit of happiness at work is a valid motivation. This too is not new: as long ago as 1910 it was the *coup de foudre* that struck John Spedan Lewis, heir to the John Lewis drapery business, on the top of a London omnibus and led him to devise his revolutionary plan to create the profit-sharing John Lewis Partnership. John Lewis was the first, and remains the biggest, family business voluntarily to abandon its dynastic inheritance by handing over the wealth in the company to its workers. Until his autocratic elderly father died in 1928, Spedan Lewis was unable to put it into practice except in a small way at the Peter Jones store on London's Sloane Square, which John Lewis senior allowed him to run autonomously.

Spedan Lewis was a deep thinker, a manager decades ahead of his time. He understood that 'the essence of good management was a contented workforce'. When he came to issue what we would now call a mission statement about his pioneering industrial concept, it ran: 'The supreme purpose of the John Lewis Partnership is simply the happiness of its members.' As the new era developed, Spedan Lewis wrote: 'The Partnership's supreme purpose is to secure the fairest possible sharing by all its members of the advantages of ownership: gain, knowledge and power; that is to say, their happiness in the broad sense of that word so far as happiness depends upon gainful occupation . . .' He was later to sum this statement up more succinctly: 'Partnership is justice. Better than justice, it is kindness.'

Job security as a component of happiness was clearly at the heart of Spedan Lewis's philosophy, and the current chairman of the John Lewis Partnership, Sir Stuart Hampson, is adamant that the principle makes for a good test of management. Hampson takes the happiness principle so literally that he holds 'happy hours' with his directors, asking them how the business is doing in terms of happiness. 'I am convinced that is the secret of sustainable success,' he says. While fashionable business thinking is urging everyone to forget the lifetime career and prepare for a life of constant change and challenge, moving from company to company on short-term projects, Hampson sticks to his belief that the John Lewis way is good for business performance as well as worker motivation.[15]

Spedan Lewis's vision of happiness and partnership in business was revolutionary for 1910 and remains rare enough 92 years later, but Andy Law's view of the same principle is something else again. Law is a founder of St Luke's, the creative communications company housed in a former Victorian toffee factory on the edge of east London. The company's chief business is advertising, but it also makes documentaries and short films. It is owned in equal proportion by every employee after they have completed six months' apprenticeship and proved that they can add value to the company beyond just doing their job. Law's book about his great experiment, *Open Minds*, tells how St Luke's chose to change the 'DNA' of business by spurning organisational convention. He describes the nature of St Luke's as one which 'furiously seeks a new, better, more fulfilling and fairer role for business in the lives of its employees – who are all also its shareholders – and in the lives of the people it touches, whether purposely or inadvertently'.

Ask yourself what matters

Open Minds begins with 'Ten Ways To Create A Revolution In Your Company':

1. Ask yourself what you want out of life.
2. Ask yourself what really matters to you.

3. Give all your workclothes to Oxfam and wear what you feel is really you.

4. Talk to people (even those you don't like) about (1) and (2). (*You should be feeling very uncomfortable now. You may even be sick. This is normal.*)

5. Give up something you most need at work (desk, company car, etc.).

6. Trust everyone you meet. Keep every agreement you make.

7. Undergo a group experience (anything goes: parachuting, holidaying).

8. Rewrite your business plan to align all of the above with your customers.

9. Draw a line on the office floor and invite everyone to a brave new world.

10. Share everything you do and own fairly with everyone who crosses the line.

(*You should be feeling liberated. Soon you will have, in this order, the following: grateful customers, inspired employees, friendly communities, money.*)[16]

The culture of St Luke's is run and maintained by a trust called QUEST (Qualifying Share Ownership Trust). Law explains: 'It is a financial system that permits the equal shareholding scheme to happen once a year . . . and is the barometer of the company. When things get hot it can cool matters down and when the company is too cool (lackadaisical, conventional) it can turn the temperature up. The QUEST is the nearest thing we have to a regular governing force . . . Despite the influence of the QUEST, it is often made up of people with little or no management skill. But that's fine, because they are not voted in for those skills. They are voted in because they are trusted. It's as simple as that. They are trusted to ensure the shareholders are properly represented. They exist to remind everyone that the

company has a wide and widening franchise of
employee owners who are keen to exercise their right to
contribute to the democratic running of the company.'

St Luke's has become a landmark for its iconoclastic
structure – 'the Amoeba Growth Principle' which splits
off working groups when they become bigger than 35
and forms new ones – and its off-the-wall practices such
as the monthly 'Flag Meeting', a lively and often
raucous session where the month's achievements are
reviewed and someone gets to state publicly his or her
'five favourite things' in life.[17]

The St Luke's approach might well not work in a
different business sector, but companies don't have to be
as revolutionary as this to be inspirational. Jeffrey
Pfeffer, professor of organisational behaviour at
Stanford Graduate School of Business, is driven by the
conviction that the single most important factor in
whether companies succeed or not is the way they
manage their people. In *The Human Equation: Building
Profits by Putting People First* (1998), Pfeffer highlights seven
practices that distinguish successful organisations: job
security, careful hiring, decentralisation and teamwork,
good pay dependent on collective rather than individual
performance, lots of training, low differentials in both
status and pay, and systematic sharing of information.
He claims that putting these practices in place can
improve performance in almost any company by 40%.
But people do have to work harder, smarter and
shoulder more responsibility.

Why, then, do so few companies pursue the practices
identified by Pfeffer as key success factors? And why are
so many still downsizing, outsourcing, instituting
performance pay and substituting the employability
argument for job security? Pfeffer believes the
fundamental answer is that, in an era of stock options
and quick fixes, managing through people takes time
and is hard work. Too many companies fail to take an

holistic approach or retreat at the first setback. But he is adamant that companies 'gain a tremendous advantage by being different: they will attract and retain a better workforce and capitalise on the skills and knowledge developed by it'.

John Seely Brown offers management a deceptively simple solution. 'I would argue that one of the greatest skills today is listening, and that is why the learning organisation doesn't work because management is very bad at listening. We expect to talk, we expect to lead, and we don't understand that the essence of the thing is listen, learn and lead. You've got to listen to the back talk in your own group. And it does require a kind of calmness in being able to listen – Donald Schon, one of the fathers of the learning organisation, stressed this.'[18]

But is calmness something that managers can any longer hope to experience in a world spinning at Internet speed?

Powerpoints
- Tomorrow's company increasingly needs to become a living, learning, social organism that benefits its employees, shareholders, customers and surrounding community in equal measure.
- New concepts of human and intellectual capital in the Internet economy are changing the way in which people are managed. Talented individuals can auction themselves as economic units.
- Companies can 'rent' talent as needed, but if they want to retain employees in the era of the footloose Generation X and the talent wars, they need to rethink how they are recruited and managed.
- 'Adaptive leadership' is emerging as a new idea of leading without formal authority, a concept that fits the reluctance of many knowledge workers to be directed in the old way.
- Trust is also the goal of 'fair process', a new

management theory stating that productivity and innovation can be unleashed if employees understand how decisions are made in the company.

- Tomorrow's most successful companies will explore new kinds of 'moral contract' and individual-organisational relationships so as to harness corporate loyalty along with individual autonomy.

- Personal qualities of empathy and spiritual self-awareness are going to be required in the leaders of these organisations. Attention is increasingly paid to fulfilment, even happiness, in the working life.

- The rarest skill in management is the ability to listen – that's why the learning organisation still hasn't happened. The essence, says Internet visionary John Seely Brown, is to 'listen, learn and lead'.

NOTES

[1] author interview, October 2000; Tapscott, D., Ticoll, D. and Lowy, A.: *Digital Capital*, Nicholas Brealey, 2000

[2] Davis, S. and Meyer, C.: *Future Wealth*, Harvard Business School, 2000

[3] *FT, The Business*, 13.5.00

[4] author interview, London 1999

[5] author interview, London 1999; Handy, Charles and Elizabeth: *The New Alchemists*, Random House, 1999

[6] Mercer, David: *Future Revolutions*, Texere, 1998

[7] Tulgan, Bruce: *Winning the Talent Wars*, Nicholas Brealey, 2001

[8] author interview, Harvard, September 2000: Heifetz, Ronald A.: *Leadership Without Easy Answers*, Belknap Press, Harvard University, 1994

[9] author interview, INSEAD, 1997; Kennedy, Carol: 'From competing to value innovation', *MBA* magazine, December 1997

[10] author interviews; Kennedy, Carol: 'The roadmap to success: how Gerhard Schulmeyer changed the culture at

Siemens Nixdorf', *Long Range Planning*, Vol. 31, No. 2, 1998

[11] author interview, London Business School, 1999

[12] Goleman, Daniel: *Working With Emotional Intelligence*, Bloomsbury, 1998

[13] Overell, Stephen: 'Quest for a Soul Friendly Workplace', *FT*, 15.10.00; 'Monk on a Mission', *Evening Standard*, 26.6.00; *The Times*, 18.11.99; *Mail on Sunday*, 9.1.00

[14] *FT*, 20.10.00

[15] Kennedy, Carol: *The Merchant Princes*, Hutchinson, 2000, published in paperback as *Business Pioneers*, Random House, 2001

[16] Law, Andy: *Open Minds*, Orion Books, 1998

[17] ibid.

[18] author interview, September 2000

CHAPTER SEVEN

MANAGING AT NET SPEED

The Internet, we were constantly told until recently, 'changes everything'. Five-year business plans belong to history, or are only relevant for bankers and investors. Budgets that used to be planned on an annual basis may now have to be adjusted monthly or even weekly. As the Web puts customers in direct touch with companies, more and more decision-making has to be pushed out to frontline operators, collapsing old reporting structures and forcing the abandonment of centralised control. Strategy has to change radically too. When your nearest competitor is one-eighth of a second away, such exercises of the mid-1990s as Gary Hamel's 'industry foresight' – anticipating markets and customers five to ten years ahead – become largely academic, and Hamel himself has moved from foresight to a concentration on continual innovation.

Speed is the buzzword of new-economy management. Start-up companies have developed from raw idea to market launch in just ten weeks, and the life-cycle of the average business model is now put at two years. With the same technology available to all, entry barriers are being continually lowered and incumbent companies have to be ready to change their entire market strategies at short notice. Some companies are having to retool strategy every few weeks because of what customer feedback is telling them. 'Strategic planning used to be based on a build-then-sell model,' says John M. Jordan, director of e-commerce research at global consultancy Ernst & Young. But now 'customers are calling the shots, telling companies what they want, and companies have to respond to those desires or lose out. It's a whole new way of thinking about strategy.'

A strategy expert at IBM's Advanced Business Institute likens the difference between old and new to that between a bus following a set route and a taxi, going where the customer wants it to go. The acquisition-driven Cisco Systems (40 companies were acquired in two years at the end of the 1990s) has been remaking its strategy almost annually, according to *Business Week*. To cope with suddenly collapsed timeframes and swarming competition, companies have had to revise their management systems, using a variety of techniques including multiple scenarios of the kind military planners employ before battles – or the equally prolific kind that nature, in the living systems model, throws out in evolutionary experiments to ensure survival. At Solutia, the chemical company spun off from Monsanto, strategists plan four different short-term outcomes for any initiative, with 'signposts' or triggers built in to indicate when to change course. By this means the company can abandon or change a particular strategy within hours, whereas previously it would have tried to make the strategy work regardless of the reactions of the marketplace.

Similarly, the president of Sun Microsystems holds weekly sessions with his key decision makers to run a check on which strategies are working and which aren't. They are called 'whackometer' sessions because they confront all the ways in which Sun's competitors might be about to 'whack' it in the marketplace. Sun believes this helps it think strategically and prevents complacency. A Californian software and e-services company called Portera Systems changes strategy weekly after Monday-morning sessions in which sales reports are analysed to see how the market is responding to Portera's products. In online consumer businesses, budgets may have to be revised weekly to keep up with strategy changes. At Accompany.com, a Silicon Valley-based online buying club, such strategy changes are communicated within hours to the entire organisation, using emails and groupware, to encourage all employees to feel fully engaged in the decisions and 'ready to fly'. Accompany.com also has a policy of hiring only people who thrive on speed and ambiguity in their working life.[1]

What has really changed?

Outside the Internet sector itself, though, how far has the new technology 'changed everything' for managers? The great British economist Arthur Marshall wrote in his *Principles of Economics* more than a hundred years ago: 'The full importance of an epoch-making idea is often not perceived in the generation in which it is made . . . A new discovery is seldom fully effective for practical purposes till many minor improvements and subsidiary discoveries have gathered themselves around it.' Some thoughtful commentators today draw the analogy between information technologies as a transforming invention in business and the spread of electricity at the turn of the nineteenth and twentieth centuries: it took all of four decades between the first major exhibition of electrical power at the Philadelphia Centennial Exposition of 1876 and its complete dominance of industrial life.

In the same way, it may take another generation (in today's foreshortened sense of that word) for the digital technologies to be fully exploited, and for the management of them to become second nature. Until a generation of managers emerges who use computer capability as instinctively as we all use electricity, much of the world's business will be directed by people who are learning new skills rather than exercising them intuitively. How much do they feel pressured by talk about 'managing at Net speed'? And where are the Big Ideas to help them adapt? Business already demands a fluidity in management responses that is a complete break with the traditional model formulated by Henri Fayol, the nineteenth-century French mining engineer who first attempted to codify managerial activity: to forecast and plan; to organise; to command; to co-ordinate and to control.

The existence of a global tool like the Internet, though still in its adolescence, makes for an unprecedented capacity to transform the way in which we work, learn, play and manage, and to do so at speeds unimaginable even a decade ago, so its eventual dominance will take place much faster than the transition to electricity. Since the power of chip technology doubles every 18 months, the pace of that transformation won't be comfortable. And the advent of optical communications, with data of all kinds transmitted in light over glass fibre, means that business will soon be transacted at, literally, the speed of light. A single strand of glass fibre thinner than a human hair can already carry on it every telephone call, email and web page in the world.

Since the first wave of e-business market frenzy has crashed back on itself, with technology stocks collapsing and dot-comets falling to earth like so many burned-out satellites, forecasts of 'hyper-growth' in e-business-to-business look less exponential (it had been projected that trade in this area in the US alone would double every year on a curve from $43bn in 1999 to $1.3 trillion in 2003, with Europe following later in the decade). But the technical potential remains unchanged. Lou Gerstner, chief executive of IBM, has predicted the 'storm' that will arrive 'when the thousands and thousands of institutions that exist today seize the power of this global computing and communications infrastructure and use it to transform themselves'. Businesses will not achieve their goals of innovation, says Gerstner, until they integrate Internet technology into all their processes – cost structures, marketing, sales and the supply chain.

Outside the Internet companies the main impact so far of the Web and its capacity to collapse and streamline processes has been in revolutionising customer relationships and cutting supply-chain costs: billions of dollars are being saved by major industrial companies such as General Electric and Ford by purchasing through online exchanges. Jac Nasser, Ford's chief executive, has said that the Internet is transforming car manufacturing as radically as did the first Henry Ford's assembly line. Huge added-value opportunities are also being picked off in formerly mundane service industries such as utilities: two UK water companies, for example, have used remote-control Web technology to expand their business from supplying domestic taps to treating water systems around the world. But the potential still to be realised is going to involve seismic shifts in strategic thinking, and anyone running a business now, whether in the old or new economic sectors, has to understand what is different and possible through technology, even if they don't yet understand the mechanics of it.

John Chambers, chief executive of Cisco Systems, says that most people haven't yet grasped the biggest payback application of the Internet: the way that key data about the business is immediately available throughout the organisation. 'I can now close my books in 24 hours,' he said in an interview in *Business Week* in the summer of 2000. 'I've known for a month what my earnings are for this weekend. I know my expenses, my profitability, my gross margins, my components . . . Once I have my data in that form, every one of my employees can make decisions that might have had to come all the way to the president.' Product-line managers, he added, could see exactly what their gross margins were, whether they were below expectations and why. 'Quicker decision-making at lower levels will translate into higher profit margins. So instead of the CEO and CFO making fifty to a hundred different decisions a quarter, managers throughout the organisation can make millions of decisions. Companies that don't do that will be non-competitive.'[2]

'Richness and reach'

One of the Internet's biggest effects on business strategy will be its ability to blur the boundaries between niche markets and mass consumption, known as the difference between 'richness' and 'reach'. The 'connectivity' of information networks between customers and providers, suppliers and employees, is exploding the need for a market strategy to concentrate on one or the other. Where the old business-school matrices used to describe strategy trade-offs – exclusivity for premium pricing or the lowest-price option – in reality customers now have access to both richness and reach, and competitive advantage is not what it was. This fundamental change means that organisations as well as strategy have to be re-engineered.

Stan Davis and Christopher Meyer, the two Ernst & Young consultants who point out that once-internal management processes such as pricing policy are now 'migrating into the marketplace', say: 'Learning to change as fast as the marketplace means that customers are, in effect, designing your organisation. When your organisation changes as fast as your business, that's as it should be. What seems like the risk of reallocating your resources is really the opportunity to keep pace with the market. What feels like chaos is effective adaptation.'[3]

Those forcing-grounds of big management ideas, the US business schools and global consultancies, are only just beginning to wrestle with the practicalities of managing this chaos. A research programme into managing emerging technologies run by America's oldest collegiate business school, Wharton at the University of Pennsylvania, found that the accompanying 'disequilibrium, profound ambiguity and a rate of change that often defies standard analysis' directly challenge the still entrenched belief that a manager's job is to control and manage uncertainty. Ultimately, say George Day and Paul Schoemaker, the editors of a series of Wharton papers, managers of emerging technology businesses have to develop 'the ability to live with paradox and its associated ambiguities. Simple, absolute answers are few and far between.'[4]

Two senior members of the Boston Consulting Group, Philip Evans and Thomas S. Wurster, contend that the old rules of strategy still apply, but at a more refined level. It isn't a comfortable process, they admit. Deconstructing what is going on in a world of connectivity 'is the opposite of what most managers are trained to deal with'. It is disconcerting and mentally exhausting. 'With the partial exception of pure information businesses, the strategies themselves are essentially the same: scale, market share, cost, innovation, capabilities, competencies and the rest. But the objects of those strategies are different. And the task is therefore one of identifying these new objects and then rethinking and reapplying the old principles of competitive advantage.'

In a much-praised book on Internet strategy called *Blown to Bits*, Evans and Wurster set out a dozen principles that make chilling reading. Here are just the first three:

- No business leader today can presume that the business definitions in his or her business will still be valid a few years from now.
- Deconstruction is most likely to strike in precisely those parts of the business where the stakeholders have most to lose and are least willing to recognise it.
- Waiting for someone else to demonstrate the feasibility of deconstruction hands over the biggest advantage a competitor could possibly wish for: time.[5]

In Internet time, as the Boston Consulting pair say, 'everything is a sprint', and the race goes to the first competitor to get a business strategy right. It is no longer an option to learn from others' mistakes and then piggyback successfully into the market. Today, companies have to make their own mistakes and keep trying. 'Fast follower' strategies 'may work in marathons, but not in sprints'. This belief is debated by some who have watched first-mover online companies lose hundreds of millions of dollars of investors' money, but it is widely held among cyber consultants.

The three-clicks culture

What does this mean for the average manager's daily work? Internet time is generally reckoned to work on a ten to one ratio, meaning that business in the e-economy is transacted ten times faster than in the old economy. But it's not quite as simple as that. In Silicon Valley they reckon a day is now a week of pre-Net time, a week is a month and a month is a year. It's a 24/7 world, and if, as Net entrepreneur and author Mark Breier puts it, you are not moving forward at that pace, you're just falling behind. 'Internet time not only means doing business fast but doing it anytime the customer wants and for as long as he wants it,' writes Breier.[6] Not only that, but the

Net player is never far from his or her beeper, fax machine, email or cell phone. Talk about information overload!

Managers are suddenly very exposed. Their office doors might as well be made of glass, and email means they can no longer hide behind defensive lines of secretaries. In many businesses, the customer now has as much undiluted power as if he or she had a direct line to the marketing director. In response, the company has to develop a whole corporate culture that works in Net time. Peg Neuhauser, Ray Bender and Kirk Stromberg, co-authors of a book called *Culture.com*, say Web site designers understand that most Internet users have patience for no more than three clicks of the mouse in their search for a product, service or information. If they do not find what they want by then, the fourth click takes them somewhere else – to a competitor. Thus, the book argues, if companies must develop strategies based on a three-clicks concept of Net time, they need a three-clicks culture to support it.

A key chapter headed 'Making the Jump to Warp Speed' describes how a company called Acxiom formulated a 100-Day Project to change its pace and business strategy so as to create and market its new B2B software in 100 days instead of one year. Acxiom identified two main areas of learning: how to organise and make decisions at high speed, and how to create a safe culture with a high level of employee trust in the new ways of doing things. A number of key lessons emerged, such as:

- Launch and learn rather than learn, then launch. 'Second to market is not good enough any more.' A start-up like Amazon.com would probably not have secured a foothold in that market behind the leader.
- Go for both speed and quality: it's not an either-or choice. (This is not a new finding: Jim Collins and

Jerry Porras, authors of an outstanding management study called *Built to Last*, found that sustainably successful market leaders have consistently succeeded at apparently contradictory goals.) Decide those functions or products for which 80% quality is acceptable and those requiring zero defects, and develop guidelines for employees. Clients can help in developing 'quick and dirty' prototypes.

- 'Create a culture that supports risk-taking . . . better to destroy your own cash cows and replace them with the next generation of products than to have the competition come along and do it to you.'
- 'To speed up decision-making in your organisation, count the number of meetings it takes to make a decision and the number of sign-offs each requires.' Cut in half the number of committees, the number of people on each and the time allotted, and slash the number of sign-offs.
- Change your approach to decision-making. Time-box it, as Procter and Gamble does – set a goal for a project's completion that is three or four times as fast as 'normal' speed.[7]

It's never too late to learn speed

Some very old-economy companies discovered the speed ethos long before the Internet ruled the world. In the early 1990s Percy Barnevik, then the much-admired chief executive of Asea Brown Boveri (ABB), the Swiss-Swedish engineering conglomerate, was energising his managers to make rapid decisions. 'I'd rather be 70% right and fast than 100% right and slow,' he used to say.

But it's never too late. Even the biggest oil-tanker-like companies can learn to turn on a dime, as GE proved with its quickfire conversion to e-business (see Chapter 3), and as IBM discovered when its chief information officer, Steve Ward, devised the idea of the Speed Team in November 1999. As the story was unfolded in a *Fast Company* case study, Ward saw that if Big Blue didn't re-set the clocks of its worldwide IT group to Internet time, nimbler start-ups would be taking business from it, particularly in Web-linked applications. The team comprised IBMers who had managed innovative Web projects to completion in remarkably short times, and was led by two people with particular reputations for getting rapid results: Jane Harper, director of Internet technology and operations, and Ray Blair, director of e-procurement.

Their first decision was to send an appropriate message throughout the company by limiting the Speed Team's life to six months, winding up by June 2000. Next came an analysis of fast, successful projects to determine any shared characteristics, and to find out where the 'speed bumps' lay that had hampered the progress of others. Inevitably, in a company the size and complexity of IBM, bureaucracy came into it. One of the factors slowing things down were the rules governing application development. These had been devised for good reason, to safeguard quality, but they worked on a 'one-size-fits-all' basis. Ray Blair saw that tailoring the process to each project would put some on a fast track without sacrificing quality. Within a year, by skipping several steps of the application system, Blair had moved nearly $2bn worth of IBM purchasing to e-procurement and saved the company $80m. In the second year, he anticipated savings of $250m. The time for approving purchase requisitions shrank from two weeks to 24 hours.

The Speed Team also drew on the culture of one of IBM's leading-edge divisions, its WebAhead lab in Connecticut, where new technologies are prototyped. WebAhead had a sort of Great Groups or garage-culture attitude to its work and saw itself as doing 'cool stuff for IBM'. Its team worked in a shared office with rows of people round long tables. It used instant messaging technology and wireless networking to communicate with clients and other IBM colleagues. An innovation called the Video Watercooler simulated the sort of spur-of-the-moment meetings staff have at the water cooler or coffee machine – informal, time-saving, keeping people up to speed on projects more frequently than they could by scheduled video conferencing.

Jane Harper, who ran the 20-strong WebAhead lab, was already pulling out key lessons from the lab's work. One was the realisation that speed is its own reward, because people love seeing their projects completed quickly. Another was the need to recruit individuals geared to speed – not everyone is. As a result, she has been expanding IBM's internship programme for software engineers, catching likely engineering candidates from Harvard and Stanford universities before the start-ups get to them.

IBM identified six 'success factors for speed':

- strong leaders;
- team members passionate about speed;
- clear objectives;
- strong communications;
- project-tailored approach to processes; and
- a timetable geared to speed.

Above all, the Speed Team found that everything depends on how you view time. Treat it and measure it as a tangible resource as important as money and people, and its use improves. As with any change-management technique, targets can be divided into quick hits to encourage people (such as a 'speed rating' at staff performance appraisals) and longer-term initiatives requiring big corporate changes in policies, procedures, even values. An online 'town hall' system harvested useful feedback and good ideas, such as the need to master information overload, a major barrier to speed.

Naturally, the Speed Team couldn't afford to waste time in its own meetings throughout the six months of its existence, so it evolved a set of five rules that other companies could adopt with profit:

(1) Do your homework: come to meetings properly briefed and prepared.

(2) Focus fast: structure meetings and stick to the topic, using emails to explore side issues with colleagues.

(3) Don't waste time on side issues: deal with matters deserving of further discussion in conference calls later.

(4) Don't mind your manners: saying 'move on' or 'go to the next point' saves time, especially when most are in agreement.

(5) Encourage fast follow-up: post action notes from the meeting on a database within an hour so that everyone knows what is to be done next.[8]

As the IBM team discovered, a lot of business processes act as barriers to speed because they put quality ahead of speed. But there doesn't need to be a choice if, like IBM, you tailor procedures to projects and don't try to squeeze everything into the same mould. At Barclays Global Investors, the fund managing division of Britain's Barclays Bank headquartered in San Francisco, Bill Drobny has evolved a methodology for getting projects quickly to completion which depends on fitting the right person to the right team role. Drobny, in his late thirties, is BGI's personable manager of strategic projects, a title that enables him, as he says with a smile, 'to do a bit of everything – marketing, strategy, finance and technology'. Effectively, he is the e-strategist and chief business planner for the half of the company that operates in the US. Projects were getting bogged down because people were trying to do too many of them, resources were being diluted and there was a reluctance to make decisions about what *not* to do. Now BGI has an internal project clearing-house to qualify those worth doing.

In a sunlit office high above San Francisco's financial district, Drobny explained his model, which revolves around five key roles: the ***sponsor***, or money partner, a heavyweight executive who is solidly aligned with the company's strategic goals and gives the project corporate credibility; a ***business owner*** or line executive who champions the project and makes the day-to-day decisions; the ***project manager***, ***technical experts*** and ***support staff***. 'You need to have money, you need to have decision-making, you need somebody who is worried about the deadline, and you need tools to do it.'

When Drobny launched his anatomical dissection of projects that were running into the sand, he found that roles such as project manager and business owner were often being combined in the same person, with the result that whenever there was a conflict in decision-making, the person didn't know what to do. 'You can't have people cross their roles because they get biased towards what they do best,' says Drobny. An absolute essential is that the project manager should be obsessed with deadlines rather than quality, he argues. 'If someone comes to me as project manager, I say, "Are you a deadline person? Does a deadline make you more excited than anything else in the world?" If they say no, I say, "Don't talk to me about being project manager. Because if you're more interested in the quality than hitting the deadline, you're going to hurt the project." If he's a quality guy, make him business owner; they are the people who keep going over and over a project to ensure it's right. People try to make the project manager an administrative function. It can't be like that. A project manager has to be someone who kicks all the other people around.'

Drobny, who describes himself as 'a resource that people can choose to use' when they are facing problems with a project, says his is a model that will 'make you feel better because you'll finish something and the fact of finishing something is most important. The problem is usually not that a project fails but that it doesn't do anything, it just goes on sucking in resources.' If someone gets stuck in progressing a project, they can come back to the model and use it to check what's missing in the roles or skillsets required. But it needs people who can fill the roles and who fit culturally with the organisation.

BGI had a conservative, risk-averse tradition, which may have been appropriate to its principal function of managing retirement funds, but which had got to the point of near-paralysis in some decision-making. Now its culture is 'very entrepreneurial', says Drobny, and the company even lures back quite a few 'retreads' who have gone off for a while to work in dotcoms but miss the combination of corporate structure and ideas-driven culture. 'The environment here is very invigorating; there is a high level of discussion and conversation. You go into meetings and all of a sudden you are being mentally challenged and wonder if you can get your head round this.' Drobny now hopes to get his project-driving model spread throughout the organisation. 'I'm trying to empower others. I don't particularly need to own the model, I want to make it something they can own. What this is about is rapidly transferring a tool that people can run with. If everybody did it the whole firm would be more efficient.'[9]

The challenge of managing at Internet speed has naturally produced a few instant how-to books. Mark Breier, a former marketing vice-president of Amazon.com and chief executive of a software retailer, was mightily impressed when fresh out of college by a business best-seller called *The One-Minute Manager* by

Spencer Johnson and Kenneth Blanchard (1982). Going back to it nearly twenty years later as the head of an Internet company, Breier found himself thinking, 'the way things are going these days, it's hard for me to find a free minute'. So he sat down, rattled the keys of his word-processor and produced – yes, *The Ten-Second Internet Manager*. In the fast track of today's information superhighway, he informs us in the introduction, 'my old friend *The One-Minute Manager* would probably be found face down with tyre tracks up his back'.

In the main, Breier's book is a smartly packaged exercise in time management, with good tips on handling email overload, having 'power coffees' instead of breakfasts or lunches, and getting faster action by being 'very specific' on targets. 'Don't tell your technical crew you want "faster" page load speeds, tell them you want pages to load in less than four seconds.' He shares with IBM's Speed Team a belief in hiring 'fast people', whom he says you can identify by their physical restlessness and fast way of walking, and he likes Microsoft's and Amazon's interview technique of asking off-the-wall questions to test candidates' powers of quick thinking. 'I've been known to ask candidates to tell me how many stoplights there are in the city of San Jose, or how many sesame seeds there are on a Big Mac bun ... What I look for is what Yahoo's CEO, Tim Koogle, calls "similitude", meaning that you don't have all the facts so you have to come up with an educated guess ... I'm paying attention to the process rather than the answer. Internet managers are hit with dozens of questions every day that have no easy answers, and so are the people who work for you. If they're going to be able to keep their heads above water at all, your key people have to be able to make decisions that are fast and smart. Winning on one count isn't enough.'[10]

Henry Mintzberg, the Canadian strategy guru, carried out some celebrated studies a generation ago analysing how managers make decisions and how, in practice, they spend their working days. The results, published in a book *(The Nature of Managerial Work*, 1973) and in a famous *Harvard Business Review* article ('The Manager's Job: Folklore and Fact', 1975), were revealing. Mintzberg found that managers were constantly firefighting, their time hopelessly fragmented by interruptions and crises. They were juggling as many as fifty projects and often disposing of issues in ten minutes or less, yet the adrenalin produced by this ceaseless reaction to events gave them the glowing if misleading feeling that they were achieving a great deal.

If management in the 1970s was like this, what on earth are the pressures and forced reactions of the Internet age doing to managers, and are they, too, registering a distorted view of their own capabilities through making decisions in slivers of time? As yet, there seems to be no modern equivalent to Mintzberg's research. It's a safe bet that the results would be even more unsettling.

Learning from the 'Nintendo Kids'

There are those who believe that the managers most likely to be able to cope with Internet sprint time will come from a generation to whom the technology is instinctive rather than learned, and whose reactions have been honed by making split-second decisions in computer games. Professor Kenichi Ohmae, the Japanese strategy guru, calls these 'the Nintendo Kids', and he thinks the best environment for managers today is to be surrounded by Nintendo Kids, working in 'Resonance Zones' – that is, wherever new-economy entrepreneurship and innovation is happening, whether in Cambridge, Silicon Valley, the 'cyber frenzy' of Singapore or Ireland.

Don Tapscott, a rising 'cyber-guru' from Toronto, is

another who takes this view. Tomorrow belongs to the Net Generation, he says, because they are best fitted to manage in the digital age. Noting that Procter and Gamble, among a raft of leading old-economy companies, has introduced 'reverse mentoring' by young people to help older executives manage the Internet and tap into cyber culture, Tapscott believes the Net Generation can make speedier decisions because 'they have grown up changing their minds and making this sort of decision through playing interactive computer games. They have a different way of processing information.'

Professor Garth Saloner, head of Stanford's e-business and commerce department and an astringent observer of Silicon Valley management, dismisses this idea out of hand. 'A manager is a manager – the essence of Web management you can learn in a day,' he says. 'The Nintendo Kids have speed but haven't got a clue what they are doing. I would happily entrust them to go out and create something cool with a bunch of money they were given, but I would not in a million years entrust them with the management of a serious enterprise. By contrast, a 50- or 60-year-old manager who's been through this ten times can make decisions in a nanosecond because they are based on experience, and they are good decisions. I've sat by these folks and seen it happen.

'You have to know when you can pull a trigger in 30 seconds, and how do you know that if all you've been doing is to produce some cool software that all your friends like? Older managers do find it difficult to adjust to Net speed, but they are still better able to do it than someone with no experience. These are very different skills from founding a technology business. But when you've created a Netscape, you don't want a kid running it. You want someone who knows how to do a deal, how to manage.

'Who would you rather fly with – someone who has piloted a bunch of really old, stodgy aircraft not nearly as cool as those we are now flying but who has done it for years, or someone who has just trained six months on a Stealth jet? Quick reflexes are nice, but tons of experience are worth more.'[11]

Are there perhaps useful analogies for Net-age management training that can be drawn from the world of a pilot or a racing driver? Bedded-down knowledge and simulations of all the scenarios likely to be encountered in the air or on the track are, after all, what enables the captain of a 747 or a Formula One driver to take emergency decisions, when needed, with nano-second instinct. John Seely Brown thinks it's an interesting comparison, but one that operates in reverse for management because 'a pilot's life is 99% boredom and 1% terror', which means more or less learning procedures by rote. 'That's almost old-style manage-ment. The new-style management means things are happening every day that have to be acted on and managed. Managers are in a constant interpretative stance, making sense of what's going on. You have to read the papers and think, what are the implications of Ford's problem [in the summer of 2000] with electronic ignition, is it going to cause a backlash in technology, and so on. You have to be constantly thinking, what does this mean for my company, what does it mean for my competitors?

'In the aviation analogy, you spend half your time flying the GPS system and half without navigational aids. You spend as much time off the map as on the map. You have to find your navigational aids as you plough ahead. It's a cognitive, political, emotional role, grounded in the emotions of your people. If you're an explorer you don't know what's round the corner anyway. You have to have your wits about you. Today's managers have to have their wits constantly honed.

Today's managers have to operate in diversity. It's essential to get a management team with different points of view, or you'll be screwed. Group-think is important.'

The key, says Seely Brown, is to 'construct an environment where people are constantly learning, constantly challenged and really turned on. In the past the world stayed the same, so you could take twenty years of experience and use that as the basis for your decisions. Now you have to trust your current understanding of the world – certain parts don't change, certain parts do. Managers fail now by either being way too modern, hip-shooting all the time, or way too conservative, thinking, "We can't afford that acquisition." Today you have to think rather than intuit, think your way through a situation. It's exciting for those who like to be on the edge.'[12]

Maybe it's time for a re-run of another Mintzberg study into the role of left-brain, right-brain thinking. Over the two decades before he published *Mintzberg on Management* (1989), the Montreal professor who also taught at France's INSEAD school of management had researched the functions of the brain in the making of strategy, finding that chief executives who were the most successful at strategic thinking favoured the right-hand, or intuitive, side of the brain rather than the left-hand, or analytical, side. Mintzberg concluded from this that there was more than logical planning behind successful strategy or the running of an organisation. 'Effective managers seem to revel in ambiguity, in complex, mysterious systems with little order,' he wrote. Perhaps the demands on Internet managers are tilting the balance back towards fast, analytical, left-brain skills.

'Brains don't speed up'

Surprisingly, one of the most driven managers in the Internet economy, Andy Grove of Intel, who named a book after his most famous saying, 'Only the paranoid survive', now takes a relaxed view of the current obsession with speed. 'This business about speed has its limits,' he told *Business Week* in the summer of 2000. 'Brains don't speed up. The exchange of ideas doesn't really speed up, only the overhead that slowed down the exchange. When it comes down to the bulk of knowledge work, the twenty-first century works the same as the twentieth century. You can reach people around the clock, but they won't think any better or any faster just because you've reached them faster. The give and take remains a limiting factor.' His left brain and right brain are telling him different things, Grove says. 'The left brain is the technology side, and it's very excited. My right brain is a manager's brain. I've lived through forty years of management, and people haven't changed in those forty years, so I'm a little sceptical. Our fundamental organisations haven't changed on paper. On the fringes, there is more looseness in the organisation, but more hasn't changed than has. Things have changed, but the left brain says they should be galloping. The right brain says there have only been slow, gradual changes in the way we operate organisations.'[13]

Sumantra Ghoshal, professor of strategic and international management at London Business School, thinks that individuals will have to take decisions faster but that is nothing new – it has been necessary before in history. The difference, he suggests, will be 'a broadening of the decision-making processes, so that the decisions *emerge* faster. Who takes the decision and how it is taken will have to change to cope with the need for rapid response.'[14]

Some clues on the qualities needed in senior managers today can be deduced from the hunt for chief executives in the business-to-business online exchanges or marketplaces, a sector that is rapidly proliferating as industries vie with each other to strip out supply-chain costs. These exchanges are likely to be generating thousands of billions of dollars' worth of trade within a few years and are often joined as partners by companies which have spent decades as bitter competitors. Professional headhunters, when asked by London's *Financial Times* in late 2000 for the personal qualities they hoped to find when looking for chief executives for industry-led exchanges, pinpointed exceptional strategic thinking and deal-making skills, allied to experience in implementing partnerships between multinationals in mature industries, thorough industry knowledge and a flair for e-commerce. Acknowledging that such a paragon might well not exist, the recruitment experts thought the answer was to offset any weaknesses through selection of the whole management team.

Russell Reynolds, a leading international executive search consultancy, gave priority in its CEO criteria to technological expertise, but several others plumped for management skills over 'web DNA'. Joseph Laughlin, chief executive of GlobalnetXchange, the online marketplace for the retail industry, said an understanding of e-commerce and technology was necessary 'but you don't have to be an expert. You've got to surround yourself with experts.' More important, he considered, was the ability to build partnerships and implement decisions rapidly, and here the responsibility of the CEO among the exchange's partners should be paramount. Chief executives who need to consult a number of equity partners before making a decision would not be able to operate at Internet speed. 'If you can make quick decisions and execute, you're probably going to be one of the survivors.'[15]

Powerpoints

• The difference between old- and new-economy strategies has been likened to that between a bus and a taxi – follow a pre-set route or go where the customer says.

- The ability of the Internet to blur the boundaries between 'richness' and 'reach' means customers now have access to both, eroding old competitive advantage principles such as low-cost versus quality.

- Management skills now have to be far more fluid and agile. They will be under ever more pressure from the technology. Optical communications work literally at the speed of light.

- Online companies develop a 'three-clicks' culture – customers lose patience after three clicks when searching a Web site. This speeds up everything from market entry to the way decisions are made.

- It's never too late to accelerate. Set up a Speed Team like IBM, based on analysing the fastest, most successful projects and learning why 'speed bumps' held back others.

- The Speed Team's key finding: treat time as a measurable resource, as important as money or people, and its payback improves.

- Barriers to speed can result from a one-size-fits-all approach to quality. Project management becomes faster and more efficient if people are fitted to the roles they do best.

- Find the fast thinkers by asking bizarre interview questions that force them to come up with an educated guess. In Net time, managers are hit every day with dozens of questions that have no easy answers.

- Some 'legacy' companies are already bringing in Net Generation 'reverse mentors' to help older managers adapt. But you don't have to be a Nintendo Kid to make good decisions quickly – experience counts.

- 'Today's managers have to operate in diversity,' says John Seely Brown. 'Get a management team with different points of view. Group-think is important.'

- Don't get unduly distracted by the speed mania. Andy Grove of Intel says the management of people hasn't changed much in forty years.

NOTES

[1] *Business Week*, 1.11.99

[2] *Business Week*, 28.8.00

[3] Davis, S. and Meyer, C.: *Future Wealth*, Harvard Business School Press, 2000

[4] Day, George and Schoemaker, Paul: *Wharton on Managing Emerging Technologies*, Wiley, 2000

[5] Evans, Philip and Wurster, Thomas H.: *Blown to Bits*, Harvard, 2000

[6] Breier, Mark: *The Ten-Second Internet Manager*, Piatkus Books, 2000

[7] Neuhauser, Peg; Bender, Ray and Stromberg, Kirk: *Culture.com*, Wiley, 2000

[8] Kirsner, Scott: 'Faster Company', summarised from the May 2000 issue of *Fast Company* magazine. All rights reserved. The full story can be accessed on www.fastcompany.com/online/34/ibn/html

[9] 'Getting it Done: BGI – a model of effectiveness', *Fast Company*, June 2000; author interview, September 2000

[10] Breier: *The Ten-Second Internet Manager*

[11] author interview, Palo Alto, September 2000

[12] author interview, San Francisco, September 2000

[13] *Business Week*, 28.8.00

[14] author interview, 1999

[15] Maitland, Alison: 'Plenty of room up top,' *FT*, 3.10.00

CHAPTER EIGHT

GURUS OF THE NEW ECONOMY

Managers in the new economy have few maps to guide them, and even fewer mapmakers. While the dotcom start-ups of the last two years have learned the hard way that a bright idea plus venture capital is not enough if you can't manage the business plan, the financials, the market and the people, there are, as earlier chapters have shown, new skills and models to be learned, and little has yet been formulated about them in theory.

Such gurus of the Internet as exist are still stronger on the technology of it than on the strategy or business management. So, in Japanese style, guru figures tend to be found in the technology industry itself, in businesses that have proved their success. Top of the list, naturally, is **Bill Gates** of Microsoft, still the world's richest man despite losing the equivalent of a small country's GDP when the technology stockmarket bubble burst in 2000. Gates has now quit the executive direction of Microsoft to be its technical visionary and innovator-in-chief, his real passion, but his managerial style and corporate philosophy has already been set out in the second of his best-selling books, *Business@the Speed of Thought*, published in 1999.

Gates is a phenomenon, and not merely for his stupendous wealth. The opposite of charismatic, with an awkward presence that has had some of its rough edges smoothed by maturity, marriage and parenthood, he still looks the archetypal computer geek, with a schoolboy haircut, big glasses and a passion for the technology. Yet even when he was chairman and chief executive of the world's biggest company, as one management writer observed, 'he reads voluminously, even in odd moments, specialises in "multi-tasking" (doing many things at once) and somehow contrives to give the running of Microsoft his full attention, while also spending much time on public relations'. (Most old-economy managers complain they have no time for reading outside the business press.) On one flight to London for a conference appearance, he sent more than three hundred emails back to Seattle, and the recipients knew that he expected a reply to each within hours.

Yet even Gates's mega-brain failed, as he acknowledges in his latest book, to foresee how fast the Internet, 'a network for academics and techies, would blossom into the global commercial network it is today'. From 1998 he was reorienting his business towards this 'new universal space for information sharing, collaboration and commerce', saying that it combined 'the immediacy and spontaneity of the TV and phone with the depth and breadth inherent in paper communications'. He realised that the true breakthrough to using the Net would come when it was accessible away from the desktop, through portable and mobile devices that would enable people to control their work and life wherever they were, from calling up business data on their WAP phone to organising grocery deliveries and regulating the domestic central heating from the car fifty miles away.

Within business organisations, Gates urges companies to follow Microsoft's own example of installing a complete 'digital nervous system' that will 'enable a company to perceive and react to its environment, to sense competitor challenges and customer needs, and to organise timely responses'. Changes in organisational structure include contracting out whatever does not belong to the company's core competencies – and employing only a small permanent staff with others hired as needed – expanding quickly from small bases, transferring work geographically wherever it can be done best or most cost-effectively, refocusing everything on the customer, and speeding up all processes.

'Almost all the time involved in producing an item is in the co-ordination of the work, not in the actual production,' Gates has observed. And he has perceived, astutely, that speed of delivery changes the essential nature of what a company does. 'When the increase in velocity of business is great enough,' he writes, 'the very nature of business changes. A manufacturer or retailer that responds to changes in sales in hours instead of weeks is no longer at heart a product company, but a service company that has a product offering.'[1]

Microsoft's self-perpetuating success thus far has been built on a principle which is simpler for an icon of the new economy than for lesser-known companies: namely, recruiting the best brainpower around. Microsoft's talent scouts rove the world looking for it, and Gates devotes – or did while he was chief executive – a large part of his time to interviewing potential high-flyers. Gates is famous for applying the technical term 'bandwidth' – the volume of data that an electronic communications system can carry at one time – to the human intellect. In his view, the way to build a knowledge company, a term he prefers to the looser 'learning organisation', is to hire the best human 'bandwidth' and then allow people to build their knowledge into the shared operations of the company.

Microsoft's hiring policy looks for abilities that reflect those of the founder: ability to grasp new knowledge and ask the right questions, a limpet-like concentration on the task in hand, ability to interpret software 'language' at a glance and photographic powers of recall. As Randall E. Stross observed in *The Microsoft Way* in 1996, 'All else being equal, the company that recruits the largest number of . . . the alphas among alphas is most likely to win the biggest sweepstakes.' But Gates knows that a collection of the brightest and best still does not make a focused commercial organisation. That relies on the company reacting as fast and as purposefully as an individual of high mental bandwidth – shared knowledge is corporate power. 'The ultimate goal is to have a team develop the best ideas from throughout an organisation and then act with the same unity of purpose and focus that a single, well-motivated person would bring to bear on a situation.'

To achieve this, projects are set up that share knowledge across the organisation and become an integral part of the work. Like Thomas Edison and many latter-day IT wizards, Gates believes in a cross-fertilisation of ideas among 'a critical mass of high-IQ people' to get the company as a whole 'working smarter'. Training is absolutely basic to this scenario – available online and at every employee's fingertips, including feedback systems. There is also, Microsoft employees will tell you, a 'just do it' culture of decision-making, within certain known parameters, that is felt to be energising and genuinely empowering.[2]

Microsoft's future was clouded for a year by the federal anti-trust lawsuit that ended in June 2000 with Judge Thomas Penfield Jackson ordering Microsoft to be split into two companies, but in June 2001 the company won a landmark victory on appeal. Gates's perception that the future belongs to mobile communications may, however, not be enough to retain Microsoft's dominance, which was based on older, desktop uses of technology. Smaller, nimbler companies specialising in the latest wireless technology will make inroads. But the phenomenon of Microsoft is still with us and Gates's book does provide practical ideas for the building of a successful, knowledge-rich e-business.

These are his twelve key steps to creating a 'digital nervous system':

(1) Insist that communication flows through the organisation over email, so that you can act on news with reflex-like speed.

(2) Study sales data online to find patterns and share insights easily. Understand overall trends and personalise service for individual customers.

(3) Use PCs for business analysis, and shift knowledge workers into high-level thinking work about products, services and profitability.

(4) Use digital tools to create cross-departmental virtual teams that can share knowledge and build on each other's ideas in real time, worldwide. Use digital systems to capture corporate history for use by anyone.

(5) Convert every paper process to a digital process, eliminating administrative bottlenecks and freeing knowledge workers for more important tasks.

(6) Use digital tools to eliminate single-task jobs or change them into value-added jobs that use the skills of a knowledge worker.

(7) Create a digital feedback loop to improve the efficiency of physical processes and improve the quality of the products and services created. Every employee should be able to track easily all the key metrics.

(8) Use digital systems to route customer complaints immediately to the people who can improve a product or service.

(9) Use digital communications to redefine the nature of your business and the boundaries around your business. Become larger and more substantial or smaller and more intimate as the customer situation warrants.

(10) Trade information for time. Decrease cycle time by

using digital transactions with all suppliers and partners, and transform every business process into just-in-time delivery.

(11) Use digital delivery of sales and service to eliminate the middleman from customer transactions. If you're a middleman, use digital tools to add value to transactions.

(12) Use digital tools to help customers solve problems for themselves, and reserve personal contact to respond to complex, high-value customer needs.[3]

Big Ideas for new businesses have tumbled out of the first generation of Internet pioneers: David Filo and Jerry Yang of Yahoo! with the first practical search engine; Jim Clark with graphics technology and the Netscape Navigator browser; Sabheer Bhatia with Hotmail, the first Web-based email service; Jeff Bezos with Amazon.com, a whole new business model for retailing; John Seely Brown's 'hot group' at Xerox PARC (Palo Alto Research Center), which invented most of the basic tools of today's technology, only to see the parent company let them slip into other hands. Big management insights to rival Theory X and Theory Y, empowerment or the hierarchy of needs are, as we have seen, much thinner on the ground. In practical organisational terms, too, there has been very little that is new apart from the virtual company. Even Gates's digital nervous system is essentially a technology application of re-engineering principles.

Aside from Gates, at least three other individuals who have helped shape the digital economy deserve mention for new ideas in management and business models. **Michael Dell**, who started his personal computer company with $1,000 capital when he was a student of biology at Austin University in Texas, designed an entirely new marketing model by cutting out the dealer middleman and selling direct to the customer over the

Internet. This principle, using customer feedback to improve products, build machines to order, deal with complaints swiftly and manage inventory on a just-in-time basis, made Dell Computer Corporation and its founder phenomenally rich, especially when other companies, like Apple, were suffering from 'channel-stuffing' – over-selling to dealers to boost quarterly figures and then seeing profits collapse when the surplus wasn't sold. 'Think about the customer, not the competition' has been Dell's mantra. Competitors, he says, represent the accumulated habits of the past, while customers represent your future growth.

Larry Ellison of Oracle, obsessively striving to overtake Gates in the top league of the world's richest men, has turned the tiny database software company he founded in 1976 with two partners and $2,000 each into a global giant challenging Microsoft and IBM for Internet software supremacy. Oracle has set out to make itself indispensable to all kinds of e-business and periodically launches bold new products such as the first Internet database and the first full-featured Internet portal for business users, bundling an email service together with business news from top providers such as Forbes.com, shipping reports, credit ratings, analysts' reports and financial news. Up to now, claims Oracle, there has been no single Web site that gives business users everything they need. In February 2001 it launched a service to deliver software over the Web by subscription instead of selling it as a CD. The product would be maintained by application service providers. While the subscription model is so new that its sales are starting from zero, Oracle executives are confident it will account for half the sales revenue in three to five years – and it could be unimaginably profitable because of its low costs and good margins.

Ellison, who was born in 1944, once said he learned a valuable business lesson from the Japanese and their attitude to competitors. He quoted a Japanese executive as saying, 'In Japan we think anything less than 100% market share is not enough. In Japan, we believe it is not sufficient that I succeed; everyone else must fail. We must destroy our competition.' The words were attributed to Ellison in a US newspaper report, exacerbating his arrogant, fighter-pilot image (he flies jet warplanes as a hobby). But Ellison's management style within Oracle is intensely team-oriented. He doesn't believe in fostering internal tension, creative or otherwise, and he has said the secret of recruitment is never to hire anyone you would not want to have lunch with three times a week.

Bill Gross of Idealab is frequently held up by the strategy guru Gary Hamel in his seminars as a role model of innovation. The structure of Idealab's Internet incubator model has been briefly described in other chapters and it was a pioneer in a field that now proliferates. Gross, born in 1959, has built a multi-billion-dollar corporation in five years out of the idea of creating Internet businesses from great ideas. Idealab's Web site solicits ideas, and the company prototypes dozens of them with inexpensive Web sites masquerading as portals. If enough customers 'hit', the prototype goes live and the customer gets his or her order; if not, those customers who do respond are reimbursed. Casting bread on the waters in this way paid off handsomely in Idealab's first years, creating businesses such as Cars Direct and eToys, though some have suffered in the general e-commerce collapse. Start-ups are also given office space, infrastructure and the chance of funding. When they grow to more than seventy people, they have to move out of the big aircraft-hangar space inhabited in Pasadena by Idealab and set up their own offices. Idealab also invests in other Internet-related companies and an Idealab partner sits on each board.

Gross has a 'One Per Cent' rule – that start-ups should give each employee a minimum 1% of the equity, which of course restricts staff numbers to a hundred. This, he told *Wired* magazine in September 1999, produces something like a chemical reaction. 'It unleashes new energy! I urge someone else to do this in other industries. I think this is the new model for business in general ... Every 10,000-person company should be broken up into 100-person companies.'[4]

Gross also had an Idealab investment ceiling of $250,000, and his abandonment of this limit in 1999 was the first of a series of bad financial decisions that has since led to the company dumping its planned IPO (Initial Public Offering) in 2000 and burning through nearly $1bn of funding raised for the project. It also over-expanded geographically, opening expensively designed new offices in Boston, New York and London, but has recently retrenched and intends its branch offices to become self-sufficient with strategic partners. Gross is still fizzing with creative ideas himself, one of the latest (in spring 2001) being a business based on domain names, New.net, that he claims will destroy the 'com' monopoly and 'revolutionise the Internet'.

Andrew Grove of Intel, the world's largest computer chip-maker, was once called the world's best manager by *Fortune*. Born in 1936 and in at the birth of Intel when it was set up in 1968 by two of his colleagues at Fairchild Semiconductors, his personal Big Idea, introduced in his managerial autobiography *Only the Paranoid Survive*, is Strategic Inflection Points – SIPs. These are the events, usually but not always technical, whose impact may be barely sensed at the time but which permanently change the fundamentals of a business. Examples would include the effect of automated telling machines on the banking industry. Another is 'the possibility that all entertainment content can be created, stored, transmitted and displayed in digital form may change the entire media industry'.

SIPs can't always be recognised right away and the problem is that they won't wait until you do recognise them, so that means relying on instinct and judgement more than data. 'If you run a business,' writes Grove, 'you must recognise that no amount of formal planning can anticipate such changes. Does that mean you shouldn't plan? Not at all. You need to plan the way a fire department plans: it cannot anticipate where the next fire will be, so it has to shape an energetic and efficient team that is capable of responding to the unanticipated as well as to any ordinary event.'[5]

In 1985, when Japan's onslaught on the US memory chip business was at its height, Grove responded by switching Intel into microprocessors, a courageous decision involving thousands of redundancies and a complete change of strategic direction. A few years later, Grove demonstrated his ability to firefight the totally unexpected and potentially devastating when a flaw was discovered in Intel's Pentium processor, which had been promoted in a costly advertising campaign and was at the heart of its marketing. He committed further heavy expenditure in order to replace every flawed processor, and a technical débâcle which could have damaged the company's reputation was defused while keeping customers impressed and loyal.

So far, the theorists of the Internet have tended to be either technologists or philosophers, without the practical application of business strategy. But the Net is such an unparalleled device for shrinking time and space, for breeding new business opportunities and for enlarging the sum of human knowledge and understanding, that we are only at the dawn of thinking about its possibilities. The following are the leading minds so far to be interpreting the implications of the new age. Appropriately, they are headed alphabetically by the man without whose visionary experiments with retrieving and sharing information in the primitive computer systems of 1980 the whole of computer technology, and global businesses such as Microsoft, would be struggling in a mapless world.

Tim Berners-Lee, the English-born, Oxford-educated inventor of the World Wide Web.

Berners-Lee is, or appears to be, a paradox in the business world he has created, where unimaginable fortunes are made overnight. If he had commercialised his invention, he could have approached the Gates league for wealth, but he chose instead to turn the Web technology over to the public good. Since 1994 he has worked quietly at the Laboratory for Computer Science at the Massachusetts Institute of Technology, and as director of the World Wide Web consortium, a body that monitors its global development.

Berners-Lee, born in 1955, read physics at Oxford, where he built his first computer with the aid of a soldering iron, an M6800 processor chip and an old television set. His first job was at Plessey Telecommunications in Dorset, England, and he then worked on software systems for a local computer company before joining the European Particle Physics Laboratory in Geneva, part of CERN, the European Centre for Nuclear Research. It was here that his 'lousy memory' and a desire to organise his data prompted him to experiment with writing a new kind of computer program that would allow the user to make a 'random association between absolutely anything and absolutely anything'. Quirkily, he called it 'Enquire', after the Victorian vade-mecum for the household, *Enquire Within Upon Everything*, which he remembered from the bookshelves in his parents' home.

Enquire remained unpublished, the germ of something much bigger, and Berners-Lee came back to

Britain for three years, returning to CERN in 1984. Now he had a business application to prompt further work on his retrieval program as he sought to find a method of preventing the loss of knowledge in organisations such as CERN where there was a high turnover of staff. At the same time, CERN was becoming the largest Internet site in Europe, and in 1989 Berners-Lee had his *coup de foudre*: to run hypertext – non-linear writing or texts containing links to other texts – across the Internet, making it a global phenomenon. He then interposed a piece of software called a browser between the user and the Internet servers, transforming the Net into a vehicle for mass usage. In an astonishing burst of creativity over 12 months, Berners-Lee had by 1992 invented everything needed to operate what he called the World Wide Web, and the fuse was lit for the explosive growth of the Internet.

Berners-Lee has been hailed by *Time* magazine as one of the hundred greatest minds of the twentieth century. Beyond his technical brilliance, he has a vision of the Web as a powerful force for social change, individual creativity and cultural freedom, and has sacrificed immeasurable wealth in pursuit of that vision. If the Web, as he points out, removes geographical barriers to cultural mixing, that challenges Europe, for example, to communicate more between its diverse languages and cultures. Not only did Berners-Lee shift the use of the Internet from a handful of technocrats to the mass of humanity, he also realised that it needed to be governed by standard protocols – still, globally, in many respects a dream rather than a reality. To this end he invented the URL – Uniform Resource Locator – to identify each information sender. Information would be exchanged by the HyperText Transfer Protocol (http) and documents set in Hypertext Markup Language (html), giving us the formula for every email and Web site address in the world.

In his memoir and philosophical credo, *Weaving the Web*, Berners-Lee says the Web offers infinite opportunities to dissolve hitherto established social, cultural and economic boundaries, and for creativity and rationality to be integrated across ever larger and more diverse groups. The question he poses in his final chapter is whether the Web can 'scale up' the way knowledge is advanced in a small group of people by brainstorming, the ability to solve problems intuitively, without applying a well-defined logical method.

'A larger company fails to be intuitive when the person with the answer isn't talking to the person who has the question. It is important that the Web help people to be intuitive as well as analytical, because our society needs both functions ... Scaling intuition is difficult because our minds hold thousands of ephemeral tentative associations at the same time. To allow group intuition, the Web would have to capture these threads – half-thoughts that arise, without evident rational thought or inference, as we work. It would have to present them to another reader as the natural complement to a half-formed idea.' To make this work, he says, writing, link creation and browsing must be totally integrated so that individuals can make the shortcut link when they notice relationships that are relevant. 'For this to be likely, the Web must be well-connected, have few degrees of separation' – rather in the way that researchers try to hold as much in their minds as possible and go to sleep hoping to wake in the night with a brilliant synthesis of the problem.

'We want to be able to work this brainstorming approach on a much larger scale,' he continues. 'We have to be sure to design the Web to allow feedback from the people who have made new intuitive links. If we succeed, creativity will arise across larger and more diverse groups ... among ever-larger interconnected groups of people acting as if they shared a larger intuitive brain.' The analogy of the Web as a global brain fascinates him, and although he does not pin any great hopes on it, he is generally optimistic that it will drive global co-operation. 'I feel that to deliberately build a society incrementally, using the best ideas we have, is our duty and will also be the most fun . . . people seem to be naturally built to interact with others as part of a greater system.'

Berners-Lee draws a parallel between the Web and Unitarian Universalism, a church-based movement that takes its pick of practical philosophy from all religions. 'The experience of seeing the Web take off by the grassroots efforts of thousands gives me tremendous hope that if we have the individual will, we can collectively make of our world what we want.'[6]

Key reading Berners-Lee: *Weaving the Web* (London: Orion Books, 1999)

Manuel Castells, economic historian and sociologist of the Internet, described by *The Economist* as 'the first significant philosopher of cyberspace'.

Castells, born in Spain in 1942, holds the chair of sociology at the University of California, Berkeley, and is an adviser to numerous UN agencies and governments. A graduate in law and economics from the University of Barcelona, he established a European reputation for his work in urban sociology before taking up an appointment at Berkeley in city and regional planning in 1979.

In 1983 he began his ground-breaking study of economic and social transformations associated with the information technology revolution. Over the next 15 years his researches covered North and South America, Europe and Asia, and were eventually distilled into the monumental three-volume work *The Information Age:*

Economy, Society and Culture, published between 1996 and 1998. The trilogy has led to his being compared in significance to Max Weber, who identified the moral and philosophical springs of the first industrial revolution in *The Protestant Ethic and the Spirit of Capitalism,* and he published a further study of the Internet's influence on business and society in 2001.

Castells is a scholar rather than a guru-professor in the mould of those produced by Stanford and Harvard business schools, and his books are fairly impenetrable for the business reader. He offers no prescriptives or principles for navigating the wild waters of the Internet, other than subscribing to chaos theory as it operates in the global economy, which he believes will eventually produce a new order out of disorder – 'but we cannot see that order now'. Although he sees national governments increasingly working together as a result of the new connectivity, he takes a gloomy view of the global economy as out of control and operating in an unpredictable way, likely to undermine the social fabric. A wild form of capitalism is sweeping the world, leaving social safeguards in a shambles, he concluded in the first volume of his trilogy, *The Rise of the Network Society.* 'The labour movement is powerless except in certain public service areas. Welfare and institutions of social protection have been lost. There is a downward spiral of the conditions of work and the environment. I am not necessarily saying that the global economy will destroy the world. But that is happening now.' The social consequences of these transformations will have to be addressed if the world is not to collapse into a violent and unwieldy division between those who can work the new system and the billions who will be left out.

Castells later took a more positive view of social developments, saying in a series of lectures at Oxford University in 1999 that while new Internet applications were predominantly driven by commerce in the US, in

Europe its possibilities would also be defined by public services and social movements, allowing for a broader range of global options. 'Mobile Internet leadership will be shaped by Nokia and Ericsson, and its norms, usages and customs will be European. These are the ones which will be taken into the US.'

Key reading *The Information Age: Economy, Society and Culture* (Oxford: Blackwell – Vol. 1, *The Rise of the Network Society*, 1996, revised edition 2000; Vol. 2, *The Power of Identity*, 1997; Vol. 3, *End of Millennium*, 1998, revised edition 2000); *The Internet Galaxy: Reflections on the Internet, Business and Society* (Oxford University Press, 2001)

Esther Dyson, premier techno-guru of the Internet and, like Berners-Lee and Castells, another who believes in its power to change the role and relationships of individuals within society.

Dyson, born in Zurich in 1951 to an astro-physicist and a mathematician, entered Harvard University at the age of 16 to read economics and has been a prodigy ever since. Starting her career as a fact-checker at *Forbes* business magazine, she has become one of that elite whose names are constantly bandied about and is known to be linked with the world's leading research institutions and technology companies, yet few could tell you exactly what she does or what her publications are about. Among her many activities is leading ICANN, a new international agency for setting core policy for the Net's technical standards and governing its system of domain names. Her online company EDventures.com, which focuses on and invests in emerging technologies and businesses, also runs high-profile conferences and publishes an influential industry newsletter called *Release 1.0* (the name comes from the computer industry's term for an early model still improving). In 1997 she wrote a book on the Net's impact on life called *Release 2.0* (the industry's term for a market-tested, supposedly perfect product).

In 1994, she was among the first to explore what the Net's influence might be on intellectual property, still a wild frontier that poses threats to creative minds as well as opportunities to spread knowledge. She invests in cutting-edge companies and sits on the boards of at least a dozen. Her days begin at 4.30am and on average she is on a plane somewhere every other day. She has a lot of irons in Eastern European fires, especially Russia, where she is a member of a Moscow health club (needless to say, she speaks fluent Russian). In one of the continual updates to her book, she offers reassuringly down-to-earth tips for making the most of the Net in one's life. These include 'disclose yourself: let others know what you stand for', 'trust but verify: use the Net to check the credentials of strangers and organisations', and 'ask questions: the Net is the most likely place to find someone with an answer'.

Key reading *Release 2.0: A Design for Living in the Digital Age* (New York: Broadway Books, 1997)

Nicholas Negroponte, first of the cyber-gurus with his 1995 book *Being Digital*, a founder of the pioneering tech-age magazine *Wired* and founder-director of that Mecca of multimedia invention, MIT's Media Lab.

Negroponte, a graduate of MIT in computer-aided design and a member of its faculty since 1966, has written little in recent years and is not as high-profile as he was, but he will have a lasting place in technological history with the Media Lab, for which he was instrumental in raising $50m funding in 1985. Currently supported by around 170 corporations anxious to keep a toehold on the future, the Media Lab focuses exclusively on research into future forms of human communication – what Negroponte calls 'man-machine symbiosis'. One of its recent ventures has been the 'Things That Think' programme, experimenting with computer technology incorporated in clothing and shoes, for example, and intelligent doorknobs that let a homeowner know who is outside. The Lab is acknowledged as the seedbed of multimedia and digital video.

It is now involved in a major new global research consortium called Digital Nations, in which researchers at the Lab will collaborate with others around the world aiming to bring the capabilities of digital technology to bear on improving education, reducing poverty, enhancing healthcare and supporting communities in their development. Together with the Center for International Development (CID) at Harvard, it is working on a new generation of technologies and applications that enable individuals to learn, design and create in new ways, helping them become more active and creative participants in their societies. It will focus primarily on those sections of the world's people least provided with technological support – children, the elderly, developing nations. The consortium, says its prospectus, 'will test out ideas and technologies in pilot projects around the world, helping individuals and communities develop innovative strategies in domains ranging from commerce to agriculture to healthcare – and more broadly, transform the ways they learn and develop. [Its] ultimate goal is a world full of creative people who are constantly exploring, experimenting, and inventing new opportunities for themselves and their societies.'

As with the other Internet visionaries, there is a lot of idealism in Negroponte's creation, perhaps more than any other technological revolution in history. One hopes that it will survive the pressures of global capitalism, or manage to bend them to a mutual self-interest.

Key reading *Being Digital* (Alfred A. Knopf, 1995)

Tom Peters, first of the 1980s generation of management guru megastars and still the most durable.

Peters has reinvented himself for the digital age. Co-author with Robert H. Waterman in 1982 of *In Search of Excellence*, which identified eight habits common to America's 'excellent companies' of the day and made both ex-McKinsey consultants multi-millionaires, Peters is the world's highest-paid and best-known speaker on the business circuit, his seminars guaranteed to pack out despite outrageous fees. His books have become steadily more eccentric in their presentation and language, full of exclamations like WOW! and YIKES! and odd diagrams, as if he is trying to bring the impact of a live presentation to the page.

In his latest book and its offshoots, he has latched onto a major idea running through many writings about the knowledge economy: that the individual is now capable of playing as big a role as a business entity as the company or corporation. With talent wars raging, and brainpower at a premium, plus an outpouring of human assets from companies that too rashly downsized when faced with recessions in the early 1990s, individuals with scarce skills can capitalise as never before on what they hold in their heads. The era of Me.inc or Me.com is here. *The Brand You50* grew out of an article in *Fast Company* magazine in 1997 and offers 'fifty ways to transform yourself from an employee into a brand that shouts distinction, commitment and passion'. It is one of three books under the umbrella title *Reinventing Work*. At the end of 2000 Peters signed a multi-faceted business agreement with Dallas-based jobs.com Inc., linking his *Reinventing Work* series with the company's Web-based job and career service.

Peters was the first major guru of the old school to

have his own Web site, tompeters.com, and can be relied on to continue as his own inimitable brand of business 'infotainment'.

Key reading *Reinventing Work*: *The Brand You50*, *The Project50* and *The Professional Service Firm50* (Alfred A. Knopf, 2000)

John Seely Brown, chief scientist and director of Xerox's famous PARC (Palo Alto Research Center).

An intellectual leader and social observer of the information revolution as well as a practical technologist and entrepreneur, Seely Brown is, from 2001, reducing his commitments at PARC and spending more time advising and investing in a San Francisco-based venture capital enterprise.

Under JSB, as everyone calls him, the PARC has changed its structure and business model entirely from the 1970s, when a brilliant 'hot group' was given the task by the Xerox Corporation of creating 'the architecture of information' and ended up inventing most of the technology tools we now use, including the first personal computer, the mouse, Graphical User Interface software (the files, folders and menus through which we scroll and click), the laser printer and the ethernet (a protocol or language for the exchange of information between one computer and another). Xerox unaccountably failed to develop them commercially and lost out irrevocably to competitors like Apple and Microsoft. Bill Gates has said that the father of both the Mac and Windows was Xerox.

Xerox learned its expensive lesson. PARC today is bridged to its parent by Xerox Technology Ventures, set up with $30m to exploit new PARC ideas. After its first ten years it had more than 12 young firms developing ideas for Xerox that would have gone elsewhere or been dumped. PARC keeps an equity stake in the new companies as well as ensuring that employees share in the equity. Its innovations are organisational as well as product-based: JSB is deeply interested in the organisation of the future and has said that the most important invention to come out of the corporate research lab in the future will be the corporation itself.

This strategy has been adopted by other corporates with rich research resources such as Lucent Technologies, which inherited AT&T's renowned Bell Labs, the world's greatest crucible of innovation. Lucent holds 25,000 patents through the Labs and continues to generate three new ones every working day. Bell Labs' New Ventures Group follows the Xerox model and after two years of existence had nine new ventures based on its technologies. One of them, in Internet technology, went from idea to marketplace in just nine months. Thomas Uhlman, Bell New Ventures' president, heads a group that will provide $100,000 to fund a business plan; if it works, up to $400,000 is then available for prototyping, with 'multiple millions' following if it takes off commercially.[7]

Seely Brown draws on some aspects of complex adaptive system thinking in his pursuit of what he calls 'knowledge ecology' – an interplay of ideas, knowledge and learning among individuals in 'a community of practice' that could provide, at last, a workable template for that management chimera, the learning organisation. But he points out drily that most champions of complex adaptive systems in nature – insect communities and the like – 'say relatively little about the importance to human behaviour of deliberate social organisation. To pursue the analogies from entomology or artificial life much further, we would need to know what might happen if bugs decided to form a committee, bats to pass a law, or artificial agents to organise a strike or join a firm.' Nor is he a blindly fashionable admirer of the virtual organisation, arguing that 'there is still life left in formal organisations and collective practice', and that such organisations have helped foster humanity's most valuable resource, its 'infinitely renewable knowledge base'.[8]

Seely Brown's interim testament is his book *The Social Life of Information* (2000), in which he roams over the history of communications from Samuel Morse to Microsoft, arguing that the social context of technology is vital for its success (the telephone only caught on after Alexander Graham Bell managed to get phones installed in public places such as restaurants) and that human interaction and conversation, human habits and judgement, are essential for the fullest potential of the information revolution to be realised. A number of Silicon Valley thinkers (such as Professor Jeffrey Pfeffer of Stanford, cited earlier in this book) are sharply aware of the arrogance of technologists obsessed with their products to the extent of damning the customer for misuse instead of questioning why the machines malfunction, but Seely Brown is unique in sending his humanist messages from the very centre of that technology.

One of the most important of those messages is about 'communities of practice' – like-minded people who do similar work, read the same journals, go to the same conferences and whose networks of interest cut across competitive organisations. This, JSB explains, is the reason that knowledge often sticks and refuses to flow round a corporation while leaking out of it to competitors – why, in short, Xerox failed to capitalise on the PC, GUI (Graphical User Interface) and the mouse while Steve Jobs of Apple picked them up and ran with them into the future, licensing and replicating. The ideas part of Xerox at PARC was a community of practice cut off from the 'toner-heads' who ran the Xerox copier business. But when the Xerox management invited the Trojan horse in the shape of Steve Jobs into PARC's premises in 1979, the creative spark found a ready way to leap the gap into the outside world.

Xerox, as Seely Brown points out fairly, was not alone in ignoring the potential of the PC; Gordon Moore of Intel saw no future in it either. Also, informal links between Apple and PARC were already well established before Jobs' fateful visit, which 'may have helped him to look beyond what Xerox intended to show . . . scientists at PARC finally felt they were dealing with people who understood them as their corporation did not.'

Seely Brown's book reflects the well-rounded man: fizzing with ideas, thoughtful and philosophical, taking a long view of history and liable to quote the metaphysical poet John Donne, the Greek sages and nineteenth-century economists along with an awesome grasp of the next technological possibilities.

Key reading *The Social Life of Information* (Harvard Business School, 2000)

Don Tapscott, Canadian management consultant and 'cyber-guru' who has a genuine claim to be a thought leader of e-business.

Tapscott's books *The Digital Economy* (a phrase he coined, along with 'paradigm shift' and 'the Net Generation'), *Growing Up Digital* and *Digital Capital* marry deep technical knowledge and social insights to practical business applications.

His latest idea, business webs or 'b-webs', extends John Seely Brown's communities-of-practice concept into the Internetted world of global business. B-webs are communities of mutual business interest linked by the Internet. Sometimes structured, sometimes fluid and amorphous, they are business platforms of suppliers, distributors, service providers and customers that come together 'to create value for customers and wealth for their shareholders'. They will be the new business model, superseding the old vertical corporation, Tapscott argues, because the cost of communications and transactions is constantly reducing on the Net and 'no company can be a world-class provider of everything'. Companies such as Schwab, eBay, Microsoft and Cisco Systems operate as b-webs, co-opting partners with complementary skills, and in doing so have outrun the rules of competition in their industries.

In *Digital Capital*, Tapscott identifies five different types of b-web, each defined by its leading partner:

(1) **Agora** Named after the assembly centres of ancient Greek cities, which evolved into commercial marketplaces, and used to describe the kind of Internet business, such as eBay, where buyers and sellers meet in cyberspace and the site operator only facilitates the transactions. Agoras fundamentally change pricing mechanisms because these are determined by the market.

(2) **Aggregation** Here one company, typically a retailer or wholesaler – for example, Wal-Mart – takes a lead by positioning itself between producers and customers, setting prices and discounts in advance.

(3) **Value Chain** Where design and delivery of an integrated product or service meets a specific customer need or market opportunity, and the seller sets the pricing. Cisco Systems is a prime example, sitting at the top of a $12bn Web-run value chain. It designs the core technologies, co-ordinates processes across the b-web, markets and manages the relationships, while b-web partners manufacture, fulfil and provide customer service onsite.

(4) **Alliance** High-value knowledge partnerships without a controlling partner, such as online research initiatives, games and development communities like the PalmPilot and Open Source innovation initiatives.

Alliances have great networking advantages. 'The more customers who buy PalmPilots, the more developers who decide to create applications,' writes Tapscott. 'The value cycle is continuous and accelerating.'

(5) **Distributive Network** The b-webs that 'keep the economy alive and mobile' – including data network operators, banks and new logistics companies. They service the other types of b-webs by allocating and delivering goods or resources from providers to users. 'The more customers who use a Distributive Network (e.g. a telephone network), the more value it provides to all its customers.' Tapscott says that distributive networks have both high and low value integration; high because they often involve a critical performance benchmark, e.g. a courier service or bank, and low because the flows of traffic are unpredictable. They are also characterised by being both hierarchical ('tight network management is critical') and self-organising because the fluctuating ratio of supply and demand determines price, as in electricity and financial capital.

One of the book's most interesting chapters concerns 'human capital' and its acquisition or management via b-webs. Here Tapscott is working in the same territory as Stan Davis and Christopher Meyer in *Future Wealth* and Bruce Tulgan in *Winning the Talent Wars*, predicting the increasing extension of 'employees' beyond the boundaries of a company. He quotes a Cisco vice-president as saying, 'We have 32,000 employees, but only 17,000 of them work at Cisco.' And he suggests that the human capital assets of Amazon.com include countless authors and readers who participate online in book reviews, commentaries or exchanges of views via the Web site; publishers; distributors, and literary critics. People now advertise their talents for sale on auction sites such as eBay and the Talent Market at Monster.com, and companies with small professional core staffs can outsource projects to the cream of global talents, if they are skilled enough to tap into them.

This means the whole HR function will have to change and shift its thinking away from corporate silos of pay, perks and working conditions to a far more fluid ability to bargain for the best short-term 'employee'. Rather than recruiting, Tapscott suggests, 'HR managers should think about amassing internetworked human capital ... Companies must court human capital to anticipate needs, develop and maintain reserves, make processes digital and networked, and develop new performance measures. Electronic recruiting, already an important new facilitator, is a multi-billion-dollar market.'[9]

More than any other commentator on the Internet economy, Tapscott has plugged directly into the 'Net Generation', which he calculates is 88 million strong in the US and Canada alone. He draws on the experience of computer-savvy youngsters for his book *Growing Up Digital*, which he wrote on the Internet in collaboration with a research team and several hundred Net users, children and adults, on six continents (Web site: www.growingupdigital.com). As an example of what this generation holds for the future of business, he cites Michael Furdyk, a 16-year-old from Toronto at the time the book was written in 1998. Michael had already set up two Net companies, having begun his digital career at 12. He considered going to university, but when he asked to take a course in entrepreneurship, the university replied that he didn't have the necessary educational qualifications. Tapscott told Michael that, rather than attending the course, he should be teaching it!

'We can learn from him and his generation, and they are an unprecedented force for change,' writes Tapscott in the introduction to *Growing Up Digital*. 'Imagine being Michael's employer. Michael has grown up in a culture of innovation, collaboration and networking which will replace the culture of the traditional firm. Imagine Michael as a consumer. He'll purchase his first car online. He'll shop for many things, from groceries to his first mortgage, on the Net. He'll change our thinking about the brand, advertising, the establishment of prices, and most of what is known about merchandising.' Soon, says Tapscott, 'this generation will be assuming positions of growing influence in the business, cultural and political arenas. Their comfort with the new media, and their mastery at its exploitation, guarantees that this generation will be an increasingly powerful voice in all debates. Ultimately, of course, it will become the dominant voice – dominating the twenty-first century.'

Key reading *The Digital Economy: Promise and Peril in the Age of Networked Intelligence* (McGraw-Hill, 1996); *Growing Up Digital: The Rise of the Net Generation* (McGraw-Hill, 1998); *Digital Capital: Harnessing the Power of Business Webs* (with David Ticoll and Alex Lowy) (Nicholas Brealey, 2000)

The true gurus of the Net Generation, when they emerge, are likely to be a different breed from the showmen-speakers of the 1980s and 1990s like Tom Peters, Michael Porter and Gary Hamel. Their seminars may well be online and interactive, and their ideas are likely to be aired and receive research feedback through their Web sites or online subscription services rather than reach their management audiences by the traditional slow route: business school to *Harvard Business Review* article and reprint to blockbuster book to international lecture circuit.

The business school as a nursery for gurus is also changing, with more online courses being launched and virtual alliances designed for the Internet such as Cardean University (named after the Roman goddess of portals), which was launched in the summer of 2000 to provide courses for people in full-time work who want to learn in the evenings or weekends. It plans eventually to offer full degrees. Cardean, with a staff of 500 based in Chicago and three Nobel economics laureates on its advisory board, is a consortium of five eminent educational institutions: the London School of Economics and four US universities – Columbia, Chicago, Stanford and Carnegie Mellon. Barclays Bank was the first big corporation to sign up 1,000 of its employees for courses. Larry Ellison of Oracle and Michael Milken, the former junk-bond king, are among the private investors who put up $80m initial backing for the venture.

Cardean's founder and chief executive Andy Rosenfield does not think that learning via the Internet will suffer in comparison with that in the classroom: 'the key part is making people do, think, interact with each other, ask questions and form groups, and we think that the Internet is ideal for that'. His colleague Professor Gary Becker, who won a Nobel prize for his work on the economics of human capital, believes the Net will radically change the way of teaching for a significant number of people, not least in modernising economies such as China and India.

But one issue that has yet to be tested is whether the exclusivity that certain universities such as Stanford and Harvard enjoyed in the past, and still enjoy, with their faculty stars and professor-gurus, will survive the open market and global access of the Internet. At the end of 1999 *Business Week* published a league table giving the top choices of management development executives for certain types of in-demand course. Top choice for information systems and e-commerce was MIT (Sloan School of Management), top for innovation was Stanford and top for global business was INSEAD. Future choices may be much harder to make.

Notes

[1] Gates, Bill: *Business@the Speed of Thought*, Penguin Books, 1999

[2] Stross, Randall: *The Microsoft Way*, Little, Brown, 1997; author interview, Microsoft UK

[3] Gates: *Business@the Speed of Thought*

[4] *Wired*, September 1999

[5] Grove, Andy: *Only the Paranoid Survive*, HarperCollins Business, 1997

[6] Berners-Lee, Tim: *Weaving the Web*, Orion, 1999

[7] *The Economist*, 20.2.99

[8] Seely Brown, John and Duguid, Paul: *Structure and Spontaneity: Knowledge and Organization*, a development of ideas that first appeared in the article 'Organizing Knowledge', *California Management Review*, 1998

[9] Tapscott, Don: *Digital Capital*, Nicholas Brealey, 2000

CHAPTER NINE

THE HOLE AT THE HEART OF SILICON VALLEY

If you do as most visitors to Silicon Valley don't, and instead of braving the roaring tangle of freeways out of San Francisco take the trundling Caltrain that runs all the way down the Valley twice an hour, you get a very different perspective from the popular image of the richest piece of real estate on the planet and the epicentre of a global business revolution.

Just a quarter of a century ago, this was a region of fruit orchards, and from the train the string of sleepy towns hardly seems to have changed since the 1970s: clusters of low, red-roofed houses with a vaguely Spanish look, tree-lined streets of suburban quiet, dusty railroad stations with so little traffic that local high-school students amble casually across the track knowing they will be warned by the clanging bell of the approaching double-decker train. The town names are world-famous – Menlo Park, Palo Alto, Sunnyvale, San Jose – but the technology powerhouses that make them famous – Hewlett-Packard, Oracle, Cisco, Intel – are invisible from the tracks, hidden away in landscaped campuses off the freeway.

There is a similar gap in the business world's image of Silicon Valley as a role model for the new economy. Its huge success in proving the 'cluster' theory – drawing scientific and engineering strength from Stanford

University at its heart, and constantly spinning off phenomenally successful businesses built on the latest 'new new thing' in technology – has led to a perception that it must also have something to teach the old economy in the way new-economy businesses are managed. 'Bring Silicon Valley inside,' the strategy guru Gary Hamel advises the managers who attend his expensive seminars to learn the secrets of ceaseless innovation. And it is true that Silicon Valley companies are exceptionally good at reinventing their businesses to keep on top of the curve of change. Hewlett-Packard changed from being a maker of electronic instruments and test equipment (a business it has now spun off) to becoming a computer manufacturer that caught up with the PC revolution in time to become the top US consumer brand, and is now a leading printer company. Intel has moved with agility from microprocessors for PCs into equipment for computer networking and consumer electronics. Cisco is broadening its customer base from networking equipment to the whole e-business consultancy market. But with a few exceptions, there is a hole at the heart of Silicon Valley: its acute dearth of management skills.

The original Valley trailblazers, William Hewlett and Dave Packard (who were persuaded by their engineering professor at Stanford, Fred Terman, to start their business in a nearby lockup garage in 1939 instead of going back east) were renowned for their management innovations. As well as being pioneers of profit-sharing, they were among the first industrialists to recognise that knowledge workers could not be managed in the same way as Taylor-era technicians and were quick to understand the importance of good human relations on productivity and the bottom line, teaching that was only beginning to break through Taylorism in 1939. The partners invented 'management by wandering around', and the 'H-P Way', as their corporate philosophy was known, became a bible for enlightened managements. Today, however, only the profit-sharing – now stock options – ethos seems to have been inherited by their entrepreneurial successors.

'Silicon Valley is great at building technology, terrible at building companies,' says Jeffrey Pfeffer, the out-spoken professor of organisational behaviour at Stanford and an acknowledged authority on the management of human relations. 'There are four key things that characterise how companies are managed in this Valley,' he continues, ticking them off on his fingers. 'One, a free labour market with a turnover of 30–40%, which makes no sense. Two, contracting out – the idea of the virtual corporation. That makes no sense either; you own nothing of your core technology. Three, giving stock options, which encourages wrong behaviour and risk-taking and does not build commitment. Four, the idea that people should work all the time – 80- to 90-hour weeks are unsustainable!' And this is not the extent of bad Valley management, in Pfeffer's acerbic view. Most technology companies, he thinks, have 'complete contempt' for their customers. 'If any other appliance in your home failed as regularly as your PC, you would not accept it, but these companies' helpdesks will always blame you, the user! The engineer always knows best. If the auto industry was run like the PC industry, Toyota would be unprofitable and GM would be very profitable because GM would be selling the upgrades!'[1]

The need to become ambidextrous

John Seely Brown, the bearded, charismatic chief scientist at Xerox Corporation's famous PARC and the nearest thing to the Valley's resident guru, said even before the dotcom implosion that the new economy had an 'astronomical amount to learn' from the old economy. 'There is so much hype and rhetoric out

there, saying everything is new in the new economy –
that's bullshit,' he said in the autumn of 2000. 'There is
a need to become ambidextrous in terms of knowing
how to innovate constantly, challenge the status quo,
motivate people and at the same time understand best
business practices in terms of how you operate very
complex business systems. There is a need to
communicate, to create architectures and provide an
enabling structure for people to be creative in. We need
serious management that knows how to operate teams
of a thousand people, that knows the financials.
Successful dotcoms are now searching out old management methods.

'What we are seeing is the growing need for real
leadership, an understanding of what technology is and
where it's going. We need to master technology and
what it means in terms of new ways to work, to learn, to
organise. I would claim that the role of leadership in the
new-new economy – the hybrid between old and new –
is greater than ever before, because you have to count
less on business processes doing all the work. You now
have to have elegantly minimal processes that enable
rather than constrain. Those processes provide the
backbone for people to be incredibly creative, to
improvise and innovate, but to do that the strategic
mission has to be as clear as can be, and for that to
happen, communication has to be in someone's gut, not
just in their head. Posters on the wall no longer cut it –
it has to be internalised in ways that haven't been done
before. The whole issue of communication and
leadership is with us in spades.

'There is a profound war for talent, to attract and
retain stars. One has to understand the social and
psychological dynamics of the workscape better than
ever, so that people are able to create meaning for
themselves as well as wealth. If all you do is give
everyone stock options as the stock goes up and up, that

enables CEOs of dotcoms to think they are great leaders, but the test is when the stock drops 70% one day, 10% the next and 10% the next. Then come back a month later and see how many people are still there. The number of CEOs who say to me, John, the DNA I've created in my company – this team is behind me 150%! Go back a month later when the stock price has gone from 100 to 20, and people are leaving in droves. Most options are worth nowhere near what employees think anyway; they are based on the fact that one company out of ten might be successful.'

A company in the 'new-new' economy that Seely Brown regards as truly 'ambidextrous' in its ability to adapt (and he declares his interest: he is on its board) is Corning, a 150-year-old glassmaker headquartered in upper New York state, as far as you could go geographically within the US from Silicon Valley. It has completely reinvented itself and is now a high-tech Internet company and the world's biggest supplier of components for optical networks, the backbone of the digital economy. 'It has an incredibly serious management team that constantly embraces challenge, learning and change,' says Seely Brown. 'Every one of the management team is deeply marinated in new technology and it consistently turns out both leading-edge and lowest-cost products. It is simultaneously a low-cost provider of yesterday's technology and the most radical innovator at the cutting edge of today. It has a lasting DNA; the company has stayed together through good and bad times. It has the hottest group of research talent in terms of inventing the future, so people want to work there, and its CEOs (until recently mostly from the founding family) have stressed the value of values and of walking the talk.'[2]

Much of Silicon Valley is not yet ambidextrous in this sense, but there are signs that it is learning a new balance by bringing in professional managers from outside its own culture. The world of higher management was astonished when George Shaheen, the drivingly ambitious chief executive of Andersen Consulting, quit the rich global consultancy (now called Accenture) to lead WebVan, an online grocery delivery service. But WebVan's selling point was good, old-fashioned logistics – clicks need bricks to warehouse the stock and vans to deliver it to customers – and there was nothing new about the managerial skills needed to tie the package together effectively. (Despite Shaheen's reputation and a promising business model, WebVan's rash expansion plans were scuppered by the technology slump and in July 2001 it filed for Chapter 11 bankruptcy protection.)

Lighthouse companies illuminating the future

Some Valley companies have managed to get it consistently right. The exemplar everyone mentioned with reverence until its fortunes nosedived in 2001 along with other technology stocks was Cisco Systems, the data-networking giant that at its peak was valued higher than Intel or Microsoft. Cisco is essentially a virtual company, built on a canny acquisition strategy that absorbs each new business – selected for shared values as well as strategic fit – by means of an efficient 100-day integration programme. Managers are rewarded on a basis of how well they retain the new companies' human capital; one in four of Cisco's staff came from its wave of acquisitions at the end of the 1990s. Outside its direct acquisitions, Cisco also operates within a web of some 10,000 business partners.

'Cisco is really good at managing Internet human capital,' says Don Tapscott, the Canadian strategy consultant who has deconstructed successful Web companies to see how they work. 'One of its executives described that as its core competence, and said, "We are good at managing eco-systems." Cisco has a whole new vision of the corporation, and that has shaped its managers.'

Stanford's Jeffrey Pfeffer, one of whose respected books is called *The Human Equation*, is another Cisco admirer. 'Why is Cisco so successful?' he asked rhetorically in the autumn of 2000. 'Because it takes seriously the idea that its people are its most important asset. In John Chambers it has a CEO who actually listens rather than talks. He almost never says anything except to ask a question; he's always learning. Also, part of Cisco's core culture is that it will do what the customer wants rather than what the engineer wants!'

Yet the paradox of Cisco, along with other well-managed icons of Silicon Valley, has been that it doesn't really know why it got successful or how its successful structure evolved – one proof that the best 'next Big Ideas' in management are being forged in the furnace of doing rather than thinking; at the cutting edge of industry rather than in the faculty rooms of business schools. While researching 200 companies with two colleagues for his latest book *Digital Capital*, Tapscott found that no one could articulate their management process. 'We had to do reverse engineering to discover it. Even Cisco couldn't tell us.'

But it is these 'lighthouse' companies, says Tapscott, whose experience will shape many of the management ideas of the future, and in time some leading thinker will come to formulate them in Harvard and Stanford case studies. Ideas often have to wait until their time has come, he points out: knowledge management, for example, had to wait for a new generation to come along to whom it was obvious to share knowledge – the Web generation – before it could be made to work as a management process. Earlier corporate generations were bred to think of knowledge as power and turf and were reluctant to yield any of it.

Tapscott takes a different perspective on whether youth or experience is best fitted to manage in the digital age, agreeing with Kenichi Ohmae rather than Seely Brown and Garth Saloner that the 'Nintendo Kids' have an inbuilt advantage. He thinks the young have the edge because they have grown up making snap decisions through playing interactive computer games and therefore 'they have a different way of processing information'.

John Chambers, chief executive of Cisco, falls firmly into the old-/new-economy generation, his first job in 1977 being with IBM, just in time to learn from Big Blue's near-fatal mistakes such as failing to cater for the smaller customer. He also learned the value of a strong corporate culture like IBM's, although the days of a sales force in three-piece suits with rigid quotas and company songs were already long gone. From his experience at IBM Chambers brought a key principle to Cisco: listen to what the customer wants, not to what the company thinks the customer wants. From a subsequent stint at Wang, which crashed with thousands of lay-offs in 1990, he brought a second key principle: avoid destroying people's jobs, though that had to be sacrificed in 2001. From both companies he learned principle number three: stay ahead of the curve and don't try to cling on to a technology that is past its best. These three foundation stones underpinned a company that has been universally admired for its customer-focused ethos, as a place where employees are respected and as a talent magnet.

Chambers's fourth guiding philosophy, and one rare in the ego-driven jungle of Silicon Valley, was team-work. He anchored this principle in the company by introducing a system of rewards tied to team-based success, both intrinsic and project-based. Managers at Cisco are rewarded for building top-quality teams as well as on measurements of customer satisfaction. 'I learned a long time ago that in team sports or in business, a group working together can always defeat a team of individuals, even if the individuals by themselves are each better than your team,' says Chambers. Effective teams, he believes, are also essential for decentralisation, and Cisco had to be decentralised to achieve his four-step business plan: (1) to make Cisco a one-stop shop for network providers; (2) to systemise the acquisition process; (3) to define industry-wide networking protocols; and (4) to choose the right strategic partners.

Decentralisation by creating five business units to handle Cisco's major networking products and treating them as start-ups within the organisation was the only way Chambers could grow the business at the speed he wanted. All this had the desired result of bringing Cisco closer to its customers, and of motivating employees with a sense of their value to the business. 'As decision-making capabilities spread outward and downward, more and more people within the organisation had the capability to make a difference,' writes the technology editor and publisher David Bunnell in his account of Cisco's phenomenal rise, *Making the Cisco Connection*. 'Naturally, this affected customer relations as well as Cisco's capability to adapt with the technology.'[3]

John Chambers is only the third chief executive at Cisco since it was founded in 1984 by two Stanford alumni, business school MBA Sandra Lerner and computer scientist Leonard Bosack. Their electronic courtship by primitive email (they eventually married and divorced) prompted the invention of the 'router', a small black box that links different computer systems and now forms the core technology for global Internet communication. Appropriately for a data networking business, Cisco is now itself a company built on networks of alliances, a model of what Don Tapscott calls 'b-webs', the first big contribution the new economy has made to organisational theory.

It is also a model of older virtues, a lesson to any new-economy business that some truths about management cannot be ignored. David Bunnell distils what Cisco is about down to three basic principles: 'fanatic about customer service, obsessively frugal and committedly honest'. Somehow it also manages to marry these mundane characteristics to corporate charisma. When Bunnell asked people at Cisco what it was like to work there, one response was: 'It's electronic heroin!' Cisco has, until recently at least, managed to sustain that most difficult of fusions, the small, dynamic start-up feel within the giant corporation – 'a federation of entrepreneurial teams', as Bunnell puts it. It has done this despite life on the San Jose campus being cocooned in the kind of corporate welfare culture pioneered by the Cadbury brothers at Bournville in the 1870s, updated to the twenty-first century (sports clubs and gyms, free popcorn and soda machines, free car washes, everything from self-defence classes to dry-cleaning facilities provided onsite).

Despite some disaffected voices in 2001 complaining that Cisco was becoming staid, its achievement under Chambers has been to balance the risks of equilibrium – life in the corporate cocoon – with a healthy input of mavericks and non-conformist thinking. It was a risk that Chambers recognised soon after taking the helm, telling an industry journal: 'You've got to have the mavericks in Cisco. You've got to have people who challenge you.' But he added that mavericks too had to play on the team, and then, switching metaphors, likened his managers to a flock of wild ducks. 'I don't expect us to fly in formation. I just want us to go south at the same time of year, and when it's time to go north, to go north at the same time of year.'

While Cisco piles on the stock options like any other Silicon Valley company – along with bonuses for pleasing customers – there is nothing new-economy about its people management or its obsessive attention to customer care. Professor Bob Sutton of Stanford teaches his students of management science and engineering how, every night, Chambers sits down and ponders a dozen or so customers who are having serious problems. The ritual not only produces solutions but continuously serves to remind the CEO that things can and do go wrong in the most successful companies.

The ability to manage mistakes

In fact, what consistently successful companies in both new and old economies tend to do is manage mistakes, and try to turn them to good use. Idealab, the Internet incubator company based in Pasadena, California and Sunnyvale, Silicon Valley, has built a huge business on learning from experimental but short-lived mistakes. Under its youthful founder, Bill Gross, it is continually setting up prototypes on the Web and testing concepts in the marketplace. A rapid rate of churn allows Gross to discard the losers quickly and concentrate on developing the most promising businesses. Successful companies are then linked in a network that shares ideas and information.

Idealab's rapid-response strategy has much in common with a form of scenario planning favoured by leading Valley companies which deflects successful businesses from holding on to good ideas beyond the point where they need to change. It's known as 'trigger-point' planning, a term that comes from game theory, and involves laying out multiple scenarios marked with trigger points that tell companies when scenarios are about to change and new strategic decisions are required. Examples of triggers could be cost, market share, competitor action or the advent of a new technology.

Triggers ring alarm bells and force a change in

management thinking; a Valley strategy consultant describes them as akin to stop orders in the stock market. What makes trigger-point planning useful for any company operating in the unpredictable chaos of the new economy is that it acknowledges the fact that 'the future is not what it was' – that forecasting in the old way is virtually impossible. But it does mean that all possible scenarios have to be thought through and planned for in advance, so that the triggered reaction is fast enough to do its job.

Hewlett-Packard, the original Silicon Valley company founded in 1939 (the site of the famous garage, at 367 Addison Avenue, Palo Alto, is now designated by the state of California as 'the birthplace of Silicon Valley'), uses trigger-point planning throughout the organisation, to be prepared for sudden shifts in the market and to seize the moment to change. The latest beneficiary of the system was the spin-off of H-P's test-and-measurement division as a separate listed e-services and solutions company called Agilent Technologies, although its acceptance was largely as a result of Carly Fiorina, who came in as CEO in 1999, doing a Jack Welch and converting H-P to e-business. The venture coincided with Fiorina's drive to reinvent H-P and adapt its inventor's culture to the Internet age under a set of rubrics known as 'Rules of the Garage' (see Chapter 4).

H-P, however, does not always tolerate mistakes. Professor Robert Sutton of Stanford, who has studied the company for many years, is periodically told by insiders about people being put in 'the penalty box' – reassigned to other parts of the business, perhaps as a learning experience. This may well be intended to help them overcome the effects of whatever mistake prompted the move, but it has also led to a number leaving the company. Sutton's colleague and co-author on several books, Jeffrey Pfeffer, instead points to the US domestic airline industry as an example of how a no-blame culture can produce better performance.

At Southwest Airlines, the no-frills, low-cost operation that revolutionised its sector in the 1990s, shortfalls in performance such as flight delays or slow turnarounds are regarded as team problems to be solved by team action and ideas. The emphasis is on solutions rather than scapegoats. By contrast, when American Airlines was run by the aggressive Robert Crandall, there was a culture of strict accountability: someone or some group had to be found responsible for a flight delay or other defect. In such a culture, Sutton points out, no one is willing to jump in with ideas about how to fix the problem, for fear of getting blamed if it doesn't work. 'The two facts are that Southwest has the best on-time record and it turns around planes faster than anyone else,' Sutton has said. 'Firms that are good accept a high failure rate, they anticipate that failure is going to come and there are certain things they don't do. They don't get obsessed with blaming individuals and looking for scapegoats. They don't use it as a reason to create a climate of fear.'[4]

Sutton likes to tell the familiar, if apocryphal, story of Thomas Watson Sr, founder and CEO of IBM, being approached by a junior executive who had been in charge of an unsuccessful $10m venture within the company and who offered to resign. Watson refused to accept his resignation, reportedly telling the manager: 'We just spent $10m educating you.'

The inescapable truths of good management down the decades – respect and trust for the human assets – are proved over and over again by the starriest new-economy companies. The absence of these values is particularly disastrous in the new economy because technology has spread power and information away from the top-floor executive suites to every level of the organisation and there is no longer any hiding place.

SAS Institute, the world's biggest privately owned software business, which provides statistical analysis tools essential to the understanding of data mining, is famous on a frivolous level for the jars of M&Ms (chocolate button-like sweets) that sit on every employee's desk and are regularly replenished at a cost of some $55,000 a year. But its wider emphasis on a good work/life balance, its philosophy that no one should be expected to work more than a 35-hour week and its $50m annual budget for staff 'perks' such as free healthcare on campus are the elements that have enabled SAS to retain its key talent in the incessant brain-drain to the dotcoms. They have kept its staff turnover to an impressive 4% in an industry where the norm is 20%.

Being two-thirds owned by its founder, Dr Jim Goodnight, SAS Institute was until recently an exception to the industry standard of keeping people loyal by throwing stock options at them. Goodnight's reluctant decision in the late summer of 2000 to go for a partial flotation is an acknowledgement that even this 'nearest thing to a workers' utopia in America', as *Fortune* described it, has to bow to the get-rich-quick mentality that powers Silicon Valley. When SAS is finally part of the stock market, it will be fascinating to see if Goodnight can carry through his strongly declared intention for its culture or corporate DNA to remain the same.

'E times I'

If good Silicon Valley management is as dependent on traditional values as the best cases seem to demonstrate, what is it about the Californian model that attracts such interest from the business world, apart from the frequent creation of great personal wealth and the technological advances on which we are now all dependent? The answer, in a word, is innovation. Gary Hamel, the Palo Alto-based strategy guru and consultant who defined the concept of core competencies in the mid-1990s and taught managers 'industry foresight' by working out how they could reinvent their markets five to ten years ahead, has spent several years studying how businesses of all kinds could 'bring Silicon Valley inside' their organisations and thereby haul themselves into a competitive position in the new economy.

The Einstein-like formula he has evolved for business success in the twenty-first century is 'E times I' – E, of course, being the established presence of electronic commerce and I representing innovation. 'E is already over,' he said during a transatlantic telephone interview in spring 2000. 'We already know the impact that electronic commerce is going to have on the world. It's going to give people more choice, bring more individuality to the list, but we know how that's going to play out. Ninety-five per cent of the investment most companies will make in e-business is going to be totally wasted, because most of it will simply be part of an arms race: my competitor is investing in order to respond to their customers in 24 hours, so I'm going to invest to respond in 18. And then they are going to do it in 12, so I'll have to do it in six. You have to do it, but it creates no unique competitive advantage. My argument is that it's E times I that creates new wealth today. Yes, you have to understand e-commerce, but pretty soon e-commerce is going to be no more interesting than e-electricity.

'For the first time in history our tools are nearly as good as our dreams, and what will separate winners from losers is not the tools, because they are available to everybody, but the quality of one's dreams. For me, that is the next big competitive advantage for organisations.

'One of the questions I ask every divisional director or MD or CEO is: how much energy and effort has your company expended over the last three or four years on getting better, taking costs out, getting quicker to market, improving customer service, being more efficient? Most will say 70 to 80% of our time. They will say we've done the whole ERP thing, turned our organisation upside down, broken through the functional chimneys, Webified our supply chain and customer interface and now we're investing in customer response systems. I say, fine. Now, how much of your energy and effort and capital has been devoted to getting different, to becoming what I call an industry revolutionary? And typically they will say, oh, we're going to have an offsite meeting next month for two days and worry about it then. And I ask them, why do you think getting better was so much work and getting different is going to be so easy? The fundamental blind spot people have is this: they understand why quality and re-engineering and ERP were so difficult and took so much time and effort, but they somehow think that innovation should be an easy thing.'

Hamel likens the critical nature of innovation in the early twenty-first century to that of the quality revolution in the last half of the twentieth. The difference is that companies now cannot afford to take 20 or 30 years to recognise its importance, as happened within US industry when it ignored the first messages from its own prophet of quality, W. Edwards Deming, in the 1950s. Deming then took his crusade to devastated post-war Japan, which embraced it wholeheartedly and went on to hammer US markets in automobiles, copiers, cameras and electronic goods in the 1980s. Today, the battleground is between incumbents and insurgents, and where incumbents once had a year or two to catch up on competitors, says Hamel, 'increasingly, if you miss something today you will never catch up'. More alarming still, the speed of market change and new entries means that 'any company more than a day old is an incumbent. You can be rendered irrelevant almost overnight.'[5]

So what Silicon Valley can teach the world, argues Hamel in his seminars and latest book, *Leading the Revolution*, is how to foster continual innovation, how to make the critical shift from stewardship, however efficient, to entrepreneurship within an organisation. The Valley may be deficient in management skills, but in Hamel's words it is 'the distilled essence of entrepreneurial energy'. Out of perhaps half a million people in the Silicon Valley 'gene pool' contributing actively to the generation of new business in 1998, Hamel wrote in *Harvard Business Review* the following year, there were 41 initial public offerings or flotations with a combined market valuation by January 1999 of $27bn, representing some $54,000 of new wealth creation per head in a single year.[6]

Silicon Valley has no monopoly on brainpower, Hamel argues, but it attracts it because of the prevailing ethos, where ideas are prized as the fuel of wealth creation and where every other office on Palo Alto's prestigious Sand Hills Road is a venture capital company, able and willing to supply the combustion to the fuel. It follows that to apply the same wealth-creating principles to an established business requires applying the same factors that work in the Silicon Valley environment – namely, dynamic internal markets for ideas, capital and talent. It is not so much a question of resource allocation as of resource attraction, Hamel contends, that gives the Valley its magnet-like ability to draw brainpower and investment to its 50-mile corridor south of San Francisco.

Silicon Valley is estimated to account for one-third of all the venture capital raised around the world, with $5bn invested annually there, most of it raised locally. Within its area, before the dotcom implosion of 2001, were some 6,000 firms, a quarter of which had been founded by Chinese or Indian expatriates between 1990 and 1996. *The Economist* has called it the world's best example of Schumpeter's 'creative destruction' theory, as old companies die and new ones emerge. With Stanford University as its intellectual engine-room, it is also the ultimate model of Michael Porter's 'cluster' theory, in which businesses in associated or complementary industries assist each other to make the area an economic powerhouse.

Several leading old-economy companies have already embarked on a strategy for implanting their own dynamic internal ideas markets. Royal Dutch/ Shell, a 'legacy' company if ever there was one, has since late 1996 been drilling for ideas as well as oil in its largest division, Exploration and Production. It has done this through a programme called GameChanger (assisted by Hamel's consultancy Strategos, so it naturally figures high on his list of exemplar case studies).

GameChanger started with a panel of laterally-thinking Shell employees given authority to allocate $20 million to innovative ideas from internal staff that they considered worth funding. Any employee from anywhere in the vast Shell organisation could put up an idea. The process was slow to ignite, which was when Hamel's consultancy was called in. Their solution was a three-day 'Innovation Lab' in which entrepreneurially-minded employees were coached by consultants to develop their ideas, to learn from new thinking in other industries, to challenge long-standing conventions in the energy business and to draw on Shell's rich reservoir of competencies.

A modest pool of $500,000 seed money was provided. By the end of the second day, wrote Hamel, 240 ideas had been generated – some for entirely new businesses, others for putting a new twist on existing Shell operations – and development teams put in place for each. Twelve of the 240 were selected for funding and subsequently a five-day 'Action Lab' took the processes further, producing finished business plans. The final stage was for each team to present to a 'venture board' composed of the GameChanger panellists and senior Shell managers, including some involved with an existing technology funding project. In *Harvard Business Review*, Hamel reported in the autumn of 1999 that out of five of the company's largest growth initiatives earlier that year, four had been generated through GameChanger.[7]

Other companies, notably Sir Richard Branson's Virgin Group, Monsanto and GE Capital, have adopted 'Silicon Valley' principles of internal markets for ideas, capital and talent. But internal resources are not enough. As Hamel says, Silicon Valley success is based not on resource allocation but on resource attraction: 'if an idea has merit, it will attract resources in the form of venture capital and talent. If it doesn't, it won't. There's no CEO of Silicon Valley. There's no giant brain making global allocation decisions. And there's also no reason resource attraction can't be made to work inside a General Motors, an AT&T or a Procter and Gamble.'[8]

If enough big corporations can import the free movement of ideas and capital that characterise the world's high-tech Mecca, and if it works on a large enough scale, this could turn out to be Silicon Valley's most lasting contribution to new management thinking.

Powerpoints
- The new economy is learning that the older virtues of management are as valuable as keeping ahead of the technology curve.
- Some of the world's most successful companies, like Corning, are 'ambidextrous', blending old and new technical and management values and attracting the hottest research talent.

- Internet companies can do it too: Cisco has kept down the high talent turnover typical of the Valley. It rewards managers in terms of how well they retain the human capital in acquisitions – what's measured gets done.

- 'Lighthouse' companies like Cisco are learning on the curve and don't yet know what makes them management models. Some of tomorrow's best ideas will come out of research into today's working practices.

- Cisco's chief executive John Chambers brought three key lessons to the company: listen to what the customer wants, not what the company thinks he wants; avoid destroying jobs; don't cling to a successful technology that's on its way out.

- Trigger-point planning is a new scenario technique that works by deflecting companies from holding on to good ideas beyond the point where they need to change.

- Manage mistakes and learn from them. Idealab tests hundreds of prototypes in the market and is ready to discard the many that fail for the few that win big. Successful companies in old- and new-economy sectors have no-blame cultures.

- One Big Idea Silicon Valley could bequeath to traditional business practice is to replicate itself within companies through establishing internal markets for ideas, capital and talent.

Notes

1 author interview, Stanford, September 2000
2 author interview, San Francisco, September 2000
3 Bunnell, David: *Making the Cisco Connection*, Wiley, 2000
4 *Red Herring*, May 2000
5 author interview, February 2000

[6] Hamel, Gary: *Leading the Revolution*, Harvard Business School Press, 2000; *Harvard Business Review*, September/October 1999

[7] Hamel, Gary: 'Bringing Silicon Valley Inside', *Harvard Business Review*, September/October 1999

[8] ibid.

CHAPTER TEN

AND THE NEXT BIG IDEA IS . . .

No word has been more over-used in management over the past ten years than 'change', invariably preceded by the adjective 'radical'. Change is necessary, we have been incessantly told, change is essential for life and growth, change will be the silver bullet to cure all business ills. That slippery concept 'change management' has become the main propellant of every consultancy business. Companies have been sold huge and costly programmes to 'transform' themselves on the back of warnings that they have to change or die. Sometimes they die precisely because of the changes forced upon them, as with the infamous case of Figgie International, one of the largest manufacturing conglomerates in America, brought to virtual bankruptcy by two leading firms of consultants in the mid-1990s. Its tragedy is told in the book *Dangerous Company* by James O'Shea and Charles Madigan, and is a terrible warning to managements in thrall to the lust for change.

The perceived need to change – over and over again, like the rewound daily round of the hapless character in *Groundhog Day* – is what creates and sustains the boom in Big Ideas, whether generated in business schools, consultancies or corporate offices. Consultants have a wonderful carte blanche in that almost any external or internal circumstance can be cited as the reason why radical change is necessary – the need to expand, the need to retrench, impending recession, impending boom, the need to merge, the need to demerge, competition, globalisation and, overwhelmingly since 1998, the electronic revolution.

It comes, therefore, as a refreshing shock to find the chief executive of the world's largest food company, Nestlé, early in 2001 going against the entire flow of the radical-change industry and advocating slow, evolutionary development. Austrian-born Peter Brabeck, 30 years a Nestlé man from frozen-food salesman to CEO, told a *Harvard Business Review* interviewer who asked him what was wrong with radical change, 'What's so good about it?' It might be fine for a crisis, he conceded, but not every company was in crisis all the time. Nestlé was very sceptical of management fads and the gurus who promoted them, he added. 'When you run a business you must be pragmatic. Big, disruptive change programmes are anything but that.' Abrupt change imposed a traumatic impact on running the business, provoked fear in the staff and made too many demands on management's time. A case could even be made, he suggested, that any kind of one-time change programme gave a worrying signal about the way the company was run. 'If you take preventive care of your health and you've taken the time for check-ups, you won't wake up one day to find you have cut off your leg.'

Evolutionary rather than revolutionary change was desirable, said Brabeck, and the keys to that were collaboration and regular communication with people. Once a month, he sits down with a dozen or so employees for lunch, without their bosses. They are encouraged to talk freely about how their work is going, whether they feel they are getting the information they need, and if they have questions about where the organisation is heading. New opportunities such as China, which Nestlé expects to be its biggest market in ten years, meant focusing on 'people, brands and products' – the things that make the difference. It would not take a revolution. 'I know that assertion may disappoint many people, but the truth is, in business, you can win the war without killing off half the army.'[1]

Brabeck did not mention the word, but it's a safe bet that when he made that final comment, he was thinking of re-engineering and the havoc it has wrought, not only on the thousands of people scooped out of their jobs in the cause of 'streamlining' processes but on the motivation and trust of their colleagues who survived – this time – and hence on the cohesiveness and per-formance of the business. If the day of the Big Idea is drawing to a close, re-engineering was the Big Idea that killed it, the light that failed. The results were deva-stating; even the idea's co-inventor, Mike Hammer, admits that up to 70% of re-engineering efforts failed to achieve the desired goals, while in 1995 independent research in the UK put the rate as high as 90%. Billions of dollars of investment were wasted for short-term balance-sheet gain, along with thousands of working lives. Hammer and Jim Champy, his co-author, were right to say that in most cases the technique was applied for the wrong reasons and in the wrong way, but an idea touted as such a magic bullet should surely have been designed more cunningly, so that it could not have been misused by two-thirds of its practitioners.

Champy and Hammer have not, however, given up. Like Freddie Kruger, the razor-fingered ghoul of the *Nightmare on Elm Street* movies, re-engineering rose from the grave just as this book first went to press. The pair's massive best-seller, *Re-engineering the Corporation*, was scheduled for reissue in the autumn of 2001, revised, updated and with new case studies – presumably this time writing the people dimension back in. It will be an interesting test of the lingering power of the Big Idea on managers thirsting for prescriptives to see just how far it flies this time around – and, if it does catch on again, whether the catalyst will be recession in the US economy rather than the merit of the idea itself, proving that panic can always drive out wisdom. (Hammer had a new book out in 2001, *The Agenda*, which offered prescriptives for 'rethinking' business processes.)

Small is beautiful again

If evolution rather than revolution is the answer, then maybe the future of management innovation lies in small experimental ideas rather than big radical ones. For all the now-derided new-economy hype (Hasso Plattner, chief executive of Europe's largest software company, SAP, says 'there was never a new economy. It is still the same economy, one where you only survive if you show results'), business today is undeniably a different animal from that of 1990. Silicon Valley management may not be a model for the world, but companies in all sectors are having to adjust to strategies dictated by the new electronic tools. In doing so, they are inevitably influenced by the management of Internet start-ups and incubators and their suck-it-and-see ways of trying out new concepts. That, too, militates against the Big Idea. Managing at Internet speed, there just isn't time any more to take something like re-engineering through the change process.

The pursuit of management lessons from outside business has been throwing up dozens of small ideas, some of which were explored in earlier chapters. As Richard Dawkins suggests about scientific analogies, these can be useful if treated as a different way of looking at business problems, rather than adopted as a benchmark in their own right. But the process is some-times in danger of degenerating into emperor's-new-clothes farce, as when management educationists introduce, in all seriousness, courses that aim to teach personal development skills through singing pop-songs and horse whispering. Manchester Business School was offering an executive course based on the latter early in 2001, on the grounds that studying such communication techniques with animals helped establish leadership, build trust and turn individuals into team players.

In the real world, however, the world with which business must deal through its employees, customers, investors and, increasingly, its wider 'stakeholders', a profound change is beginning to take place in public values, and here there are the glimmerings of a Big Idea struggling to be born which will shape the future management of business. As yet the forces behind it are unfocused, unformed and hopelessly fragmented, a loose and lumbering alliance composed of disillusioned voters, environmentalists, animal-welfarists, sceptical shareholders, principled opponents of global poverty and unprincipled rent-a-mob agitators.

It can be sensed in the movement for ethical investment, now a feature of several major institutions; in the new agenda for corporate social responsibility; in the counter-culture 'summit' first held in Brazil in January 2001 so that disadvantaged nations could challenge the complacent World Economic Forum at Davos with its one thousand global business chiefs and assorted political, scientific and media grandees; and among the older, middle-class participants in the rough anti-globalisation demonstrations of the last few years. The fact that such people – computer engineers, lecturers, suburban housewives – could turn out in May 2001 in London alongside masked hooligans, knowing that the event might degenerate into street mayhem like it did the previous year and would therefore attract a massive police presence, is indicative of an anger at something in the corporate world which they feel unable to express at the ballot box or in any other effective way.

On a more cerebral level, there is the Royal Society

of Arts project to define the values of 'tomorrow's company' and a growing number of seminars advising senior
executives on how to monitor public criticism of their
industries and find out what subversive activities are
being directed at their company on the Internet.
Greenpeace, the environmental protest group, got hold
of BP-Amoco's new sunburst logo even before the company had rolled it out officially, and mounted its own
Web site which required attentive reading before revealing itself as a 'vigilante' site, not the genuine corporate
article. Do you know what your staff are saying about
you in chatrooms when they surf the Web late at night
in their own homes? asked a guest speaker from BP at an
Institute of Directors briefing in the spring of 2001.
Directors who previously thought about reputation
management, if at all, only as briefing City analysts after
a dire stock-market performance or as part of crisis
management after an environmental disaster are suddenly being confronted with a whole new agenda.

Nor are annual general meetings the deferential
affairs they once were, with the company report nodded
through on the way to the coffee and cakes. More and
more institutional shareholders, the ones with the voting
clout, are protesting against remuneration committees
that hand out multi-million-pound bonuses to senior
executives who are simply doing the job for which they
are already paid handsomely. When fully 22% rebelled
at United Business Media's AGM in the spring of 2001,
defying its powerful executive chairman, the corporate
governance leader Sir Ronald Hampel, one institutional
investors' body said such actions could presage an
'avalanche'.

Big business under siege

All these manifestations are reinforcing other
dissatisfactions with big corporations that have been

around for some years. The 'green' movement has grown enormously since Rachel Carson launched her attack on the pesticide industry in 1961 with *Silent Spring*. It now encompasses serious concern over the ransacking of rainforests for Western DIY stores, the growth of Third World debt to the industrialised West, global warming and climatic change, the toxification of rivers and oceans by chemicals and industrial effluvia, the depletion of natural resources and fossil fuels, the risk of a future 'water war' between have and have-not nations, fears about genetically modified foodstuffs and a generalised suspicion that big business is careless in what it does in the pursuit of profit. In many ways, with the global growth of concern about the future of the planet, industry seems to present a more repellent picture of spoliation and exploitation in 2001 than it did in 1901, when heavy manufacturing was belching chemicals and thick smoke into the atmosphere and colonies existed to strengthen the trading position of already rich nations.

This gathering anti-globalist, anti-capitalist movement barely existed before the 1990s. Its catalyst was the fall of the Berlin Wall in 1989, which brought multinationals pouring into formerly communist countries in search of new markets and cheaper sources of labour and materials. In this latter-day gold rush, they did not always consider the best interests of the host communities, or the fact that their presence was not an unmitigated blessing. When General Electric acquired a former state-owned lighting company in Hungary and proceeded to lay off half the workforce as part of a rationalisation enabling it to win markets against other lighting companies, it was seen as a betrayal by people desperate for a better life under capitalism. GE's shareholders were the major winners, though the company would argue that there were training benefits for the employees that survived. Today, even George Soros, the epitome of capitalist prowess and beneficiary of global markets, believes that anti-globalisation is a serious movement, to be taken seriously despite its anarchic fringe.[2]

Simultaneously with these rumblings of grassroots discontent, a number of serious commentators have been viewing the corporation as an instrument of growing power for social transformation, even rivalling that of government. In 1997, the strategy guru Richard Pascale addressed the issue at a conference in Prague, arguing that international corporations were moving into the same key role in society that national governments had occupied in the late nineteenth and early twentieth centuries, and the Church in the Middle Ages. 'Increasingly, the wellbeing of nations is determined by the competitiveness of its corporations,' said Pascale, introducing his keynote theme of organisational renewal as a core competence before moving on to his work with the Santa Fe Institute on complex adaptive systems and their parallels with human organisations. 'If a nation's portfolio of companies is able to compete effectively on the global stage, this will determine its balance of payments and in turn the strength of its currency,' he argued. 'Above all, the competitiveness of a nation's companies determines the size of its unemployment. Corporations are seen as the vehicle through which high employment can be sustained. As a result of this phenomenon, national policy is increasingly subordinated to what allows the companies within a nation to compete effectively.'[3]

Other management analysts see more specific influences. Andrew Wilson, director of the UK's Ashridge Centre for Business and Society, has argued that in the global marketplace, shoppers now exercise more influence over Western democracies by the consumer goods they buy than they do as voters in their national elections. Wilson's case is that by choosing, for example, products from companies with a good record in ethical practices and 'fair trade' policies with their suppliers in developing countries, and boycotting others with more questionable practices, consumers are effectively casting votes that will influence corporate behaviour, and eventually the livelihoods of people in poorer producer countries.[4]

Some would argue, however, that there is a lot of hypocrisy in this: if a Western company stamps out child labour among its overseas suppliers, it fulfils the ethical criteria of its own society and makes its customers and shareholders feel good, but how does it compensate thousands of dirt-poor households in, say, Bangladesh or Malaysia that suddenly lose their mainstay of income? These are deep waters in which companies, understandably, are reluctant to take too many soundings.

The rise of stakeholder ethics

Businesses have certainly been responding to a perceived need for 'social' activities within their local communities since the early 1990s. UK consultants Michel Syrett and Jean Lammiman, writing at the end of 1997, charted three distinct forms of social driver in corporations: paternalism, market demand and stakeholder ethics. They defined paternalism in this context as a feeling of obligation to give back in a disinterested fashion some of the wealth acquired from society, although in practice companies clearly hope for some beneficial spin-off in goodwill. Such activities would include arts sponsorship, providing facilities for the homeless or financing public parks or playgrounds (though supermarket chains have often played a cunning hand with town councils by offering to provide such facilities in tacit return for permission to build stores on greenfield sites). Market demand is where the company's social activity is linked more directly to its commercial activity, such as the French food retailer Danone underwriting the education of schoolchildren in healthy eating, or the technology transfer provided by Western pharmaceutical companies in China. 'Stakeholder ethics' stems from the company's basic philosophy about the people who have any kind of interest in the firm, from investors and customers and employees to suppliers and the whole local community. Anita Roddick's Body Shop is an obvious example here, having appointed a 'director for stakeholder development' and adopted a practice of publishing an annual audit of opinion about the company from a range of people with whom it has contact.

Syrett and Lammiman point out that legislation defining the limited-liability company in the nineteenth century was never designed to anticipate such late twentieth-century developments as the tidal wave of acquisitions and mergers across borders, or the global market activities of multinationals. 'With anything between two-thirds and three-quarters of the equity of publicly owned companies in North America and Great Britain in the hands of institutional investors, very real questions are being asked about who owns companies and who therefore controls their activities,' say the two consultants. Independent board directors are in consequence finding themselves increasingly expected to spend time and care on stakeholder concerns that are far wider than their basic fiduciary responsibilities to the company's investors, even if the letter of company law does not require it.[5]

To fill this legal vacuum, pressure groups, lobbyists and single-issue activists have emerged to monitor and sometimes intimidate the direction of corporate policy towards their desired ends. Occasionally the activists manage to spark widespread public disapproval of a company's stance, such as Shell experienced in its Nigerian operations in 1995 after failing to oppose the

execution of a minority-rights protester, Ken Saro
Wiwa, and again after Greenpeace campaigned against
its proposal to dump a defunct oil rig in the North Sea.
Nike and Reebok, the sports clothing manufacturers,
suffered a consumer backlash when it was revealed that
under-age labour was being exploited among some of
their suppliers in developing countries, and although
McDonald's won a libel case against two young
environmental activists who had accused it of exploiting
people and animals, it found its public image changed.
(It is no coincidence that McDonald's is a favourite focus
of aggression by street demonstrators in anti-capitalist
tirades.) More recently, the US chemical giant
Monsanto, in many ways a model of textbook management, disastrously underrated the strength of public
feeling in Europe against genetic modification of crops,
leading to a media frenzy about 'Frankenfoods' and
wholesale withdrawal by supermarkets of GM products
from their shelves.

Most of these corporations were influenced into some
kind of change by 'stakeholder' groundswells, Shell in
particular committing itself to consult more with human
rights groups in the countries in which it operates. As a
result of sharper public awareness of child exploitation
among suppliers to the multinationals, this particular
issue has moved right up the corporate governance
agenda. Boards are now being advised that it is no
longer good enough to plead ignorance that a supplier
has been contravening a company's otherwise
impeccable trading policy, as Marks and Spencer was
able to claim successfully in a court action.

Reputation management has become a fast-growing
subject for courses, conferences, consultants and
management handbooks, though as yet that reputation
is chiefly seen as operating in the firm's domestic
constituency of investors, customers, employees and
suppliers: few are thinking seriously about reputation in

other national communities where they operate, though this could be the source of future explosive reactions. Marks and Spencer's abrupt decision in 2001 to close its flagship store in Paris along with others throughout Europe – a decision that would have been astonishing had it been taken under the autocratic Sir Richard Greenbury, never mind the Belgian Luc Vandevelde, a man experienced in French employment law – was made without any local consultations or apparent concern for local employees and customers. It sparked enormous resentment and the threat of legal action in France, and could well have had an adverse effect on the international reputation of a company once respected around the world as a leading exemplar of British trading values and management practice.

A warm pool for the fish to swim in

The most likely key to corporate change in such matters will be the growing power of ethical investment. The mass of moderate protesters against global business practices is not looking to see capitalism destroyed but made more accountable – and not only to shareholders, staff and domestic customers but to underdeveloped countries where multinationals are currently not accountable to anyone. Court cases will also have their impact. The recent South African trial of 39 pharmaceutical companies, from which the firms backed down after threatening to impose patent restrictions and thus force up prices on anti-AIDS drugs, may prove a watershed in the power of multinationals to dictate market terms outside their own backyards.

These are legitimate weapons against corporate policy, but some activists are venturing outside the law. One of the most disturbing examples concerns Huntingdon Life Sciences, a UK company developing pharmaceutical drugs, and the violent intimidation of its executives and staff by animal-rights fanatics to the extent of attacks being carried out on the chief executive with a baseball bat. The perpetrators claimed their violence was justified because of the company's treatment of animals for drug-testing purposes, a claim which challenges the whole legal basis of animal testing – a UK government requirement before human clinical trials are allowed. The most alarming aspect of the case was the fact that such a tiny group could force institutions of the size of Barclays Bank and Charles Schwab to withdraw investment and brokerage from HLS because of the fear of similar violence against their staff. When legitimate pressure turns into a perceived protection racket, it opens the door into a lawless world.

There is a wider issue here, too. With the animal-rights extremists, as used to be said about the IRA in Ireland, all that is needed for a small band of violent people to exert power is 'a warm pool for the fish to swim in' – i.e. a much larger group of non-violent people who hold general sympathy for the ends of the cause, if not the means. Animal welfare has become an enormous issue in the UK over recent years, with celebrity support from stage and TV stars, and activists clearly trade on this. In forming strategies to meet objections to their activities, companies have a fine line to tread in terms of respecting legitimate public opinion while not caving in to blackmail.

Significantly, a public opinion poll held in Britain on the day of the 2001 May Day protests in London against global capitalism found that a majority of UK voters believed big corporations to be a negative force in society. It would be interesting to see, as single-issue politics rise and the old political parties lose their sway for lack of big ideas and causes, whether a proper political movement founded on an anti-capitalist platform could command any serious support from an otherwise generally apathetic electorate. At present, the international groups involved are too ill-focused, impulsive and – literally – anarchic to have a coherent platform. (One of the more ironic by-products of a day in which shops in central London boarded up their premises and lost trade to the tune of £20m – a perceived 'win' for the protesters – was that vast quantities of the plywood used originated in the Amazonian rainforests, which many of the protest groups would have fought to protect from the global timber trade.)

However, as one management consultant privately observes, in 15 or 20 years, many of the people who are now demonstrating in the streets are going to be investors, customers and managers, and their agendas are likely to be radically different from today's investors, customers and managers. The 1960s generation grew up and ditched most of its student radicalism but 1960s attitudes did change society in many ways. It is already clear that in the long term a great deal more social responsibility will be demanded from the corporate sector, and the best corporate strategists will be working on it now.

The end of the 'performance improvement paradigm'?

Richard Pascale has pointed out that 'we are at the end of a long chain of theories about management', from late nineteenth-century ideas about how people could be clustered in organisations to get work done better, through the efficiency experts to the industrial psychologists. It was not until the middle of the twentieth century that the concept of strategy was imported into business from the military, where it had been a familiar tool for centuries. 'We have just lived through 20 years in which performance has been the dominant item on the agenda,' Pascale told the Prague conference in

1997. 'It started with total quality management and progressed to process re-engineering, cycle time, kaizen and a whole variety of other concepts. The question is . . . have we used up the performance improvement paradigm? I am not suggesting that any of the concepts connected with performance improvement are irrelevant, but you have to question whether we have leveraged most of what they have to offer . . . We are at a time in history where there is a whole new chapter to be written in management thought.'[6]

Until about the mid-1970s, Pascale reminded his audience, there had been relatively few management ideas, so most of them had a long shelf-life. 'Beginning with the mid-1970s we have experienced a rapid proliferation of management techniques. The world has become more competitive. It has been a great time to be in the guru business. Companies have been eager to deal with the opportunities and constraints of a more complex and intense business environment, and they have been in the market for any management ideas that will help.'

The problem, Pascale suggested, was that all the ideas of the past half-century had been 'layered on top of business as usual'. In the US in one year in the mid-1990s, about $600m was spent on TQM alone. Yet even this great idea fell short of business expectations. And all these ideas that were stacked up like flights waiting to land at an airport – TQM, excellence, delayering, matrix management – were prescriptions for *doing* rather than *being*.

The exploration of 'being' inevitably involves dealing with live issues, with people, with fluid and ever-changing human perspectives, with 'resocialising' the organisation. This is much more difficult than restructuring processes or finding new ways to measure competitive advantage because, in Pascale's words, it 'deeply enrols people at every stage'. He believes that identifying common traits among all living systems in the universe, including the behaviour of human beings in organisations, could provide a sustainable Big Idea for the coming decades. Among other benefits it could prolong the longevity of companies (typically now less than 13 years in Europe and Japan, with US multi-nationals scoring between 40 and 50), as well as making them more productive and rewarding to work in.[7]

It is here that Pascale's thinking links up with the Dutch strategist Arie de Geus, who believes that the most successful and long-lived companies have a purpose beyond the bottom line. Pascale's theories also tie in with Charles Handy's approach, the British philosopher of work and organisations who for years has been advocating a more humanist approach to the management of business enterprises. In this vision, the company becomes an organic part of the society in which it operates, rather than a profit-driven machine, and may on occasion even choose to damage its short-term profits in order to uphold its business ethics and, in the long term, to reap shareholder approval.

Take the example of Merck, the pharmaceutical company whose drug Mectizan cures a type of blindness found in poor countries. Merck had anticipated that government or international agencies would buy and distribute it to the people who could not afford it. When this did not happen, Merck gave the drug away free, benefiting both the people who needed it and the morale of its own scientists who had developed it.[8] Coincidentally or not, Merck enjoys a high reputation among its peers in the global industry, rating number two to Pfizer in the league of most-respected healthcare companies.

Sir John (now Lord) Browne of BP-Amoco has led his industry in terms of adopting a more environmental attitude to cleaner fuels, and was the first oil chief to declare, in a speech at Stanford University in 1997, that

global warming might indeed be a reality and to pledge
his company by the year 2010 to a reduction in emissions
of carbon dioxide, a 'greenhouse gas' linked to climate
change, by 10% from 1990 levels. He currently ranks as
the UK's most admired manager, but he says simply
that 'in the end, it's just good business'.[9]

Here, as well as in the issues provoking unrest about
global business, is the raw material for a Big Idea that
could prove bigger than all the management fads of the
past century. Whatever form this idea takes, it will
revolutionise corporate governance, that drearily
named but increasingly urgent function, as it tries to
answer the question being posed by an ever more
insistent chorus: what is business, and the company,
ultimately for?

Powerpoints

- The relentless drive for 'radical change' is slowing
  down as the merits of managed evolutionary change
  emerge. Nestlé chief Peter Brabeck says you can 'win
  the war without killing off half the army'.

- Small, experimental ideas suit the new economy of
  Internet start-ups and incubators.

- New Big Ideas about business as a whole, however,
  may emerge as a result of the growth of anti-corporate
  feeling. This is a new factor for corporate leaders to
  address.

- Simultaneously, the growing power and influence of
  multinationals are leading to the corporation being
  viewed as a tool for social transformation. How it will
  use this power is a new strategic issue.

- The rise of 'stakeholder ethics' and pressure groups on
  a global scale is forcing firms to think beyond their
  domestic constituencies.

- Companies also face moral dilemmas in, for example,
  withdrawing investment or support from others
  because of intimidation by extremist groups.

- We are 'at the end of a long chain of theories about management', says Pascale. After performance improvement, do we now move to 'being' rather than 'doing' – essentially rethinking what business is for?

NOTES

[1] 'The Business Case Against Change', *Harvard Business Review*, February 2001

[2] *Observer*, 6.5.01

[3] Pascale, Richard: 'Change Management as a Core Competence', efmd FORUM 97/2

[4] Syrett, M. and Lammiman, J.: 'More than just a donation', *MBA* magazine, December 1997

[5] ibid.

[6] Pascale: 'Change Management as a Core Competence'

[7] de Geus, Arie: *The Living Company*, Nicholas Brealey, 1999

[8] Skapinker, Michael: 'Living long in dangerous waters,' *FT*, 29.1.01

[9] Guyon, Janet: 'A big oil man gets religion', *Fortune*, 6.3.00

RECOMMENDED READING

Bennis, W. and Biederman, P: *Organizing Genius*, Nicholas Brealey, 1997

Berners-Lee, Tim: *Weaving the Web*, Orion, 1999

Breier, Mark: *The Ten-Second Internet Manager*, Piatkus Books, 2000

Brown, John Seely, and Duguid, Paul: *The Social Life of Information*, Harvard Business School Press, 2000

Brown, Shona L. and Eisenhardt, Kathleen, M.: *Competing on the Edge*, Harvard Business School Press, 1998

Bunnell, David: *Making the Cisco Connection*, Wiley, 2000

Davis, Stan and Meyer, Christopher: *Future Wealth*, Harvard Business School, 2000

Dearlove, Des, and Coomber, Stephen: *Architects of the Business Revolution*, Capstone, 2001

de Geus, Arie: *The Living Company*, Nicholas Brealey, 1999

Donkin, Richard: *Blood, Sweat and Tears: The evolution of work*, Texere, 2001

Drucker, Peter: *The Age of Discontinuity*, William Heinemann, 1969

Drucker, Peter: *Post-Capitalist Society*, Butterworth-Heinemann, 1994

Evans, Philip and Wurster, Thomas H: *Blown to Bits*, Harvard, 2000

Gates, Bill: *Business@the Speed of Thought*, Penguin Books, 1999

Gleick, James: *Chaos: Making a New Science*, Viking Penguin, 1987

Goleman, Daniel: *Emotional Intelligence*, Bloomsbury, 1995

Goleman, Daniel: *Working With Emotional Intelligence*, Bloomsbury, 1998

Grove, Andrew S.: *Only the Paranoid Survive*, HarperCollins, 1997

Hamel, Gary: *Leading the Revolution*, Harvard Business School, November 2000

Howkins, John: *The Creative Economy: How people make money from ideas*, Allen Lane the Penguin Press, 2001

Kanigel, Robert: *The One Best Way*, Wiley 1996

Kelley, Tom: *The Art of Innovation*, Currency Doubleday, 2001

Kennedy, Carol: *The Merchant Princes*, Hutchinson, 2000, published in paperback as *Business Pioneers*, Random House 2001

Kennedy, Carol: *Guide to the Management Gurus*, Random House Business Books, 1998

Lammiman, J. and Syrett, M.: *Innovation at the Top: Where do directors get their ideas from?* Roffey Park Management Institute, 1998

Lammiman, J. and Syrett, M.: *Entering Tiger Country: How ideas are shaped in organisations*, Roffey Park Management Institute, 2000

Law, Andy: *Open Minds*, Orion Books, 1998

Leonard, Dorothy and Swap, Walter: *When Sparks Fly*, Harvard Business School Press, 1999

Lewin, Roger, and Regine, Birute: *The Soul At Work*, Orion Business Books, 1999

Lipman-Blumen, J. and Leavitt, H.J.: *Hot Groups*, OUP, 1999

Micklethwait, John, and Wooldridge, Adrian: *The Witch Doctors*, Heinemann, 1996

Mikel, Harry, and Schroeder, Richard: *Six Sigma: The breakthrough strategy revolutionising the world's top corporations*, Currency Doubleday, 2000

O'Shea, James, and Madigan, Charles: *Dangerous Company*, Nicholas Brealey, 1997

Pascale, Richard: *Surfing the Edge of Chaos*, Texere, 2000

Pfeffer, Jeffrey: *The Human Equation*, Harvard Business School Press, 1998

Pfeffer, Jeffrey, and Sutton, Robert: *The Knowing-Doing Gap*, Harvard Business School Press, 2000

Ridderstrale, J, and Nordstrom, K: *Funky Business*, ft.com, 2000

Syrett, M and Lammiman, J: *Management Development: Making the Investment Count*, Economist Books, 1999

Tapscott, Don: *Growing Up Digital*, McGraw-Hill, 1998

Tapscott, Don; Ticoll, David; and Lowy, Alex: *Digital Capital*, Nicholas Brealey, 2000

Tichy, Noel M. and Sherman, Stratford: *Control Your Destiny or Someone Else Will*, HarperCollins, 1993

Tulgan, Bruce: *Winning the Talent Wars*, Nicholas Brealey, 2001

Waterman, Robert H., Jr: *Frontiers of Excellence*, Nicholas Brealey, 1994

Zohar, Danah and Marshall, Ian: *SQ- the Ultimate Intelligence*, Bloomsbury, 2000

INDEX